5/2014

Music in American Crime Prevention and Punishment

Music
in American
Crime Prevention
and Punishment

LILY E. HIRSCH

The University of Michigan Press
Ann Arbor

Published in the United States of America by
The University of Michigan Press
Manufactured in the United States of America
♾ Printed on acid-free paper

2015   2014   2013   2012   4   3   2   1

A CIP catalog record for this book is available from the British Library.

Library of Congress Cataloging-in-Publication Data

Hirsch, Lily E., 1979–
      Music in American crime prevention and punishment / Lily E. Hirsch.
         p. cm.
      Includes bibliographical references and index.
      ISBN 978-0-472-11854-0 (cloth : alk. paper)—ISBN 978-0-472-02874-0
(e-book)
      1. Music and crime. 2. Music—Social aspects—United States. 3. Music—
Psychological aspects. 4. Performing arts—Law and legislation—United
States. 5. Criminal justice, Administration of—United States. I. Title.
      ML3917.U5H57 2012
      362.88′17—dc23   2012025922

Acknowledgments

I would like to thank many institutions and individuals for their role in the completion of this book. First, I thank the library staff at Cleveland State University for their work with OhioLink to obtain some of the diverse literature on which this interdisciplinary study depends. Thank you also to the members of my rather large fall 2010 graduate seminar on music and Romantic aesthetics. Through their engagement and thoughtful discussion of complex material, the students in this class helped me think through various ideas and themes in this book. This book also benefited from the support of various faculty members at Cleveland State. I am especially indebted in this regard to Charles Hersch, a political scientist and closet musicologist, for coffee chats at different stages in this project's development. I also greatly appreciate his response to an early draft of the work, completed during a long week of jury duty. For his attention to my use of legalese and encouragement to continue work on this topic without a legal degree, I thank law professor Kevin O'Neil. I extend a similar note of thanks to my brother, Martin Hirsch, Esquire, and my dear friend, attorney Melanie Jean Vartabedian. I am grateful to both for their careful attention to several sections of this work.

I owe special thanks to Bryan Gilliam for his continued support of my work. Though this project seems a great departure from the research I began at Duke University on musical politics in Nazi Germany, Bryan has remained an outstanding advocate and adviser. His encouragement strengthens my work on any and all topics. Orin Starn has similarly been an enduring presence in my constellation of academic star-mentors. I am indebted to him for his comments on an early version of this work and his thoughtful take on the book's focus. The advice of Robert Fink was also invaluable as I worked to bring out salient themes and explored new ways of thinking about contemporary applications of Romantic aesthetics as well as canon formation in popular music.

The project itself benefited fundamentally from conversations and email exchanges with several individuals involved in the book's case studies. Thank you to Judge Paul Sacco, Judge Wayne Miller, Karen Cade, Clint McKay, Margaret Chabris, Zachary Brown, and Arnold Shapiro for providing direct insight into specific examples of music's operation in crime prevention and punishment. For more practical help, I am indebted to Taylor Roelofs for his technological expertise and to Carrie Mallonée for her musical know-how. I also thank George Nemeth, who once again proved indispensable as proofreader and foil. The anonymous reviewers assigned by the University of Michigan Press were similarly significant. Their thoughtful responses to the manuscript were extraordinarily helpful as I worked to improve this book. I owe thanks to the editorial board as well and to all those involved with this project at the University of Michigan Press. Above all, I am indebted to editor Chris Hebert. My first book benefited so tremendously from his guidance and advice. I was confident that this project would be best served by a second collaboration. I am lucky he was up for the job.

Sections of chapter 1 of this book previously appeared in "Weaponizing Classical Music: Crime Prevention and Symbolic Power in the Age of Repetition," *Journal of Popular Music Studies* 19.4 (2007): 352–58. I am grateful to *Journal of Popular Music Studies* for permission to reprint this material. Thank you also to the Taylor and Francis Group and *Popular Music and Society* (http://www.informaworld.com) for permission to reprint in chapter 2 portions of my article "'Do You Really Want to Hurt Me?': Music as Punishment in the United States Legal System," *Popular Music and Society* 34.1 (2011): 35–53. I offer my special appreciation to the editors of this particular volume of the journal, Bruce Johnson and Martin Cloonan. Their work and encouragement has had a significant influence on this project and my own thinking about "the dark side of the tune."

Finally, I am forever indebted to my supportive friends and family. Vickie Kosarik showed great patience when I thought out loud about this project, in addition to other related and unrelated topics, during our Friday lunches. Jim and Cyndi Roelofs have always expressed welcome interest in all of my academic writings. My parents, Marlena and Barry Hirsch, truly believe I can do anything. And finally, thank you to my husband, Austin Roelofs. My love for you is constantly expanding with all that I do and all that we do together—every new adventure. Our greatest adventure will no doubt be parenthood. Special thanks to Elliana Grace Roelofs for waiting until I completed the writing of this book to arrive and change my life forever.

Contents

Introduction   1

1. Classical Music in Crime Prevention   12

2. "Sound for Sound": A New Approach to Punishment
   in Noise Abatement   29

3. Rap Lyrics as Evidence   50

4. "The Music Made Me Do It": Obscenity and Incitement
   in Legal Valuations of Music   68

5. Music in Prison   85

6. Music as Torture   110

   Epilogue   132

   Notes   139

   Sources Consulted   175

   Index   197

Introduction

In the case of *People v. Kelly* (2007), the Supreme Court of California had to contend with the role of music at trial. Douglas Oliver Kelly had been convicted of first degree murder. In the sentencing phase, the prosecution offered as victim impact statement—evidence admitted during the penalty phase of a capital crime—a video montage of the victim, Sara Weir, whom Kelly had also robbed and raped. In the opening slide of the videotape, Weir's birth and death dates, 1974 and 1993, respectively, appeared on the screen. The jury then heard slow music begin in concert with a narration by Weir's mother. Chronological snapshots from Weir's life emerged one by one on screen—a picture of Weir on Halloween, another of Weir playing the piano with her grandmother. During these scenes, Weir's mother identified the soft music the jury heard as the work of the Irish musician Enya, music Weir had often enjoyed. After almost twenty minutes, the video concluded with a picture of men riding horseback in southern Alberta, a place significant to generations of Weir's family. Weir's mother offered a final comment: "As time goes by, I try very hard not to think of Sara in terms of this terrible crime that we've had to deal with here in the court, but rather think of her in a place like this. . . . [T]his is the kind of heaven she seems to belong in."[1] With the jury's eventual guilty verdict and recommended sentence of death (then imposed by the court), the defense cried foul play. Noting music's powerful influence on emotion, the defense argued that the inclusion of music in the video montage could have unfairly swayed the jury. Did Enya ultimately condemn Kelly to death?

In *Salazar v. State,* the Texas Court of Criminal Appeal had dismissed a similar video tribute to a murder victim, set to music characterized as "emotional," including the songs "Storms in Africa" and "River" by Enya as well as the song "My Heart Will Go On," performed by Celine Dion. The court insisted that "the punishment phase of a criminal trial is not a memorial service for the victim."[2] While victim impact is admissible, music within such testimony or video offering is perceived as a danger at court. As the California Supreme Court ruled in *People v. Prince* (2007), the medium of music "itself may assist in creating an emotional impact upon the jury that goes beyond what the jury might experience by viewing still photographs of the victim or listening to the victim's bereaved parents."[3]

In these cases, the court attempted in this way to enforce a divide between the law, perceived as a realm of objectivity, and music, treated as a space of subjectivity.[4] This aim relates to a general correlation between, on the one hand, the law and logic and, on the other hand, music and unreason or emotion. In "Sounds of Prejudice," attorney Erica Schroeder explains, "Music's powerful effect on emotion makes it a dangerous addition to the supposedly logic-and-reason-based setting of the courtroom."[5] Despite the horrendous crimes at times displayed and decoded at court—events that have incited fear and outrage in communities as well as irreparable despair in the lives of families and friends—the legal system "is expected to float free of this emotional intensity, an island of pure deliberative reason."[6] Legal authorities insist that "in judicial inquiry the cold clear truth is to be sought and dispassionately analyzed under the colorless lenses of the law."[7] Consequently, "emotion" has been labeled inappropriate and "corruptive" as a category of exclusion within legal discourse and practice.[8] The law thus distinguishes between reason, the premise of the justice system, and emotion as two oppositional categories.[9] To uphold this ideal—or at least the appearance of such a division—there exists at trial "the antisympathy instruction." The judge may instruct the jury that it "must not be swayed by mere sentiment, conjecture, sympathy, passion, prejudice, public opinion or public feeling."[10]

Yet emotion, like music, does not preclude reasoned thought. In fact, emotion is embedded within rational deliberation and can even have positive rather than corruptive repercussions. While evidence shows that clients may suffer harsher verdicts as a result of a jury's emotional response to "irritating" attorney behavior, a jury's generally positive mood may also aid thinking and decision making and lead to more utilitarian judgments.[11] Emotions can therefore be harmful as well as helpful in court.[12]

Rather than denying emotions a place in the legal process, this varied potential deserves study and consideration. After all, despite the theoretical divide, in practice the law is essentially confounded by emotion. As law professor John Leubsdorf concludes, "[E]vidence law does not privilege reason over emotion but remains firmly and complexly ambivalent."[13] Indeed, every aspect of the legal process is permeated with emotion despite legal efforts to combat passion. The law focuses on issues of emotional impact: various types of loss—divorce, murder, suicide, robbery—as well as myriad moral questions. Emotion cannot simply be extracted or excluded from such issues.[14] Furthermore, the law actually sanctions emotion in several ways: for example, in the "heat-of-passion" defense, extenuating circumstances can reduce the severity of criminal charges or sentencing. Of course, victim impact statements also rely on emotion.[15] During victim impact testimony, the victim's family members may offer a description of how the crime has affected their lives.

> He cries for his mom. He doesn't seem to understand why she doesn't come home. And he cries for his sister Lacie. He comes to me many times during the week and asks me, Grandmama, do you miss my Lacie. And I tell him yes. He says, I'm worried about my Lacie.

Heartbreaking, this testimony in *Payne v. Tennessee* offered by Charisse Christopher's mother described the impact of the murders of Charisse and her two-year-old daughter on her surviving three-year-old son. The statement was admitted as "simply another form or method of informing the sentencing authority about the specific harm caused by the crime in question."[16]

There are multiple questions of impropriety regarding victim impact statements, including the implication that all life is not equal—that the life of a hardworking mother is more valuable than the life of a childless man, for instance.[17] But in *People v. Kelly*, Kelly's defense focused specifically on the role of music, arguing on appeal that music transformed victim impact testimony from informative and thus admissible to emotional or prejudicial and thus inadmissible. Had music here violated the court's false polarization of reason (law) and emotion (music)?

In redress, the California Supreme Court affirmed the initial verdict, stating, "Any error in the inclusion of background music . . . was harmless in light of the trial as a whole." Such a conclusion is similar to the view that art in general is inconsequential in relationship to the law. The professor of law and philosophy Robin L. West, for example, distinguishes law and literature by citing the imperative in law, a command, as it contrasts with the expressive in literature. Law, according to West, is "a product of power," while literature, as art, is not.[18] Along these lines, the court in *Kelly* continued, "These days, background music in videotapes is very common; the soft music here would not have had a significant impact on the jury." In this way, while admitting the possibility of error—emotional excess created by the inclusion of the music—the court sidestepped the issue by categorizing the error as inconsequential, more "probative" than "prejudicial." The U.S. Supreme Court recently had the chance to review this decision but turned down the opportunity to clarify its opinion of such testimony.[19] The justices have thereby left open the issue of music's "prejudicial" effect in sentencing. This refusal to consider the impact of music is more common than one might suspect in the judicial system, even in cases that directly concern music. Though evidence indicates that the court viewed music with distrust, the court in *Kelly* ultimately evaded the issue. Why? Should music be excluded from such statements? What does this evasion say about music's roles in court? How do we understand music's place in the legal system?

This complicated case represents one of many examples of music's operation in American crime prevention and punishment. Yet despite some individual discussions of music and crime deterrence in sociological, business, and legal literature, there is currently no book-length study of music's roles in this context. *Music in American Crime Prevention and Punishment* fills this void. This book differs significantly from previous work on music and the law—work that traditionally concentrates on music's place within copyright law or intellectual property law, which regulates and protects "rights in the creations of the mind." Among the best studies in this regard are Richard L. Schur's *Parodies of Ownership: Hip-Hop Aesthetics and Intellectual Property Law* and Joanna Demers's *Steal This Music: How Intellectual Property Law Affects Musical Creativity.*[20] My focus, in contrast, primarily involves criminal law—the rules of behavior or conduct established to protect the public at large and the standards set out and enforced by the state to punish transgressions of those rules.[21] In so doing, I study music in action rather than as a species of property. Indeed, though the prevention and punishment of crime may not seem to invite music's involvement, music operates—acts—in this regard to startling ends, and these ends directly affect people in complicated ways. My study thus has surprising implications for the maintenance of law and order and for the people purportedly protected by legal responses to crime.

Given the repercussions for society's safety and the processes and state institutions that counter crime, the potential applications of this study are extraordinary. But my approach to this new concentration on music in crime prevention and punishment also offers unique insight into contemporary societal valuations of music and the meaning of music outside the concert hall. To access this potential disclosure, I approach this topic by asking several questions: How does music influence the criminal-legal process? How does this process influence music? What larger societal repercussions does this mutual engagement have? How does this interaction relate to other common uses of music in society today? Existing evidence and explanations of the commonalities of music and the law in general, though limited, offer a useful starting point and theoretical foundation for this inquiry.

Based on legal literature, remarkable links exist between music and the law. Titles of university law review articles increasingly include musical metaphors—terms such as *harmony* and *dissonance,* among others.[22] In legal writing, lawyers and legal scholars also consistently cite popular music and its artists. As of 2007, legal journals referenced Bob Dylan most frequently, with 160 citations, while the Beatles finished second with 71 citations.[23] Peter M. Mansfield, for example, begins his description of the killing of David Boim in the West Bank by two members of Hamas by quoting Bob Dylan: "Another broken heart, another barrel of a gun . . ." This line is the first of four Dylan quotations in Mansfield's article, "Terrorism and a Civil Cause of Action: Boim, Ungar, and Joint Torts," in the *Journal of International and Comparative Law.*[24] What does Dylan have to do with joint torts? Not much: This repeated citation does not highlight inherent affinity but instead points to a common rhetorical strategy. Reference to popular artists—especially artists with the enduring fame and even canonical status of Dylan and the Beatles[25]—can attract readers' attention and, in practical application in court, may create connections between lawyers and clients as well as jurors by communicating in code. That is, cultural references can index a storehouse of meaning and thus concisely communicate quite a lot in shared shorthand.[26] This attention to musical texts extends to the lives of popular artists, whose legal issues and trials have a particular appeal within the legal community. As the legal scholar Alex B. Long acknowledges, "Popular music is a popular topic in legal writing."[27] With this quotation and interest, the legal community on a surface level incorporates music into the law.

However, music and the law share more profound connections beyond such superficial attention—connections that serve the aims of this study. Both music and the law require interpretation; further, this interpretation reflects and influences social values. Prominent legal writers have theorized these ties. Legal scholars, for example, have likened the law to specific musical forms, like a fugue or round—comparing the operation of multiple voices in music to a similar polyphony within legal matters.[28] Desmond Manderson, for instance, structures his book about the law, *Songs without Words,* along these lines, titling and organizing each chapter based on a different musical genre, including the motet, requiem, and quartet.[29] The metaphor of voice here highlights the role of performance in both music and the law. Indeed, as "performative discourses," music and the law similarly require interpretation of a text, often in front of an audience. At a 1999 legal symposium on "Modes of Law: Music and Legal Theory," Manderson and David Caudill therefore argued that "a serious consideration of the nature of musical interpretation" may prove applicable to modes of legal interpretation.[30]

Earlier, the issue of interpretation in both music and law was the focus of Sanford Levinson and J. M. Balkin's review of *Authenticity and Early Music* (1988), edited by Nicholas Kenyon, in the *University of Pennsylvania Law Review.* In this article, "Law, Music, and Other Performing Arts," legal scholars Levinson and Balkin compared the early music movement, which seeks the reproduction of the composer's intentions in performance, to a disputed approach to the reading of law.[31] They discussed in this way Robert H. Bork's argument for originalism in the interpretation of the Constitution—or the view that a judge should "apply the Constitution according to the principles intended by those who ratified the document."[32] In so doing, Levinson and Balkin argued that just as the composer creates the musical score, leaving interpretation to performers, judges must interpret the commands of the legislature or constitutional founders.[33] This alignment of music and the law was not overlooked by the eminent music scholar Richard Taruskin, an original contributor to *Authenticity and Early Music.* In 1995, he recognized the "congruence between legal modernism and authentic performance practice."[34]

This back-and-forth represents one of the most striking instances of dialogue between the legal and musical disciplines. For the law, it was also an important interdisciplinary experiment. In their review, Levinson and Balkin made it clear that they were not concerned about their musical credentials and readily admitted that they were not music scholars. They countered, "But so what? Why would one believe that one must be an expert in an area in order to have interesting things to say about a given book?" This retort, according to the authors, applies to the study of constitutional law as well as music. In this way, Levinson and Balkin recognized the significance of an interdisciplinary study of the law and of the arts' relationship to it. Like music, the law has been theorized as autonomous.[35] However, such an approach ignores law's dependence on context, musical or otherwise. In applying musical debates to legal ones, Levinson and Balkin offered the legal field a bridge to end its isolation. Subsequent writers within the field have continued this mission. In her "comment on law and music," Carol Weisbrod writes, "We want to speak very directly, very clearly, about law as part of culture. Breaking through the law's 'autonomous' categories by talking about music seems to be one way to do that."[36]

The drive to theorize the law's role within culture is useful for our purposes. Such consideration can reveal the ramifications of legal interpretation beyond the law. To be sure, the law reflects and influences societal and cultural values. That is, the law responds to general community values and beliefs, which are then formalized in the law. This notion is akin to the former Yale law professor Robert Cover's position in "Nomos and Narrative" regarding the relationship between law and culture more generally. As he explains, interpretation of the law and thus the making of legal meaning "takes place always through an essentially cultural medium" and is dependent on our "interpretive commitments" or cultural values.[37] Such contextual thinking was fundamental to early work on the relationship between the humanities and law. For example, with the founding approximately twenty years ago of the first scholarly journal devoted to this connection, the *Yale Journal of Law and the Humanities,* the editors insisted, "The study of law must be informed by an examination of the socio-cultural narratives that shape legal meaning and empower legal norms; conversely, the study of culture requires an understanding of the law as a normative edifice and coercive system."[38] In other words, we must attend to the interplay between culture and the law and the impact of this exchange on both.

We can also twist this objective. By examining the law, we can find evidence of the cultural and social narratives at play and further trace the philosophical concerns that informed them.[39] Like law, music functions as a mirror and participant in wider social debates, concerns, and values. Thus, it, too, can reveal greater cultural beliefs. The law and music's interplay in the realm of cultural and social values can in some ways represent a dialogue: Music informs aesthetic values and thus the law, while the law in its participation in culture further informs music, both in practice and valuation. Accordingly, as the law professor Aaron R. S. Lorenz recognizes, music and law are "mutually constitutive social forces."[40] By extension, practitioners of the law can ultimately interrogate music to explore issues deemed legal just as music scholars explore the law to access issues termed musical.[41]

In this book, I use this potential to understand the ramifications of music's roles in American crime prevention and punishment—the effects of this interaction on legal responses to crime, society at large, and music itself—while accessing related insight into musical values today. To do so, I accept Levinson and Balkin's possibly inadvertent invitation to engage with law from beyond the field—in my case, as a musicologist. I am not the first musician or music scholar to explore the law. I have already mentioned Demers's study on intellectual property law as well as Taruskin's response to Levinson and Balkin's review. Demers and Taruskin follow the precedent of the German philosopher Theodor Adorno, who discussed distinctions between music and the law.[42] Many composers and theorists have also studied law: the composers Robert Schumann, Igor Stravinsky, George Frideric Handel, and Georg Philipp Telemann and the music theorist Henrich Schenker, among others. But with my approach to the law, goals in this context, and concentration within the law—for the most part on criminal law—my study proves a considerable departure from previous engagement with music and the law in the musical realm as well as in legal studies.[43]

With vast ground to cover, however, I cannot document in this book every instance of music's contact with crime prevention and punishment. Instead, I specifically examine case studies of music's involvement in the criminal-legal process in each stage of the U.S. criminal justice system (the processes and state institutions that enforce the rule of law, mainly criminal law), focusing on law enforcement or the police, the courts, and the prison system, including detention centers at home and abroad. In each of these case studies, I explore a gap between music's use in theory and in practice. Music's operation in theory relies on positive or Romantic conceptions of music—notions that music is solely elevated and elevating, which can be traced to the late eighteenth and nineteenth centuries and the era's prevailing Romantic aesthetic. This thinking sanctioned ideals of originality and autonomy of the composer and work and beliefs that music can enlighten, act as a window into the soul, and effect moral change. Though initially applied to classical music (generally defined here and subsequently as "European 'concert' music in its entirety" as opposed to Classical music or music of the Classical period, roughly 1750–1800),[44] these ideas of music and values associated with music persist within crime prevention and punishment in relationship to a variety of musics and at times a more general notion or abstract conception of music. For instance, law enforcement has harnessed classical music in crime prevention given its perceived ability to elicit moral transformation. The court system has similarly perceived music of various types, including ballads of the 1950s as well as classical music, as useful in punishment due to supposed powers of enlightenment. In this way, Romantic ideas have shifted in contemporary contexts to accommodate multiple genres. New discourses about popular music have also given rise to new ideals of music's value. Still, these ideals can often be argued to be fresh manifestations of earlier Romantic ruminations on art.[45] At the very least, these modern ideals grow from an impulse to elevate, to canonize, that must be connected to the Romantic era—the preeminent period of music's valorization. Throughout this study, we therefore see striking evidence to support the philosophy scholar Lydia Goehr's claim that "the view of the musical world the romantic aesthetic originally provided has continued, since 1800, to be the dominant view."[46] Yet my work also makes it clear that music does not act according to solely positive pronouncements about music. In this book, I thereby expose the rift between current Romantic thinking about music and the practical functioning of music in legal responses to crime. Moreover, I reveal how such enduring and evolving notions of music can obscure certain dangers of music's use as well as music's potential toward more practical ends within the criminal-legal process.

In chapter 1, I examine the use of classical music in crime prevention. I explore police and community leaders' use of classical music as a means to banish activity, sound, and social groups deemed unacceptable. I ask several questions: Why and how does this music repel undesirables? Does this technique rely on music's supposed ability to effect moral change, as some maintain? What does the success of this measure say about the meaning of music and societal understanding of specific categories of music, such as classical music? Ultimately, this case study offers law enforcement reasons for caution in proceeding with such sanctioning of music for exclusionary ends.

In a related case, chapter 2 investigates how authorities within the legal community have recently exploited music of various types—not just classical music—in the punishment of noise violators, once again appropriating music as a means to fight unwanted sound and behavior. By focusing specifically on a courtroom in Fort Lupton, Colorado, I interrogate the origins of music as punishment and its administration. I also explore the rift between the sentence's intended results and practical impact. But how does the use of nonclassical music distinguish this approach from the technique investigated in chapter 1? And what does the musical repertoire say about music reception today as well as possible bias in noise regulation? This sentencing pits certain musical genres—specifically, rap—against others, and this opposition should raise concerns about the courts' reinforcement of hierarchies, musical and otherwise.

In subsequent chapters, I focus specifically on issues that explicitly involve this disputed territory of rap. This focus is only logical. At trial, apprehension about music is often amplified by the specific genre of rap. This attitude, which often implies issues of race, may not be surprising. Popular music and American law have a long history of mutual opposition.[47] However, to some extent, rap, designated an "outlaw" music, has attracted greater legal hostility and involvement than other popular genres. Even in legal writing, scholars have demonstrated their trepidation in confrontations with rap.[48] In an article in the *Columbia University National Black Law Journal* (2004), Christian D. Rutherford, for example, discusses the tremendous influence of rap artists and explores the ramifications of rap's perceived promotion of lawlessness. He asks, "What happens, however, when punishment is no longer feared and a criminal record is revered?"[49] Here we see a distrust of rap related to a desire for control and a fear that certain music may disrupt the workings of a civilized society.[50]

With rap's contested legal reception in mind, in chapter 3 I explore the use of rap lyrics as evidence of crime in the prosecution of their authors. Though Romantic philosophers have conceived of music as a "window into the soul," and popular music often promotes related ideals of authenticity, this case study exposes various complications involved in rap and music more generally that undermine its treatment as a reflection of a composer's biography and thus its use as evidence in U.S. courts.

This use of music in court relates to ambivalence about rap evident in the prosecution of music as incitement to violence, which is the focus of chapter 4. In this chapter, I examine the civil suit filed by the family of police officer Bill Davidson, who blamed Tupac Shakur for inspiring the officer's murder. Though I thus venture outside of criminal law, this case grew from an earlier criminal proceeding and relates to music's operation in the punishment of crime more generally. Unlike the cases explored in chapter 3, the courts here directly engage with the societal standing of rap and thus render a more definitive verdict on the relationships between rap, Romantic notions of high art, and current canons of popular music.

In chapter 5, we continue our progression through the criminal justice system by examining the debate surrounding music's functioning in prison inspired by VH1's series *Music behind Bars*. This series elicited great criticism, including the claim that inmates do not deserve music. But have ideas that music is positive and thus belongs only in positive contexts distracted from music's practical potential in the maintenance of discipline? With this question, this chapter explores a more general appraisal of music. That is, rather than investigating specific genres of music and their interaction and operation in the criminal-legal process and thus society, chapter 5 investigates a more abstract conception of music and its roles and ramifications in incarceration.

Music's place in prison differs considerably from music's functioning in the war complex, including U.S. detention centers in Cuba, Iraq, and Afghanistan. In chapter 6, I address music's controversial use in the war on terror—specifically, the notion that music is no longer music when imposed as torture. This concentration represents the most extreme example of today's crime prevention and punishment and music's positioning therein. This focus also offers opportunity for final comment and exploration of an idea that surfaces and resurfaces throughout the book: the notion that music is and should be positive. What, in the end, accounts for this belief? How does this conviction conflict with the workings of music in the enforcement of law and order? What are the ramifications of such thinking?

In the epilogue, I return to the introduction's initial case in point— *People v. Kelly*—to model the applications of this study. I review the various commonalities that connect music's operation in the preceding chapters as they shed light on music's impact in court in *Kelly*. I ultimately contend that despite recurring Romantic rationalization of music's uses in crime prevention and punishment, music in this case and in the criminal-legal process in general has much to do with identity formation. This interaction between music and identity often implicates issues of race and class and the role of both within legal responses to crime. In so doing, music both includes and excludes in concert with American crime prevention and punishment.

This operation of music in connection with identity links music's functioning in the criminal-legal process to other common uses of music today: music at the mall, on airplanes, in factories, and so forth. By bringing music down to earth through association with contexts of the everyday, one could argue that I promote in this book a notion of music as ordinary rather than extraordinary or even otherworldly. But there is an implied valuation of music here that does a disservice to understandings of music similar to knee-jerk Romantic elevation. In this book, I carefully refrain from judgments of music inherent in ideas of the daily mundane or even from celebrating music's flexibility, its use toward positive and negative ends. My personal appraisal of music is not the point. Instead, I examine contemporary valuations and uses of music to better understand music for what it is, what it can do, and what it can reveal, while submitting to the legal community a rationale for ethical and effective harnessing of music in the prevention and punishment of crime.

1 ✦ Classical Music in Crime Prevention

In 2006, I first engaged with the use of music in crime prevention. Browsing world news headlines online, I learned of efforts to repel teens in Rockdale, a suburb of Sydney, Australia. There, in July 2006, government officials began a six-month trial program to deter local youths from late-night loitering and general noisemaking, which included roaring car engines and loud, most often popular, music. The program consisted of piping Barry Manilow's greatest hits through loudspeakers near a parking lot every night between 9:00 P.M. and midnight on Friday, Saturday, and Sunday.[1] In this way, the authorities effectively initiated a sonic brawl by fighting noise produced by teens with noise controlled by the state. At the time, deputy mayor Bill Saravinovski explained that in addition to the music of Manilow, the program would use classical music: in other words, music of "all types" that "doesn't appeal to these people."[2] This use of "daggy" (Australian slang for uncool) music to fight hooliganism has been dubbed the "Manilow Method," according to Word Spy,[3] perhaps an appropriate designation since as of March 26, 2007, Barry Manilow was No. 1 on a list of the "Top 10 Artists for the Terminally Uncool."[4] Manilow himself responded to this stratagem of coercion through music in "Manilow Unhappy with Music-as-Weapon-Ploy": "Frankly, I think if you played anyone's music for that long you'd drive any rationally minded human out of their mind." Manilow continued,

> But have they thought that these hoodlums might like my music? What if some of them began to sing along to "Can't Smile Without

You." Or lit candles when "I Write the Songs" was played? Or, heaven forbid, danced around to the infectious beat of "Copacabana"? What if this actually attracts more hoodlums? What if it puts smiles on their faces?[5]

The measure succeeded, however, and Manilow's suggestion that the teens might be attracted to his music was met with a note of sarcasm in the article's terse rejoinder: "The youths have now left the area."[6] Though Rockdale's decision to use music in this manner generated numerous articles and jokes at Manilow's expense, it was not a new idea and actually calls attention to a distinct and widespread use of music—in most cases, classical music—within crime prevention.

In fact, after reading about the situation in Sydney, I immediately recalled a similar measure in effect in my hometown of Santa Rosa, just north of San Francisco in the wine country of California. In a telephone conversation, Santa Rosa city council member Clint Mckay explained that the Santa Rosa City Council informally decided in 1996 to pipe in classical music, supplied by a satellite radio station, to clear youths from the Old Courthouse Square.[7] A teen interviewed at the time complained, "I hate the music,"[8] and this sentiment was shared by many of his peers, who left the vicinity, thus encouraging the city council to keep the measure in place.

In a more publicized U.S. example, the police department in West Palm Beach, Florida, introduced a public program of programmed classical music in April 2001 through a mounted set of speakers and CD player on an abandoned building. As reported by national newspapers, the speakers blasted a rotation of three CDs featuring the "greatest hits" of Mozart, Bach, and Beethoven at Seventh Street and Tamarind Avenue. This corner was a site of much loitering and crime, most notoriously the fatal shooting a month earlier of two Pennsylvania men who had made a wrong turn. Sergeant Ron Ghianda looked to music as remedy after he learned of the technique at a Texas seminar about music's use in nuisance abatement. The troubled corner showed marked improvement with the launch of programmed classical music there, so the strategy continued, despite a brief pause of three weeks after vandals removed speaker wires and destroyed the building's electrical meter.[9]

But how did this all begin? Where and how did this technique originate? Lately, classical music has been used as a crime deterrent all over the English-speaking world: in Canadian parks, Australian railway stations, London Underground stops, and different cities all over the United States, including my current city of residence, Cleveland, Ohio, where an ice cream shop recently initiated the strategy just a few blocks from my house. In these locales, various authorities employ classical music to reduce hooligan-ism and ward off undesirables, including, in some cases, the homeless. This represents a unique chapter in the mass culture wars—one in which law enforcement officials and other authorities exploit classical music to banish activities and sound they deem unacceptable. Legal scholars have recently recognized this use of music in crime deterrence. In the *Ohio State Journal of Criminal Law,* for example, I. Bennett Capers reviews the use of music in the government and business sector to repel and control teens.[10] Since teens seem to be the primary target of the technique, I focus in this chapter on the measure's specific effect on young people. To this end, I ask why and how classical music repels teens. Does the technique harness classical music as symbolic capital, a marker of space, or as a moralizing force? What does the success of this measure say about the future of classical music? What does it say about the role of music in law enforcement as well as society in general? To confront these questions, I ultimately consider the negative aspects of identity construction at work in this use of music. That is to say, I locate this technique's success in music's construction of not only who we are but also who we are not. In this way, I link this technique to other related means of crime prevention. With the exploitation of music's connection to identity in mind, I also, and more significantly, submit to law enforcement evidence of the harmful repercussions of music's use in this context.

Doing so requires that I start at the beginning of music's relationship to crime deterrence. But that is no easy task. With such widespread usage around the world, it is difficult to ascertain the technique's exact origins. Its genesis is further complicated by its close connection to earlier forms of background music—Germany's Weimar-era *Gebrauchsmusik* (music for use), Erik Satie's *musique d'ameublement* (furniture music), and even Georg Philipp Telemann's *musique de table* (table music). These composers had var-ious motivations for their inventions. Satie is an interesting case in point. Far from traditional, Satie may have envisioned his music as a witty challenge to composers who took themselves too seriously. However, in another explana-tion, Satie's "furniture music" was a reaction to a restaurant's loud resident orchestra. While dining there, Satie reportedly explained to his lunch com-panion, the painter Fernand Léger,

> You know, there's a need to create furniture music, that is to say,
> music that would be a part of the surrounding noises and that would

take them into account. I see it as melodious, as masking the clatter of knives and forks without drowning it completely, without imposing itself. It would fill up awkward silences that occasionally descend on guests. It would spare them the usual banalities. Moreover, it would neutralize the street noises that indiscreetly force themselves into the picture.[11]

Such a conception differed markedly from the purported use of early programmed music. The most notorious brand of programmed music is Muzak, which is credited to Brigadier General George Owen Squier's invention of a system of message transmission over existing electric power lines.[12] In the 1930s, this electric transmission, applied to music, was introduced into the workplace to "get more work out of people." Muzak's corporate pitch was strikingly direct in this regard: "We're not selling background music. We're selling the ability to motivate people in work situations."[13] In a more recent application, programmed music has been employed to enhance consumerism in malls and other retail centers. But in this example, background music is often foreground music. In other words, since the mid- to late 1980s, authorities have programmed music by the original artists rather than in arrangement or "elevator music." What links this background/foreground music with elevator music, however, is its "sourcelessness" as "ubiquitous music": "[T]his music comes from the plants and the walls and, potentially our clothes. It comes from everywhere and nowhere."[14]

In "Sounds Like the Mall of America," Jonathan Sterne, a scholar of communication technologies, describes such music as "a form of architecture." It promotes a corporate image or identity and invites a coveted clientele to enter and indulge.[15] Along these lines, a gourmet market in Dunwoody, Georgia, EatZi's, plays opera loudly. A marketing professor at the University of Cincinnati, James Kellaris, explains that "'classy' music implies 'classy' store." With this branding, he continues, "music can shape customers' time perception, lower sales resistance and increase willingness to spend."[16] In this context, as Sterne and Kellaris observe, store owners program music to encourage consumerism. But consciously or unconsciously, through their choice of music, they are discouraging unwanted elements, such as teens, who may not be attracted to opera. As Sterne maintains, "Any differentiating process—and here I return to programmed music specifically—can also alienate people."[17] In our example, the by-product of discouraging certain individuals, which is not acknowledged on the muzak.com web page, becomes the conscious primary purpose of music's employment. In other words, in crime prevention, the flip side of inclusion—exclusion—becomes the goal, a subtle turn that is not easy to localize.

In the 1960s, there were reports that certain shopping malls had begun playing the music of Mitch Miller to drive away teens. Miller, then a mainstay of family television with his sing-along renditions of enduring parlor and church songs, was seen by a new generation of youth as impossibly "square," which made him the perfect antidote to teens and their loitering.[18] However, the technique then was hardly standard or widely reported. A *New York Times* article chronicling the new trends of 1990 credited widespread deployment of music toward such exclusionary ends instead to a 7-Eleven store in Tillicum, Washington. Indeed, the authors cited the store's "discovery" that classical music "drives away loitering teenagers."[19] A January 5, 2005, article also ascribed the emergence of this measure to 7-Eleven stores—those in Canada, however.[20] When I contacted 7-Eleven corporate communications representative Margaret Chabris, she insisted that 7-Eleven was indeed the first company purposely to flip programmed music's primary function from lure to repellent. Chabris released the following statement:

> A number of 7-Eleven stores in British Columbia, Canada, were experiencing a loitering problem in 1985. It was not a problem confined to 7-Eleven, but more of a concern throughout the community. Our 7-Eleven management team there met with store personnel and psychologists to explore ways to deal with the issue of loitering.
>
> Several good ideas came out of these brainstorming session[s] that, when combined, produced a successful program to reduce the incidence of teen loitering. One of the ideas was to play "easy listening" or classical music in the parking lot. The thinking was that this kind of music is not popular with teens and may discourage them from "hanging out" at the store.[21]

Though there is evidence that music had previously been used to repel, 7-Eleven appears to be the first corporation to have sanctioned such an approach as policy.

At first, only about 10 7-Eleven stores in British Columbia employed this technique, but with success, at one time as many as 150 stores in the United States and Canada adopted it. Worldwide, companies and communities that have subsequently employed music report comparable positive results. Figures from January 2005 showed that with the installment of transmitted classical music, robberies in British subways were down by 33 percent,

assaults on staff had dropped by 25 percent, and vandalism of trains and stations had decreased by 37 percent.[22] West Palm Beach police received only
4 drug-related calls during February–June 2001, a significant drop from the
20 they received during the same period in 2000. In general, calls for service
dropped from 119 to 83. A sixty-year-old resident near the formerly troubled
Florida corner, Mamie Durham, stated, "I remember when you used to have
to walk in the street because (loiterers would) be on the sidewalk. It's cleaned
up."[23] The success in West Palm Beach and its national exposure have fueled
the perpetuation of this musical strategy. Several business and police officials
in Florida called the West Palm Beach police in 2001 for information on the
program, and, in March 2006, residents in Hartford, Connecticut, hoped
to install a system of transmitted classical music in the city's parks, citing as
inspiration the decrease of crime by 40 percent in areas targeted by music in
West Palm Beach.[24] More recently, again referring to previous success, officials and police have looked to this strategy to reduce crime at a busy transit
stop in Portland, Oregon. The Oregon legislature is currently considering a
bill that would expand this program to other high-crime locations.[25]

Classical music is often superficially selected as the most potent in these
musical programs of crime prevention. As in Santa Rosa, however, the specific type or genre of classical music selected is rarely carefully considered,
though, according to *Los Angeles Times* staff writer Scott Timberg, the music
is generally pre-Romantic, by Baroque or Classical-era composers with "a few
assertive, late-Romantic exceptions like Mussorgsky and Rachmaninoff."[26]
But why classical music?

Some in the mainstream press cite the perceived civilizing force of classical music as key to its power to scatter hoodlums. Unlike certain forms
of popular music, classical music is seen as somehow exalted with the ability to change individuals for the better. A Boston variety store owner who
witnessed the use of light classical music to fight teen loitering near the
Forest Hills subway stop maintains, "Music soothes the savage beast."[27] In
an interview in the *Los Angeles Times,* musicologist Robert Fink recognized
such motivation for the selection of classical music: "They're choosing it
because the music is still in some ways exalted. It's now 'magical': We'll spray
it around like some kind of incense."[28] Perhaps through this process, as transit police chief Fleming states in his comments about classical music piped
into Boston's subways, the city "can lift the human spirit, even the spirit of
a cynical teen-ager."[29] This idea that classical music has civilizing or ethical
properties, though extremely problematic, is a long-held belief that, Edward
Lippman notes, "seems to extend indefinitely into the past."[30]

One of the earliest philosophers of music, Plato, recognized music's potential use toward good and bad: "Music, the most celebrated of all forms of imitation . . . is the most dangerous as well. A mistake in handling it may cause untold harm, for one may become receptive to evil habits."[31] To avoid music's potential danger to society, recognized in ancient Greece and thereafter, Plato thus had advocated the censorship of musical activity and the punishment of transgressors by force if necessary.[32] During the Roman Empire, this recommendation was implemented in the position of the censor, who, among other duties, monitored singing. If singing was found insulting or "evil," the singer, according to the legal code of the Twelve Tables, 450 B.C.E., could be punished with death by clubbing.[33] But Plato extolled music's ethical effects when handled "correctly"—for example, in his discussion of music education in the third book of the *Republic,* which maintains that music education helps man become "noble and good."[34]

The opening line of William Congreve's 1697 play, *The Mourning Bride,* reiterated this positive sentiment: "Music has charms to soothe a savage breast" (a sentiment reprocessed by the Boston store owner, with slight deviation). Johann Georg Sulzer (1720–79), a Swiss aesthetician and lexicographer, refined a similar view of music. He, like many of his contemporaries, thought that all people had in them a bit of the savage (*Wilde*), "an original human being who has yet to experience the effects of the fine arts."[35] He maintained that the fine arts cultivate the ethical side of human nature, keeping that savage at bay: "It is the happy influence of the arts that tames humanity's natural savagery."[36] Among the fine arts, he believed music had a special power to this end: "The first and most forceful of [the fine arts] is that which makes its way to the soul through the ear: *music.*"[37]

During the nineteenth century, within Romantic aesthetics as conceived by Hegel, music was more consistently assigned an unrivaled, though vague, power over the soul.[38] At this time, Plato's conception of music—as moral and immoral—was cut in half, and philosophers celebrated music's redemptive powers. This thinking was not lost on Romantic composers such as Felix Mendelssohn. He wanted more than success: He wanted to further humanity, communicating ethical meaning through music.[39] This goal, a part of what the music scholar and conductor Leon Botstein terms the "Mendelssohnian Project," resulted in several compositions, including the *Lobgesang* Symphony and the oratorios *Paulus* and *Elijah.* In these works, Mendelssohn sought to promote a sense of community, foster ethical sensibilities and faith in God, and educate society about tradition. In his use of music to promote morality, Mendelssohn may have also been influenced by his grandfather, Moses Mendelssohn, and the aesthetics and theology of Friedrich Schleiermacher, who believed music should heighten emotion in the service of religious faith.[40]

This idea that music can perform good was related to a prevalent idealist aesthetic, promulgated in the late eighteenth and early nineteenth centuries, with roots in the philosophies of Pythagoras, Plato, and Plotinus. This aesthetic, in Mark Evan Bonds's general explanation, "gives priority to spirit over matter."[41] According to this thinking, art brings us closer to the infinite, reflecting a higher realm. Karl Philipp Moritz (1757–93), who was one of the first philosophers to help popularize this idea of art, wrote in his "Essay on the Unification of All the Fine Arts and Sciences under the Concept of the Perfected Thing in Itself" that by contemplating art, "we give up our individual, limited existence in favor of a higher kind of existence."[42] Beethoven, who elevated the art of composition as "tone-poet" (*Tondichter*) rather than mere "composer" (*Tonsetzer*), is said to have subscribed to this early Romantic understanding of art: "Only art and science elevate mankind to the divine."[43] Such an understanding of music would reach its heights in the work of the philosopher Arthur Schopenhauer (1788–1860), who privileged music as the expression of the noumenal realm—the will—and as such the manifestation of the essence of the world rather than merely the perceivable world.[44]

The popularity of these positive ideas of music partially explains the era's general belief in the inherent goodness of music. As the author of *Poetry and the Romantic Musical Aesthetic,* James H. Donelan, argues, "Before Mozart, Western art music had two fundamental purposes: to proclaim the glory of God in his churches and to provide musical decoration for the powerful in their courts and homes."[45] In this way, before the Romantic era, music was valued based on use. Moreover, the value of music in use was generally not high. The arts associated with contemplation and theory were privileged above music making, which, connected to the use of the hands, was related to manual activity rather than mental pursuits.[46] In the wake of the Romantic era, however, music was theorized as the ideal art. Part of music's changing valuation had to do with the sudden end of the patronage system toward the close of the Classical era.[47] For survival as an independent artist, composers had to justify and promote themselves and the worth of their art form. This promotion gave way to ideas that music both performs good and is good. With this change in status, Romantic writers also established the concept of classical music—a term introduced in the nineteenth century to classify preceding works by Bach and Beethoven, among others, as great. The initial idea of classical music therefore corresponded to other attempts to valorize music in keeping with the general repositioning of music as high art. Recognizing the specific use of pre-Romantic music in crime deterrence, Robert Fink notes the irony: "You pick classical music because it's better than other kinds of music, but the pieces you use for doing that predate classical music as a concept and come from an era when music was the lowest of the arts."[48]

But, more than that, the idea that music is a superior, civilizing force cannot and does not account for the effectiveness of classical music in repelling teens. The popular press makes it clear that teens do not change their ways or become more ethical through the magical power of classical music; rather, they take their activities elsewhere. Classical music is therefore successful not in elevating or rehabilitating hooligans but in chasing them away. Commenting on classical music in London's subways, the psychology professor Adrian North notes, "These juvenile delinquents are saying, 'Well, we can either stand here and listen to what we regard as this absolute rubbish, or our alternative—we can, you know, take our delinquency elsewhere.'"[49] Accordingly, law enforcement and other community leaders are seizing on classical music not as a positive moralizing force but as a marker of space.

Just as birds designate territory through song, authorities territorialize space through classical music by marking certain areas as off-limits and thereby creating an aural fence or "sound wall," to borrow R. Murray Schafer's terminology in *The Tuning of the World*.[50] Of course legal officials are a bit more discerning than birds in their employment of music—endeavoring to use sound to include the wanted and exclude the unwanted. In other words, authorities have found a way to use noise to unnaturally select, more like an ultrasonic pest repellent, which drives away offending rodents with sounds that do not harm unoffending house pets. This unnatural selection through music also calls to mind a device that quite literally weeds out human "pests"—that is, teenagers. A Welsh security company developed an "ear-splitting 17-kilohertz buzzer," the Mosquito, to disperse teenagers from loitering in front of stores. Most adults lose the ability to hear such high-frequency sounds and are thus immune to the device. More recently, teenagers have appropriated the idea and developed a high-frequency cell phone ring tone to circumvent rules forbidding cell phone use at schools.[51] Though there is not yet an organized appropriation among teens of the authorities' weaponizing of classical music, the use of classical music to deter youth loitering and the Welsh Mosquito share certain similarities beyond their use of sound to repel teens: Both extend "the premises of CPTED [Crime Prevention through Environmental Design] into the acoustic realm."[52]

CPTED is a concept coined by C. Ray Jeffrey and based on the assumption that "the proper design and effective use of the built environment can lead to a reduction in the fear of crime and the incidence of crime, and to an improvement in the quality of life."[53] Along these lines, CPTED is intended to influence not only the behavior of potential criminal offenders but also the outlook of legitimate users of a particular space. The awareness within design communities that environment shapes behavior is not new. For example, Greek temples in the Sicilian colony were built to keep light out as a means of producing fear.[54] But environmental approaches to crime garnered renewed interest thanks to Oscar Newman's *Defensible Space* (1972), which prompted a reexamination of CPTED.[55] The CPTED program, however, does not offer methods for solving broad issues of human behavior that underlie crime; rather, it provides solutions limited to "variables that can be manipulated and evaluated in the specified man/environment relationship."[56] As Jeffrey prefaces his influential work, quoting R. Buckminster Fuller's *Utopia or Oblivion,* "Reform the environment—not man."[57] Thus, like programmed classical music in crime prevention, this program does not target the roots of crime in the human psyche but rather specific areas, locations, rerouting crime through three overlapping strategies: 1. natural access control; 2. natural surveillance; and 3. territorial reinforcement.

The first tactic involves design strategies directed at reducing criminal opportunity. By focusing on access to doors and windows, for example, CPTED strategists can create a perception of risk. To foster a sense of organized surveillance or observation, the second strategy shifts the attention to observation. For example, CPTED proponents structure and set windows, a form of access, to cultivate the perception that the criminal will be detected.[58] The use of classical music to deter crime most closely falls under the third category. According to Crowe, "The concept of territoriality . . . suggests that physical design can create or extend a sphere of influence so that users develop a sense of proprietorship—a sense of territorial influence—and potential offenders perceive that territorial influence."[59] Landscaping is perceived as especially effective to this end: Shrubbery or trees can be planted to reinforce visually a property line, for instance.[60] Though I have not found a manual on CPTED that includes music in its discussions of territorial strategies, Crowe identifies other environmental features that may be used to affect behavior, including heat, light, temperature, pressure, and sound.[61] Underscoring music's connection to CPTED, in West Palm Beach, the police orchestrated their musical strategy in concert with CPTED recommendations: They installed better lighting and cut down trees for better visibility.[62]

It is my assertion that music reinforces territory in this way as a symbolic language by signaling to those who belong and rejecting those who do not through an encoded system of associations. As Henri Lefebvre argues, space is a product that can be marked not only physically but also abstractly, "by means of discourse, by means of sign."[63] In our example, classical music within a hierarchy of cultural practices is connected to the "uncool"—as journalist Melissa Jackson explains, "It's pretty uncool to be seen hanging around somewhere when Mozart is playing."[64] Put another way, it is not that classical music itself is unpleasant; it is the accompanying baggage, as Rob Kapilow, composer and conductor, recognizes: "They listen to this sound, and what comes with it is this whole association of its packaging, which is unpleasant: 'We don't want to be part of that elitist, white-tails, concert-going kind of world.'"[65] The authorities are likewise choosing to employ classical music not because of the actual sound of the music or inherent meaning but because of its symbolic capital: "Of all the packages that come to mind quickly, which one is furthest from our images of those thugs? . . . 'Be quiet, be well-dressed, be polite.' They're choosing the whole world of classical music and not the music itself."[66]

In this way, this strategy functions as a striking example of identity formation in the negative and legal officials' appropriation of music's role therein. Indeed, "identities are constructed through, not outside, difference."[67] Or rather, identity is formed in part by what or who we are not or perceive we are not. We thereby understand ourselves in relationship to others—that is, how we contrast. Within this process, music functions as a powerful distinguishing criterion. Musical taste and collection do play a positive role in the construction and negotiation of identity and place, as numerous studies have shown.[68] But music is far from wholly constructive in this regard. The process of identity formation can involve a rejection of the outsider as well as its associated music as a "constitutive outside." Music is thus fundamental to identity formation in both the act of identification and differentiation or dismissal. By harnessing classical music to repel and thus delineate space as Other, authorities have consciously or unconsciously recognized the symbolic power[69] embedded in values and attributes surrounding classical music and the powerful role music plays in the negative process of identity formation.

But the setting or context of listening adds an additional layer to the functioning of this technique. For example, a piece of music may soothe while the listener sits in a quiet room on a comfortable couch. But the same piece may operate differently if the listener is instead cleaning a bathroom.[70]

Within our musical strategy of repulsion, the imposition of classical music on street corners and in front of stores may similarly condition response. These settings foster a transient group listening. Though associations with classical music do not violate all teens' sense of self, and many teenagers might enjoy hearing classical music alone, programmed classical music may nonetheless achieve the desired result of rerouting these teens, at least to some extent, as a consequence of considerations related to this group dynamic, including peer pressure. That is to say, though some young people might enjoy or be indifferent to classical music at home, concerns about losing status through proximity to such associations in public might ensure classical music's deterrent effect with regard to teens. During the teenage years, peers take on heightened importance, and fear of ridicule or loss of status are powerful mechanisms for inducing conformity.[71] To be sure, a teenager with some sympathies for classical music might leave an area with piped in classical music to avoid even the risk of peer rejection. Context therefore conditions the "message" of classical music. As the sociologist Peter Martin rightly recognizes in regard to the use of music in everyday settings, "Social processes confer meaning on music, and vice versa."[72]

The listener also has a highly individualized role in this process. Teenagers' responses to classical music and its associations are rooted in their biographies and experiences, including class. To be sure, the associations with classical music—white, old, elite, rich—point to the role of class in the selection of classical music within this technique and its consequence, a role explicitly stated by the Seattle's Business Owners Association of University Avenue, which implemented measures to create "an upscale environment . . . that the youths would hate."[73] The connection between class and musical taste has been posited by the influential French philosopher and sociologist Pierre Bourdieu, who writes, "Nothing more clearly affirms one's class, nothing more infallibly classifies, than tastes in music."[74] This statement, though in need of qualification, points in part to the access to learned culture class confers. Studies on the psychology of music have recognized a connection between a pleasure response to music and familiarity or repeated hearings of a musical piece.[75] Jerrold Levinson explains, "Yet it is plain that conscious realization of thematic or structural relationships . . . commonly provide[s] a certain distinct pleasure."[76] Unless teens have become familiar with classical music through music lessons or trips to the symphony, they most likely will be unable to understand and thus enjoy a classical composition. In short, background conditions associations with music and thus, to some extent, response.

The role of class and familiarity may explain a statement by Drew Cady, general manager of the San Diego Symphony, who insists that Baroque music "seems to do the best job of driving people away."[77] For a teen unfamiliar with classical music, music from the Baroque period may sound the most foreign. To overgeneralize, in the Classical period, familiarity was important to composers. In other words, repetition and prominent, memorable melodies were significant compositional components, allowing audiences quickly to familiarize themselves with a piece. In the Baroque period, a different aesthetic prevailed, and the resulting polyphonic counterpoint and artifice of much of the era's music, especially Bach's instrumental works, hardly lent the music ready accessibility. Students in my music appreciation classes can quickly recall the first theme from the first movement of Mozart's Symphony no. 40 in G minor, K. 550, but are hard-pressed to hum any portion of a Bach fugue. The accessibility or lack thereof of many Baroque compositions may explain Cady's statement. At the very least, Cady's statement points to the potential role of familiarity and therefore class in this program of public sanitization through music.

To summarize, programmed classical music proves successful as a repellent based on associations with classical music and teenagers' interactions with these associations, conditioned by experiences and biographies, as well as on the setting of the music's playing. Authorities' exploitation of this interaction could only be possible in our contemporary times and is an instructive illustration of Jacques Attali's formulation of power's use of music as repetition.

Attali, a prominent French economist, recognizes music's connection to power: "Any music, any organization of sounds is . . . a tool for the creation or consolidation of a community, of a totality. It is what links a power center to its subjects, and thus, more generally, it is an attribute of power in all its forms."[78] In *Noise,* he writes of music in this process as silence. In this role, music is a tool of bureaucratic power, "silencing those who oppose it" through repetition.[79] The first innovation that made possible this use of music as repetition was improvement in music technology—specifically, recording. Those with power can control and possess recording technology and impose their own noise to silence others.[80] Such potential is mainly sidelined in favor of the production of youth-oriented popular music recordings. However, crime prevention through classical music is a concrete example of Attali's envisioned use of music by power and in a certain sense is a reappropriation of sound recording technology by the elite. In our case study, authorized community leaders use music broadcasting and recording technology to control space, replacing negotiation with youths or plans for rehabilitation with noise—a noise that ultimately silences.

As an exercise of such control, music's employment as repellent may inspire comparison to the use of music in torture (see chapter 6). In her 2006 American Musicological Society presentation and article "Music as Torture/ Music as Weapon," the music scholar Suzanne Cusick first informed musicologists, and in some cases the public at large, of the Central Intelligence Agency's development of "no-touch" torture, or torture through music. In detention camps in Afghanistan, Iraq, and Cuba, U.S. officials used music to undercut and crack detainees.[81] As Cusick noted, online bloggers fantasized about torture through music linked with homosexuality or the feminine, such as Gemini's "Feelings" and, interestingly enough, the music of Barry Manilow, whom bloggers responding to the Sydney case dubbed "Barely Man-e-nough!" and "Fairy Manilow."[82] But the U.S. government often favored instead aggressive heavy metal or rap, played at loud volumes (though the military also used various other types of music, including television theme songs).[83] This repertoire reflects a complex of goals, including the subjugation of the captive's sense of self, a primary objective of torture (see chapter 6).[84]

The police and other community leaders who authorize the transmission of classical music, which Sterne distinguishes from music's use in torture with the label "nonaggressive music deterrent,"[85] do not similarly aspire to undermine the personhood of teens as unavoidable physical or psychological warfare; they intend instead to demarcate space, and the selection of classical music reflects that goal. Moreover, "undesirables" have the option of leaving the area, a choice obviously denied torture victims. Music's functioning to repel thus may be more analogous to the U.S. military's use of music to dislodge Manuel Antonio Noriega from the Vatican embassy in 1989. This tactic involved the deployment of high-volume heavy metal rock as well as a bit of country music. A resident in the area, Edgar Espejo, conjectured that the strategy "could work" against Noriega, a known opera fan: "He probably can't stand it. I mean, this music is for young people, for discos. He'll never be able to sleep through it."[86] In another example, the Federal Bureau of Investigation used varied music recordings to bombard the Branch Davidian compound in 1993, hoping to dislodge the cult leader David Koresh and his followers. Music selections included Christmas carols, an Andy Williams album, the chanting of Tibetan monks, again the music of Mitch Miller, and, as a not so subtle hint, Nancy Sinatra's "These Boots Are Made for Walking."[87]

Some observers have found the specific selection of classical music to control space along these lines troubling. First, there is a potential for widespread misuse of music's exclusionary potential. Indeed, private citizens could easily co-opt this strategy. Music scholars Bruce Johnson and Martin Cloonan ask, "If public and private corporations are entitled to quarantine public spaces in this way, why may not others?"[88] This question may especially apply to those with power. For example, singer Barbara Streisand, with the power of celebrity, reportedly kept photographers away from her wedding to actor James Brolin by planting near the media encampment a parked van that blasted for hours the music of White Zombie.[89]

Beyond concerns about future appropriation, Robert Kahle, former codirector of the Urban Safety Program at Wayne University in Indiana and now president of Kahle Research Solutions,[90] sees this trend in the present as antidemocratic: "Decisions are made about how to keep the 35- to 50-year-old affluent types, while routing out kids."[91] Sterne also acknowledges "this class-polarization of public space" and insists that "we need better, more egalitarian forms of urban media design."[92] Though there are reports of drops in crime, Sterne wonders if the program has other primary goals—segregation based on class rather than criminality. He argues, "The nonaggressive music deterrent is built on the belief that people—especially upper-middle class people—should not have to encounter people of lower social classes in their daily or leisure travels."[93] Rather than a reduction of crime, the technique instead makes certain populations more comfortable. Police lieutenant John Scruggs, who brought this technique to Portland, acknowledges this potential outcome: "You may not actually be safer, but you feel safer."[94]

From this perspective, music to repel as well as other forms of primary crime prevention that focus on the offense rather than the offender are part of a larger trend in law enforcement toward exclusion and segregation. Criminologists Clive Coleman and Clive Norris explain the financial appeal of primary prevention measures: The state can pass the costs of crime prevention on to businesses and private citizens. However, Coleman and Norris clearly connect support of such measures to a "fortress mentality" with a propensity toward discrimination.[95] Primary crime prevention also seems to offer no long-term solutions to lawbreaking and hooliganism, merely causing spatial displacement that moves wrongdoing around the corner.[96]

We can see such ramifications in an earlier example of explicit criminal zoning and associated segregation: for example, the establishment of red-light districts in major U.S. cities at the turn of the twentieth century. Such confinement further involved music in the creation of Storyville in New

Orleans. This district of vice was named after Sidney Story, who penned the 1897 Storyville Ordinances, which designated a segregated district as appropriate for the city's prostitutes and associated concert saloons. The quarantine was enacted to protect "respectable" people as well as property values, conceivably affected by neighboring dens of iniquity. But the circumscribed zone and its location implied segregation on a larger level, based on social class and ethnicity. In other words, city leaders chose a site for Storyville that linked vice and prostitution with the African Americans who already lived in the neighborhood. Storyville was in this way a district for the city's explicit and implicit "undesirables."[97]

This potential for discrimination and segregation is rarely acknowledged by authorities who implement music to deter criminal activity today. In one informative interaction, I spoke with a representative at the Ohio-based ice cream store responsible for classical music's dissemination in my neighborhood. The representative subsequently asked not to be named in this study and ignored further emails I sent. When I asked her why classical music was chosen as an effective repellent, she insisted she could only give her opinion and then hesitated and stalled as she explained that classical music would not appeal to a certain "type" of person, a classification she quickly replaced with "party people." She elaborated that these people would probably prefer other types of music. Her words and her manner displayed her awareness of the problematic categorization of groups of people inherent in this system of classical music transmission. Her eventual insistence that I speak to a shop owner and seek out an official statement was to me revealing, more helpful perhaps than unreflective cooperation.

But this aural division, acknowledged or unacknowledged, may not be insurmountable or completely objectionable. Capers recognizes the anti-democratic potential of this use of music but believes it can be tailored to be more egalitarian. Theorizing his remolded musical system in New York City, he writes, "Imagine what we might learn if we piped different music in different subway stations. Imagine opera being piped through the station at Lincoln Center, folk music at the Bleecker Street station, jazz at the 125th Street station, or show tunes at 42nd Street station." He insists that "the advantage of such an approach is that it would serve to unify, not divide, to create a sense of togetherness as a component of crime reduction. It might even open eyes, and eliminate, or at least rupture, the walls that we think separate us. A lover of Purcell might find something to admire in Steve Reich. A devotee of Billie Holiday might find himself discovering Leontyne Price."[98]

Whether or not this proposed remaking of the technique would work, additional concerns remain. Shifting attention from the tactic's effects on people or society at large, some critics instead raise the issue of this strategy's implications for music or musicians. In this vein, one Santa Rosa citizen called piped-in classical music "an insult to listeners of classical music."[99] Beyond mere insult, British music columnist Norman Lebrecht railed against programmed music to repel teens: "Music is a vast psychological mystery, and playing it to police railways is culturally reckless, profoundly demeaning to one of the greater glories of civilization."[100] Such outcry will recur in reactions to many of our subsequent examples of music's roles in the prevention and punishment of crime and will be a significant focus of the final chapter. For now, it is important to highlight how classical music's status has shifted in this regard. Though classical music is still privileged for its supposed powers of elevation, authorities at the same time capitalize on classical music's loss of ultimate cultural authority by exploiting its negative associations to repel. With this change in standing, classical music can operate as crime deterrent. In other words, while authorities discuss its moralizing potential, classical music does not elevate or transform teens in practice. And, for authorities, it should not. Instead, legal officials and other authorities harness this great glory of civilization to disperse and repel by challenging teenagers' sense of self, thereby excluding them.

This strategy represents a new negative use of music's darker potential. Here, music is used to mark space, signaling inclusion to some and exclusion to others. For many teens, the decision is clear: They will take their activities elsewhere. No one has to speak or to understand the position of the Other. Music replaces direct policing and silences individuals. But does this measure have serious repercussions? Does this use of classical music harm society, creating hierarchies reinforced by sound? In the next chapter we will explore further this consideration as it concerns the related use of music in the punishment of noise violators. However, legal authorities do not favor only classical music to this end but instead use a rather diverse repertoire to fight the unwanted sound of youth, including rap. Here we see an antagonism in legal responses to crime between "good" music and rap; this qualification begins to expose complicated new musical canons as well as rap's contested valuation within criminal-legal processes and in society more generally.

2 ✦ "Sound for Sound"

A New Approach to Punishment in Noise Abatement

This second case study examines the punishment through music of low-level offenders in the U.S. justice system. Specifically focusing on municipal court judge Paul Sacco's courtroom in Fort Lupton, Colorado, I interrogate this punishment as it targets noise violators in an evolving battle for sonic space. Based in part on the testimony of Sacco and feedback forms from participants in his program of musical punishment, which have not been previously analyzed in publication, I discuss the origins of this unusual punishment and how it is administered. I then argue that the sentence's aims—including education and enlightenment—do not correspond to the contested effects. In so doing, this chapter, like the last, offers insight into hidden dangers of music's use in crime prevention and punishment as well as related valuations of music. Yet in contrast to the previous chapter, this case study suggests a more oppositional reception of various musics in society as authorities employ certain accepted music to fight unaccepted music. This exploration of music's operation in noise regulation thereby implicates more explicit concerns of prejudice and segregation—a defined hierarchy of music and associated people.

To begin this inquiry, let us turn to the long history of contestation and controversy within noise regulation to which Judge Sacco responds. By 1225, there were already complaints about noise, defined psychologically as "any sound undesired by the recipient" or simply "unwanted sound."[1] Even earlier, one of Julius Caesar's generals had voiced his frustration about the nightly noise of chariots on Rome's streets.[2] In sixteenth-century London, protests regarding sound concerned the invasiveness of traveling minstrelsy.[3] However, in many countries, widespread complaints about noise and corresponding legislative regulation did not occur until the Industrial Revolution.[4] In the nineteenth century, both Arthur Schopenhauer and Charles Dickens argued for the regulation of noise.[5] Schopenhauer insisted that "noise is a torture to intellectual people" that reduces their intellectual capabilities by interrupting the "power of concentration" on which their superior intellect depends.[6] Dickens, in his letter in Michael T. Bass's *Street Music in the Metropolis,* had similar concerns about the effects of street music on "professors and practitioners of one or other of the arts or sciences."[7] At this time, in the United States, some sought to eliminate noise, often avoiding such elitist formulations, while others heralded it as "evidence of progress."[8] In the 1900s, the first measures were instituted to actively combat unwanted sound: noise bans and "zones of quiet" in designated areas of New York City. Individuals subsequently fought noise based on general nuisance laws. The city's Department of Health was in charge of these complaints and would dispatch to investigate the scene of the complaint a sanitary inspector, a part of a special unit of the police force. The lengthy ensuing procedure was generally frustrating for all parties concerned.[9]

The case of Mrs. Richard T. Wilson is illustrative of the subjectivity and incoherence involved in policies regarding these individual noise complaints. In the spring of 1921, Francis Newton filed a complaint against her upstairs neighbor, Mrs. Wilson, who hosted late-night musical gatherings in her New York City apartment. Another neighbor, the painter Childe Hassam, complained at the trial, "I am kept awake by an absolute riot." To seek his revenge, he had imagined building "a pounding machine" over Wilson's bedroom ceiling. That is, he would fight her sound, which was not intended to disturb her neighbors, with a sound deliberately designed with disruption in mind.[10] His fantasy highlights the additional dimension of intentionality in cases of noise disturbance. And indeed, some have turned thought into deed. In 2002, Rosemary McGill reported that her loyalist neighbors in Northern Ireland "played loyalist band music for 72 hours" to antagonize nationalists in the area, a strategy she described as "psychological torture."[11]

Hassam, in contrast, relied on the courts to seek justice. However, Mrs. Wilson's defense witnesses testified that the music performed at her soirées was of great "artistic character" and therefore could not be considered noise. The judge agreed, dismissing the case.[12] For the judge, Mrs. Wilson's entertainment was legitimate sound and thus constituted music rather than noise.

Regardless of intention, as S. P. Singal has observed, noise "is the wrong sound, in the wrong place, at the wrong time."[13] Each criterion depends entirely on the individuals involved—their schedules, tastes, and cumulative experiences with music.

In the following decades, reactions to this dichotomy between noise and music continued to be highly subjective inside and outside the legal community, making it difficult to set uniform restrictions on sound. Still, with the development of recording and broadcasting capabilities, the public increasingly fought inescapable programmed sound—musical or otherwise. On March 3, 1952, the case of *Public Utilities Commission of the District of Columbia v. Pollack* brought the issue of programmed music and radio broadcasts on Capital Transit buses before the Supreme Court as a proposed violation of the First and Fifth Amendments of the U.S. Constitution.[14] In this case, the complaint had nothing to do with the value or definition of music but instead involved a demand for the right to silence. The Supreme Court ultimately allowed music on the city's buses. But two justices dissented. In his opinion, Justice William O. Douglas fought for the "freedom of no speech," recognizing the dangerous potential of programmed music in group manipulation and persuasion. He argued, "The right to privacy, today violated, is a powerful deterrent to anyone who would control men's minds."[15] This opposition was echoed in the violinist Yehudi Menuhin's contribution to UNESCO's October 1969 International Music Council meeting in Paris. There, he argued against background music on airplanes by insisting that it created a "captive audience."[16] The General Assembly eventually passed a resolution denouncing "unanimously the intolerable infringement of individual freedom and of the right of everyone to silence, because of the abusive use, in private and public places, of recorded or broadcast music."[17]

Beyond manipulation and control, this abuse can take several forms. Programmed, broadcast, or recorded music, whether intended as disruption or not, can weaken an individual's auditory system, sometimes resulting in noise-induced hearing loss. However, if a human is overloaded with sound, his or her system can begin to shut down in other ways as well. Though we rarely actively listen to every sound in our environment, our auditory mechanism is continually processing and, over time, with perpetual overstimulation, we may lose our hearing, become easily fatigued, or have trouble focusing.[18] Loud music from car stereos also represents a concrete safety risk by overpowering emergency sirens.[19] Music in our soundscape—in restaurants, stores, city squares, from car stereos, and so on—can have less tangible repercussions as well. As chapter 1 discusses, such music can create complicated hierarchies by projecting in sound markers of social difference, including taste, class, race, age and gender.[20] These effects are difficult to measure, however; the impact of noise of course varies by individual.[21]

The first major U.S. federal legislative response to noise was a 1968 amendment to the Federal Aviation Act directing the Federal Aviation Administration to regulate aircraft noise.[22] Two years later, the Environmental Protection Agency founded the Office for Noise Abatement, which worked to establish more comprehensive legislative regulation of city noise. The Noise Control Act of 1972, adopted on March 1 of that year, was intended to establish a means of coordinating federal control of noise and research into the effects of noise. The bill acknowledged "that inadequately controlled noise presents a growing danger to the health and welfare of the Nation's population, particularly in urban areas."[23] To this end, the Noise Pollution Control Act of 1972, instituted on March 14, required the Environmental Protection Agency (EPA) to establish the Office of Noise Abatement and Control to study the effects of noise on the public's health and general welfare.[24] In March 1974, the EPA published its "Identification of Levels," which recommended a maximum exposure to noise of seventy A-weighted decibels.[25] Still, according to the Noise Pollution Control Act of 1972, states and municipalities retained primary responsibility for noise control.[26]

In 1981, the EPA ended most of its noise abatement programs, and Congress halted funding for the Office of Noise Abatement. Various U.S. interest groups still call attention to the issue of noise. For example, the League for the Hard of Hearing sponsors International Noise Awareness Day.[27] But noise control in legislation ineffectively continues to rely on EPA recommendations. Without adequate federal help, the enforcement of these recommendations varies by district, based most often on zoning ordinances or nuisance actions.[28] This policing remains frustrated by contested opinions of noise. Responding to a similar state of noise regulation in the United Kingdom, Francis McManus has argued that the "fundamental problem which the government has had to confront in formulating noise legislation is that it is uncertain about the public's values about noise pollution."[29] State and local government regulation of sound also continues to contend with constitutional challenges, generally based on either the First Amendment, as a violation of expression, or the Fourteenth Amendment, as an arbitrary or vague statute.[30] Given all of these barriers and complications, how can the law adequately fight noise? How does the law in practice contend with the many legal, economic, medical, and ethical constraints involved? Once law enforcement identifies noise violators—a far-from-easy task—what are the consequences? Do these consequences accomplish their goals?

Today, New York City police have the right to seize a vehicle when the stereo's sound exceeds eighty decibels.[31] Still, noise violators, or those cited as such, are most commonly subject to monetary fines as punishment for their transgressions. In Ohio, for example, the typical fine for operating a car stereo above accepted volumes ranges from seventy-five to two hundred dollars.[32] This punishment is both deterrent and practical, generating revenue for the state.[33] However, Judge Paul Sacco in Fort Lupton, Colorado, found fines "ineffective," with "little relationship to the problem."[34] There, the parents of the often young noise violators—the average age is twenty-one—regularly paid the sixty-dollar fine in addition to the court administrative fee of thirty-five dollars; the punishment thus was of little consequence to the wrongdoers themselves.[35] In December 1998, Sacco addressed this inadequacy by inventing a new method of fighting unwanted sound, the Music Immersion Program. This program represents an additional layer of convolution within the already thorny realm of noise regulation. For our purposes, it also indicates significant appropriation of music within crime prevention and punishment. The municipal court's website explains, "Defendants who are convicted of violating the City of Fort Lupton noise ordinance are required to listen to a variety of diverse music as punishment."[36] Sacco explains the plan as "a simple knee jerk reaction," with no precedent: "I thought 'they should have to listen to music they don't like.'" In other words, if they impose "their loud music" on us, we should be able to impose "our" music on them[37]—Hassam's desire for vengeance sanctioned by law.

Sacco's program of musical immersion is conducted four times a year in the City Hall's Council Chambers. Each session takes place on a Friday night, when participants might otherwise be out socializing, and is attended by an average of ten noise violators. Participants sit for one hour without talking, chewing gum, sleeping, or breaks, and listen to a compact disc (when the program began, a tape) of classical music, country music, popular works from television programs, and pop songs by crooners, including the "repellent" Barry Manilow.[38] The September 12, 2008, set list included a musical selection for harmonica; the Captain and Tennille's "Wedding Song (There is Love)"; music by Tchaikovsky, including "Dance of the Sugarplum Fairy" from the *Nutcracker* ballet score; "The Good, the Bad and the Ugly" (main title); "Tennessee Waltz"; The Platters' "Only You"; The Crests' "Sixteen Candles"; Henry Mancini's "Mr. Lucky" and "Baby Elephant Walk"; the theme song from *Hawaii Five-O;* John Tesh's introduction for the Olympics; Anne Murray's "Moments to Remember"; a "classical" excerpt for piano; Barry Manilow's "Can't Smile without You"; Joni Mitchell's "Chelsea Morning"; Cartman's "Come Sail Away" from the cartoon *South Park;* the theme song from the PBS program *Barney and Friends* and the program's rendition of "The Itsy Bitsy Spider"; and finally Boy George's "Do You Really Want to Hurt Me?" The CD compiled for the following session, which took place on January 9, 2009, retained "The Good, the Bad and the Ugly" (main title); a musical selection for harmonica; "Tennessee Waltz"; Henry Mancini's "Mr. Lucky"; Cartman's "Come Sail Away"; and the selections from *Barney and Friends,* and added the PBS program's version of "I Love You"; a bagpipe rendition of a Scottish folk song; the Scherzo from Beethoven's Symphony no. 9; an unspecified excerpt from an unspecified opera; an unnamed piano concerto by Ravel; "An Affair to Remember"; "Who Wants to Race Me?" from the album *The Best Day Ever* by SpongeBob and the Hi-Seas; the theme song "Those Were the Days" from *All in the Family;* Bobby Goldsboro's "Honey (I Miss You)"; Bing Crosby's "Mele Kalikimaka"; "Moonlight Serenade"; Melanie Safka's "Brand New Key"; Tiny Tim's "Tiptoe through the Tulips"; "She Wore a Yellow Ribbon"; Jerry Goldsmith's theme song for *Room 222;* Willie Nelson's "You Are Always on My Mind"; and The Monkees' "I Wanna Be Free"—a sentiment most likely shared by those in attendance.[39]

Though there are violent associations with Beethoven's music,[40] these musical selections generally sample genres seen as nonaggressive (with a topical focus on feelings), associated with an older demographic or, in a few cases, a very young demographic—genres coded, for some, "feminine" and thus similar to selections exploited in the related use of music to repel and control teenagers. As Sacco observes, this repertoire challenges offenders' projection of self: "These are hard folks, guys with tattoos and metal bits, and they're part of a gang or hang out with gangs. These are some rough kids. You see some guy with shades, tattoos and all and then a Gene Autry song comes on, like 'Happy Trails,' and it's nails on a blackboard for them."[41]

During proceedings aired on CNN on November 25, 2008, noise violators sat in rows as in a classroom. A bailiff, acting as enforcer, was also in attendance, though he occupied himself with paperwork. Before the music began, the court coordinator, who starts and stops the music, reminded those in attendance, "This is very serious. . . . This is a punishment." Still, during the hour, some of the offenders laughed at certain musical selections, such as Cartman's abrasive "Come Sail Away." Others yawned or stared forward—bored, annoyed (see figure 1).[42]

Figure 1. A frame from CNN's coverage of a Music Immersion session

Upon completion of the program, violators fill out feedback forms, in Spanish and English, with the following questions: "What is your opinion of the music immersion program? Would you rather attend this class or pay the fine of $60? Which song or group of songs did you like the most? Which song or group of songs did you like the least? What did you learn if anything from this experience?" If a song receives too much positive feedback, it is replaced.[43]

Sacco's approach to noise violation is the most high-profile recent example of this use of music to punish. Indeed, CNN, CBS 4, and countless newspapers in various countries reported on the Music Immersion Program in late 2008 and early 2009. However, there are other variations on Sacco's theme. At Eastern Connecticut State University, students who commit minor infractions, including violating the campus ban on alcohol, are subject to the Alternative Restitution Program, which began in the fall of 1999. This program requires offenders to attend classical music performances as punishment.[44] In 2004, Florida judge Jeffrey Swartz sentenced motorist Michael Carreras, who had played a 50 Cent CD with his car's windows down at 5:00 A.M., to either a fine of five hundred dollars or two and a half hours of Verdi's *La Traviata.*[45] With the luxury of choice, denied in Sacco's program, Carreras opted for Verdi. Andrew Vactor, confronting a similar option, paid the fine. In 2008, a judge in Urbana, Ohio, had sentenced Vactor to either a fine or twenty hours of classical music as penalty for playing rap music on his car stereo too loudly. Vactor recalled of the rejected option, "I didn't have time to deal with that."[46]

These latter cases single out classical music, broadly defined, as somehow the most effective or at least popular means of musical punishment. In 1991, a judge in Key West, Florida, was not so sure. In this case, which predates Sacco's program as the earliest recorded instance of music in judicial punishment in the United States, Monroe County judge Wayne Miller sentenced Zachary Brown, who played reggae music too loudly, to two hours of enforced music. Aware of Key West locals, Miller knew Brown and understood that the defendant did not have enough money to pay a fine. The decision to punish Brown with music was spontaneous, an attempt to find a sentence appropriate to Brown and his crime—a specific sentence for a specific person—inspired in part by Brown's comment in court, which Miller recalls as a "dare": "I can find a message in any kind of music."[47] The judge initially sentenced the defendant to country music, but Brown explained that he was accustomed to such music, as he had previously lived in Oklahoma. To find a more effective punishment, the judge then suggested Jimi Hendrix. Again Brown responded, "Jimi's like my spiritual brother." With the defendant's ironic help, the judge eventually settled on easy-listening music, an all-strings instrumental rendition of popular songs.[48]

But how effective is this technique? What are its goals, and what does it ultimately accomplish? What role does the repertoire play to these ends? In some ways, this "punishment" is a common part of everyday life. Violators are forced to sit for a specified duration of time as another person's music plays. Most people experience something similar daily—as we sit on airplanes, in dentist offices, in elevators, or while holding on the telephone. So how is the punishment of music different? Is it really "punishment"? And if so, how does it function as punishment?

In many common everyday settings, music is programmed to avoid reflection and thus worry.[49] The music historian Joseph Lanza captures the significance of this use in his description of early reactions to the elevator: "Imagine what average turn-of-the century urban dwellers . . . felt at the sight of a conveyance capable of lifting them multiple stories in a matter of seconds. Next to roller coasters and airplanes, elevators were perceived by many as floating domiciles of disequilibrium, inciting thoughts of motion sickness and snapping cables."[50] With the arrival of the electric elevator in 1887, uniformed attendants accompanied riders to assuage fears. Music eventually would replace the attendant, performing an analogous function. The use of music in this manner relates to the comparable operation today of television in airplanes, hospitals, dentist offices, and even restaurants. The professor of cinema studies Anna McCarthy explains, "Given the pervasiveness of cultural obsessions with eating and diet, one could compare the discursive task performed by the video screens of the mediatized restaurant to that of the video screens in commercial aircraft. Both help to transform a space potentially fraught with anxiety into nothing more scary than a waiting room."[51] As common activities of distraction and entertainment that enact a progression through time—a momentum forward and through potential danger—music and television can reduce anxiety as we wait.

Operating accordingly, music accompanies a multitude of daily tasks: flying, dental work, eating, and so forth. In many of these situations, we perform additional activities: reading, surfing the Internet, talking on cellular phones, among other examples. This mode of listening represents a significant difference between engagement (or lack thereof) with music in everyday settings and the instituted punishment of music. On the whole, we do not actively listen to music while we wait or more generally in contemporary society. After all, the "dominant mode of listening today," whether music issues from personal iPods or speakers preprogrammed in sites of potential angst, is a rather distracted listening: a "ubiquitous listening" or listening "'alongside' or simultaneous with other activities."[52] In the enforcement of punishment through music, other activities are gone. This experience of listening and only listening is rare for many noise violators—as well as those who abide by noise regulations, for that matter—and this more active confrontation with music sets musical punishment apart. Yes, noise violators listen while they wait, but the mode of listening has changed and may be unfamiliar and therefore unsettling.

The choice of music also makes a difference in music's functioning, and this choice further distinguishes musical punishment from other common uses of programmed music. For example, decades ago, a woman became hysterical on a plane when the airline played the preselected song "For All We Know" while taxiing before takeoff. The lyrics begin, "For all we know, we may never meet again."[53] Of course, the listener has agency, and we never fully know how an individual will react to a particular piece. But as cultural sociologist Tia DeNora recognizes, "There are some musical materials that would undermine preferred or appropriate action frames."[54] For this reason, Muzak tailors its travel package to avoid songs of possible instigation: banned on flights are "I've Got a Feeling I'm Falling," "With a Little Bit of Luck," and "Stormy Weather."[55] Music programming on airplanes, however, can vary widely and can index complex significance beyond concerns of safety. DeNora, for example, recalls her experience of a 1997 flight from London to Los Angeles. Before takeoff, music combined with video in an airline offering called "True North":

> images of lakes and glaciers—cool and muted greys, greens and blues—were accompanied by slow, low pitched melodies and whale songs. Just before take-off the mood changed. Trumpets heralded the safety video. This decisive, upward sweeping and definite-sounding brass then faded to the background as the firm but friendly (male) voice described what we should do in the event of a water landing, etc.

The use of brass, associated with the military and thus precision and expertise, could inspire confidence in the technology of flying while drawing the passengers' attention to the safety video after the initial calm of the opening images and music.[56] Similarly, the music selected in everyday settings has specific ramifications and significance.

Such ramifications have also been recognized in studies of reactions to on-hold phone music. These studies generally demonstrate that as a medium experienced in time, music shapes time. We may stay on the line until the concluding chord, waiting for this expected release. With this distraction and goal, on-hold phone music can lead customers to estimate a shorter waiting time than groups who wait in silence. But this experience differs based on the particular musical selection. A 1990 study found that the estimation of time varies with different pieces. A customer's personal preferences and associations can also condition the response in this context. A 1993 study further concluded that people on a call to a telephone advisory service prematurely disconnected the line in reaction to styles of music perceived negatively.[57]

In this way, music eases the anxiety of waiting in concert with other activities when chosen and received appropriately. In punishment through music, in contrast to our everyday examples, tension is sought, and the musical selections and enforcement of the sentence reflect that goal. Indeed, in Sacco's program, the music should not ease the passage of time: within the context of justice, music is chosen in part to instigate, annoy, and challenge. And thus, with no accompanying activity to distract, wait time becomes punishment.

This punishment represents a literal execution of the idea of retribution—the biblical justification for punishment encapsulated in the phrase "an eye for an eye," also known as *lex talionis:*[58] an imposition of music "you hate" for an imposition of music "we hate." With his Music Immersion Program, Sacco counteracts a somewhat subjective violation with a subjective punishment. As Sacco explains, noise violators "must listen to music they don't like, because that's what they impose on others."[59] *Lex talionis* has been widely discredited in the legal profession for authorizing morally grotesque treatment. It also ignores motivation or moral culpability by punishing offenders based on ends rather than means.[60] However, in the late 1970s, some legal theorists began to support a variation of this retributionist model in the espousal of "just desserts"—the idea that "the quantum of punishment for crimes should, on grounds of justice, be proportionate to their relative seriousness." The fundamental justification for this sort of punishment is the theory that wrongdoers "deserve to suffer."[61] However, in Sacco's Music Immersion Program as well as some legal thinking about "just desserts," there is also an impulse toward education.

At the end of the January 9, 2009, musical punishment session, the court administrator stopped the music and addressed the offenders in attendance: "OK, we're done. I hope you've learned something from this."[62] Indeed, Sacco calls his method a means of "teaching manners."[63] By experiencing the pain of unavoidable music in an "offending" style, Sacco's program invites noise violators to think about their actions and perhaps gain a deeper understanding of their offense. This idea is in keeping with enduring theories of justice. In *The Theory of Moral Sentiments* (1759), Adam Smith insisted, "The violator of the laws of justice ought to be made to feel himself that evil which he has done to another."[64] Through such an approach, justice can target the roots of the crime, ensuring a moral change in the criminal. This type of sentencing is thus communicative—a means of focusing the offender's attention on the immorality of his actions.[65]

In this way, Sacco intends music to act much as silence was to operate in the nineteenth century.[66] At that time, prisons in New York (Auburn and Ossining) and Pennsylvania (Pittsburgh and later Philadelphia) enforced silence as an operation of correction in keeping with new theories of punishment.[67] Describing the Pennsylvania system, which imposed silence as well as isolation, the social theorist and philosopher Michel Foucault quotes the *Journal des Economistes* (1842): "Alone in his cell, the convict is handed over to himself; in the silence of his passions and of the world that surrounds him, he descends into his conscience, he questions it and feels awakening within him the moral feeling that never entirely perishes in the heart of man."[68] In Sacco's thinking, music similarly enacts a site of reflection and ultimately rehabilitation.

In a related claim, Sacco argues that his program educates offenders about music, much like a "music appreciation class"—exposing violators to new music and "expand[ing] their horizons."[69] "Once exposed," Sacco writes, "they are enlightened so to speak."[70] This rationale echoes the idea that classical music has elevating and even divine potential. However, Sacco does not only program canonic classical works, originally the music subject to such Romantic ruminations in the late eighteenth and nineteenth centuries. Instead, he expands in this way such positive notions of music to include other types of music: enduring ballads of the 1950s, the music of Joni Mitchell and Barry Manilow, among other selections. Such programming suggests further evolution in the legacy of Romantic aesthetics—the application of positive notions of music to popular music or, perhaps more accurately, older music of previous popularity. This expansion of terms is in keeping with characterizations of our age as postclassical.[71] As Robert Fink argues, "The canon of Western classical music is now just one among many, and not the most culturally prestigious anymore, at least in America. Other canons are forming busily, and other kinds of music are making credible plays for the top of the taste hierarchy."[72] The impulse to elevate and even canonize music persists, but classical music is no longer the sole candidate for such treatment. Notions that music is elevated from the past have changed to accommodate new ideas of what constitutes culturally authoritative music. With the end of the lone classical music canon and thus the fall of the wall surrounding classical music, classical music has fragmented, free to appear in less than classical settings—even sampled in popular music.[73] Values surrounding classical music from the past have similarly splintered—reanimated and redeployed in new settings and in relationship to other, nonclassical musics.

This evolution is evident in the handling of rock and jazz, both of which have undergone treatment designed to elevate—attempts to valorize and even canonize their respective classics—by scholars and various institutions, including schools, libraries, museums, and publishing houses, to name a few.[74] And these efforts bring new life to values surrounding the "great works" of classical music. For example, influential rock albums, such as Bob Dylan's *Highway 61 Revisited,* the Beach Boys' *Pet Sounds,* and the Beatles' *Revolver,* are celebrated based on Romantic notions of music's value, including ideas of the transcendent and sublime. Rock albums are also valorized based on ideologies of youth, rebellion, and nihilism—a seeming departure from values surrounding classical music, past and present.[75] Still, in the case of rebellion, according to Carys Wyn Jones, "it could be argued that the rock persona of the rebellious individual is simply a modern incarnation of the artist/genius," a central trope in the Romantic elevation of music.[76] New or old, discourses addressing rock's significance seek to elevate rock, just as comparable ruminations sought to exalt music during the Romantic era. Canon formation in popular music is constantly evolving, arguably at a faster pace than efforts of the nineteenth century, given the ways in which we access information, media, and music today. But the drive to establish lists of great works and, in so doing, promote music, endures.

With this in mind, it is revealing that, despite espoused goals of enlightenment, Sacco does not include celebrated rock artists such as Dylan or the Beatles on his punishment playlists. This absence, in the case of the Beatles, is highlighted by Sacco's inclusion of the Monkees, who are superficially similar. However, while the Monkees, who did not write their own songs, were created or "manufactured" to resemble the Beatles for a television program, the Beatles came together of their own volition as independent artist-geniuses.[77] The Monkees act as foil to help explain the canonic claims of the Beatles. In this way, the Beatles as well as the comparably revered Dylan may be of such a high status in Sacco's mind that they are effectively beyond punishment. Such a reading could suggest that, at least for Sacco, certain enduring rock artists are today of a higher esteem than composers of classical music such as Beethoven, who is included in sessions of musical punishment. Accordingly, Sacco's playlists support chapter 1's conclusions regarding classical music's waning authority and indicate new oppositional frameworks within popular music: Rather than the past's pitting of high and low or classical music versus popular music, new canons of popular music create value hierarchies within popular music. In a sociological study that examines responses to eighteen music genres, Bethany Bryson offers statistical evidence to bolster this claim. According to her results, in 1993 the most divisive and disliked genre in the United States was not classical music but rather heavy metal, with rap a close second. Classical music simply did not elicit the same strong reaction of disfavor—or, for that matter, favor—as heavy metal or rap.[78] But the absence of the Beatles and Dylan also calls attention to contradiction and convolution in Sacco's aim of enlightenment through punishment. Indeed, he seeks to educate through music, but it seems the music wielded to this end cannot be so exalted or possibly appealing that it could counter his goal of retribution.

Despite this tenuous balance between retribution and education, the combination of aims embedded in musical punishment is increasingly common in the legal system. For example, in 2007, Judge Patrick Carroll in

Lakewood, Ohio, sentenced a slum lord to house arrest in one of his apartments when he denied residents vital services, including gas and thus hot water and heat.[79] In another case, a burglar in Memphis, Tennessee, was ordered to allow his victim to enter his home without warning and leave with an item of comparable value to what he stole.[80] Such sentences, which seek reform through punishment, differ from traditional rehabilitation that seeks reform as an "adjunct to punishment."[81]

These unorthodox sentences are part of a trend toward increasingly inventive punishments that Jeffrey Abramson, a professor of law and politics at Brandeis University, views as "instant gratification" and at times "counterproductive."[82] In contrast, Marc Mauer, assistant director of the Sentencing Project in Washington, D.C., sees potential in alternative sentencing.[83] The Sentencing Project "works for the reform of unfair and ineffective criminal justice policies and promotes alternatives to incarceration."[84] Sacco's statistics support Mauer's program. The judge claims that the Music Immersion Program has resulted in a drop in repeat offenses—a recidivism rate of less than 5 percent.[85] However, Fort Lupton's police chief observes that offenders complete the program and then resume their normal activities; they are simply more cautious. One program graduate told a newspaper, "If you see a cop car, turn your volume down."[86] Similarly, Manuel Mendoza, a teen sentenced to the program after playing country music loudly from his pickup, insisted that he would do it again: "I'll just make sure to look out for cops next time."[87] Based on this comment, the program may not rehabilitate or enlighten noise violators, but it certainly makes them fear retribution and strive to avoid another hour of enforced music.

Still, the deterrent effects of the program cannot be accurately measured given the varied factors beyond music at play, including the punishment's enforcement on Friday night, a valued night of socialization. Nonetheless, my analysis of the Music Immersion Program feedback forms provides some insight into this issue of effect, though only forms filled out by adult offenders are available to the public. These forms are also completed on site and are not anonymous; thus, the context likely influences and even to a degree compels certain responses. Four of the ten violators whose forms are available from September 12, 2008, would rather have paid the sixty-dollar fine. However, all but one claimed to have learned a lesson: two learned that it is important to turn down the music; one cited the need to behave; one recognized only the importance of being careful while driving; and seven indicated an understanding of music as a potential bother to others—proof that either the program effectively communicated the desired lesson to some or the respondents felt obliged to mimic what they recognized as the preferred response. One of these seven, Ned Obel, wrote, "I learned that just because I like it, doesn't mean everyone else does." The offenders' overall opinion of the program was generally positive, though one was "not sure if it works" and another claimed it was boring. Respondents generally did not specify which musical pieces or genres were most and least offensive. Of those who did specify a least favorite song or genre, one person said "anything in English"; two cited the *Barney* song; another mentioned all classical, slow pieces; and one mentioned the Cartman song.[88] The favorites included the *Barney* song, the Cartman song (two respondents), and folk songs. The conflicting verdicts on Cartman's song and the selections from *Barney and Friends* highlight the subjectivity involved in the sentence of punishment through music. It also brings to mind Dave Soldier and Komar and Melamid's "most unwanted music," a twenty-five-minute piece created to include everything that the public purports to consider loathsome in music: the accordion and bagpipes; extremes of timbre, dynamics, and pitch; advertising jingles; a children's choir; atonal music; and rap executed by a classically trained soprano. For some, the resulting piece was so bad it was good—or at least humorous.[89]

Adult participant feedback forms from 2006 and 2007 generally corroborate these observations. Of the forty-two noise violators, seventeen would have chosen to attend the class, three responses were specious, and twenty-one would have paid a fine. Again, *Barney* elicited strong reactions. While most did not specify favorite and least favorite musical selection, six participants cited music from the PBS program as the least tolerable, while three cited it as the most enjoyable.

The seven feedback forms from January 9, 2009, were more hostile to the program. One respondent claimed to have "learned about some music"; four learned to turn down the volume; and one learned to "stay away from Fort Lupton." The final violator, Andrew E. Gehrig, wrote only that "Judge Sacco has no sense of humor!" If given a choice, two respondents would have elected to attend the class rather than pay the fine, while Gehrig and four others would have chosen the fine. Moreover, Gehrig defined the program as "cruel and unusual punishment": "My opinion of the music immersion program is probably not fit to be printed." Tyler North similarly wrote that the program "is very boring" and does not work. Another unnamed participant simply wrote, "I never wanna do it again." Few respondents specified favorite and least favorite musical selections. Two indicated that they did not like any of the musical selections and could not specify any piece or genre that was at all tolerable.[90] Based on these forms, it again seems that the program is successful as retribution and deterrence, though which particular aspect has that result remains unclear. Still, the program's effectiveness as moral reform or education is less apparent.

Sacco's program grows from noble goals: his desire to pay greater attention to youth offenders and even "make a connection" with them.[91] However, this idea of enlightenment or elevation through music is complicated. Can a musical punishment—or any punishment—educate? Can music annoy as retribution and at the same time enlighten? Is music here constructive, destructive, or both? If this punishment does educate or enlighten, should it? As some argue, the government as a liberal state may not have the tools or even right to educate or "coerce its citizens into embracing any particular vision of the 'good life.'"[92]

Music as punishment may be further complicated in this example by the issue of proportionality. In justifications of retribution, even when coupled or "dressed up" with ideas of communicative punishment or moral reform theory, the punishment cannot exceed the crime. Apart from considerations of constitutionality (the Eighth Amendment's Cruel and Unusual Clause), according to Ra Duff, the severity of the sentence communicates the seriousness of the crime. If the punishment is greater than the infraction, the goal of communication is nullified.[93] Though the proportionality of crime and punishment is difficult to measure—as contested as theories of punishment—the Music Immersion Program has the potential to surpass the severity of the crime by disturbing offenders' sense of self in two ways. First, by imposing music associated with the elite, an older generation, or femininity, the program undercuts violators' sense of self or projection of self as powerful, which they had previously demonstrated or realized through their imposition of "criminally" loud music. Second, by denying choice—which those offended by noise can exercise to a certain extent by leaving the area or calling the police—noise violators experience music as inescapable, a related challenge to identity. In addition to their similar use of "I Love You" from *Barney and Friends*,[94] this represents another link between the U.S. Army's program of music in torture and music's use in the criminal-legal process. Both depend on the eradication of control, which is "central to many negative reactions to music."[95] Bruce Johnson and Martin Cloonan explain that "imposed music will always tend to constitute a form of violence to a greater or lesser degree."[96] Even if a captive audience member generally enjoys the music of Beethoven, when it is imposed, he or she may react negatively. In this way, the imposition of sound is destructive as "the mirror image of censorship."[97] Like torture through music, enforced music in court can be a violation of identity as an imperialistic display of someone else's power, his or her "voice, world, and self" and thus superiority.[98] Such a breach does not depend on volume. Though the use of loud music, a strategy in torture, has a destructive physical as well as psychic impact, music at moderate levels, as in Sacco's program, can be just as damaging to one's sense of self and psychological well-being.[99] Therefore, punishment through music may indeed be harsher than the crime, thereby further undermining the possibility of moral reform or education through musical punishment.

The serious implications of Sacco's musical punishment are not always reflected in contested reactions to the program beyond Fort Lupton. Gehrig's reference to Sacco's sense of humor—or, more specifically, his lack thereof—points to more positive reactions to the program in the media and public at large. In fact, several commentators have focused on Sacco's sense of humor, finding, unlike Gehrig, a clear comedic element in the punishment. Responding to Vactor's case, one online poster wrote on October 9, 2008, "BWAHAHAHAHAHA."[100] Another poster, Terri Potratz, likewise responded with laughter.[101] Similarly, regarding Carreras's sentencing, the journalist Andrew Mueller joked, "Speaking for myself, about 15 minutes of Dido's dishwater wittering, even at a mild volume, would induce a confession to just about anything."[102]

Johnson and Cloonan consider the media's lighthearted dismissal of musical punishment "symptomatic" of the media's "trivialization of pop."[103] However, by way of explanation—not exoneration—the Music Immersion Program and related sentencing invite such reactions in several ways. Based on enduring Romantic ideals applied today to classical music as well as other musics, music is often viewed as positive—good, moral, beautiful—with the capacity to educate, comfort, and inspire joy. For many, music is thus incompatible with the negative idea of punishment. A common reaction to such an incongruity is humor. In *Reflections upon Laughter* (1750), Francis Hutcheson cited the cause of humor as "the bringing together of images which have contrary additional ideas."[104] Many contemporary philosophers share this understanding of the relationship between laughter and incongruity. However, as John Morreal recognizes, incongruity can also invoke negative emotions; as Noel Carrol argues, it can even invoke horror—the flip side of comedy.[105]

And, indeed, others responding to the incongruity of musical punishments are far from amused. In the blog regarding Vactor's case, one poster found the sentence "just plain bigotry." The author rightly recognized national and racial associations with rap music and classical music and saw the judge's use of classical music to fight Vactor's rap music as symbolically reinforcing a European standard as superior to that of Africa. Another writer agreed, calling the judge a "racist ass." Reacting to the perceived privileging of one music over another, another poster asked on October 9, 2008, "So, it would have been ok to blast his music had he been listening to Mozart?"[106] Regarding the same case, the article "Not Corporal but 'Classical' Punishment?" similarly viewed the sentence as unjust and insisted that the punishment assumed an artificial division between rap fans and classical music enthusiasts.[107]

The imposition as punishment of classical music or music more generally associated with the elite in this way augments the politics of race already embedded in the problematic policing of rap. Rap music, which originated in the mid-1970s in New York City, expanded its influence in the 1980s. During the 1980s, it increasingly included social messages and addressed political themes, such as gang violence, poverty, racism, and police brutality.[108] Consequently, rap became "a contemporary stage for the theater of the powerless."[109] Related to playwright Bertolt Brecht's idea of *Verfremdung* (alienation), this was a sort of negative theater designed to arouse dissatisfaction in the audience—art as a means to engage with rather than escape reality.[110] Significant examples of rap to this end include L. L. Cool J's "Illegal Search," NWA's "Fuck the Police," and Public Enemy's "Fight the Power" and "911 Is a Joke."[111] "White" culture responded to this denunciation, at times capitalizing on criticisms of rap by prominent African American leaders, and certain politicians in conjunction with the media portrayed rappers and rap fans as menacing and violent, often with "thinly veiled anti-Black comments."[112]

The justice system has similarly targeted rap, at times through excessive policing of rap concerts. In one example, music scholar Tricia Rose, visiting a rap concert venue, found the event a site of excessive police scrutiny and aggression: "This arena wasn't mine; it was hostile, alien territory. The unspoken message hung in the air: 'You're not wanted here. Let's get this over with and send you all back to where you came from.'"[113] In 1996, Rose argued that this antagonistic experience was an unavoidable by-product of rap concert attendance.[114] In addition to the pursuit of charges that the music incites violence (see chapter 4), the Parents' Music Resource Center (PMRC), led by Tipper Gore, encouraged state-sanctioned responses to rap by urging record companies to adopt labels that identified music, most often rap, as dangerous. The PMRC did not deem such a demand censorship.

However, Sall Nevius, part of PMRC, explained in *People* magazine, "We want the industry to police itself. If they refuse, we're going to look into legal ways to stop what we feel is a form of contributing to the delinquency of minors."[115] Major record companies chose to impose labeling in March 1990 with the "Parental Advisory—Explicit Lyrics" sticker.[116] But many rap opponents felt that this move was not enough. In 1994, representative Cardiss Collins chaired congressional hearings on the dangers of rap, which included the argument that the music of the rapper Snoop Dogg, among others, could instigate violence among the young.[117] In this way, as rap confronted the police, the U.S. judicial branch as well as the legislative branch and related parties waged an attack on rap as undesirable and even a menace to society. In these examples, this offensive sought to silence rap music, at times explicitly.

In light of this history, Stuart Laven wonders if the policing of noise—given the parallel development of rap and car stereo noise ordinances—has been wielded as just one more weapon in the dominant culture's struggle against rap: "While there is no 'smoking gun' upon which one could conclude that any particular car stereo ordinance was adopted as a way to deal with the culture of rap music and those who enjoy it, there is enough circumstantial evidence to at least negate the argument that the emergence of rap music and car stereo noise ordinances is simply coincidental."[118] This parallel has precedent in policies regarding the legality of street performance and enforcement more generally of noise legislation, including the early policing of jazz. At the turn of the century, police in New Orleans targeted jazz and its associated vice by focusing on the music's volume. They also withheld and revoked permits for live music to control the "dangerous" new sound.[119]

Rather than reacting to embedded issues of race as well as gender and class, others have instead questioned the sentence of musical punishment based again on its perceived threat to music. Clarinetist Daniel Ferreira was insulted by Sacco's program: "It's a blow below the belt to all musicians to say their lives' work can be categorized as punishment."[120] In an interview with the author, Zachary Brown, who in 1991 became the first defendant sentenced to music, similarly explained that it is wrong to use music, which is so special, in this manner.[121] Both Brown and Ferreira operate within an enduring, though expanded, Romantic conception of music that denies music's darker potential.

Daniel Sher, dean of the University of Colorado at Boulder's College of Music, conversely, was more concerned that the program might give offenders negative associations with certain music: "I hate to see somebody equate one style of music as punishment."[122] Rather than broadening horizons, according to this rationale, the program might do just the opposite. To be sure, it may in fact perpetuate negative associations with certain music, including classical music. After a young person is forced to listen to classical music as a means of punishment, how likely is it that he or she will voluntarily attend a symphony concert in the future? Such associations have further implications for society, again reinforcing through music a hierarchy that divides.

Given the various reactions and concerns regarding punishment through music, it is difficult to render an ultimate verdict on the program. However, the link between torture through music and musical punishment—the comparable loss of control—may provide evidence that the Music Immersion Program is "cruel and unusual." One way for the well-intentioned Sacco to reduce and possibly eliminate the potential negative effects of his musical punishment is to offer the option of a fine or some type of community service to ensure that the punishment targets the violators and not the parents, who pay fines. Duff further argues that, in communicative punishments, it makes sense to indulge in sentence negotiations—eliminate musical punishment as a "program" and instead, like Judge Miller, tailor sentencing to individuals: "If we are to communicate with the offender as a responsible agent, we should try to involve him in the sentencing discussion."[123]

Legal experts will decide how to proceed. However, this chapter has raised some concerns about the imposition of music in sentencing. Is the violation of enforced sound warranted as punishment and deterrent? Can the use of music in punishment be both destructive and constructive at the same time? Furthermore, does this use of music threaten once again to reinforce hierarchies in sound and ultimately divisions between people, augmenting a racial and class divide implicated in the policing of rap?

This issue of rap's relationship to noise regulation and law enforcement more generally points to additional considerations regarding music—its power and status today. While the idea that music is positive has stretched to include other musics beyond classical, this chapter shows that rap's place within this new system is far from clear. Efforts to canonize jazz and rock continue to evolve, but rap, despite considerable popularity and some serious intellectual consideration, still seems on the cusp of canon formation. Can contemporary canons include rap, or is rap somehow incompatible with general conceptions of the innate goodness of music? In the following chapters, we will further contend with legal controversies and societal valuations surrounding rap. However, in the next example, we will focus on authorities' appropriation of rap, rather than its direct policing, in cases that attempt to indict rap's artists. This concentration offers rare insight into negotiations involving a music on the verge of canonization—a significant moment of ambiguity in the history of rap and the evolution of Romantic thinking about music. At the same time, this chapter continues to undermine certain positive ascriptions of music on which these cases rely as well as their endurance in contemporary legal practice.

3 ✦ Rap Lyrics as Evidence

Shortly before the release of the enormously successful album *Doggystyle* in November 1993, Calvin Broadus (Snoop Doggy Dogg or Snoop Dogg) and his bodyguard were arrested for the murder of Philip Woldemariam, a twenty-year-old gang member from Los Angeles.[1] With his record label, Death Row Records, named to some extent for its artists' confrontations with the law,[2] Snoop Dogg seemed to respond to the charge with a short film, *Murder Was the Case: The Movie*—reusing the title of a track from *Doggystyle*. In the film, he is murdered, resurrected, and convicted of murder—a murder he committed in self-defense. The real trial began in late 1995, in the wake of the infamous acquittal of O. J. Simpson as well as the 1992 Los Angeles riots, incited by police officers' beating of Rodney King in 1991 and their acquittal for that crime. In Snoop Dogg's case, the courtroom proceedings generated television attention, concerns about the role of race similar to those generated by the Simpson case, and even charges by defense attorney Johnnie L. Cochran of police misconduct.[3] In this volatile environment, deputy district attorney Robert Grace told the jury in the prosecution's closing argument, "Murder is the crime they committed. Murder is the crime they committed"—citing the lyrics of "Murder Was the Case" from *Doggystyle*.[4] The citation of Snoop Dogg's lyrics in the prosecution's closing argument as well as his track and short film underscore the seemingly blurred line between art and life. The U.S. legal system has increasingly accepted this overlap in trials involving rap artists or wannabes, admitting lyrics as evidence against their composers.

In this way, for the prosecution, rap music, especially gangsta rap, a subgenre of rap defined in part by its misogynous themes and violent lyrics,[5] has constituted evidence of violence—proof to substantiate crime. As early as 1991, a federal court allowed such a strategy, admitting rap lyrics composed by the defendant as substantive criminal evidence.[6] After the seminal 1994 California case, *People v. Olguin,* this practice gained legitimacy, and in 2006, it was part of the prosecution's case in Albany, New York; Oroville, California; College Station, Texas; and Gretna, Louisiana. In 2008 and 2009, the California Courts of Appeal heard several cases involving contentions surrounding this use of rap lyrics, including *People v. Mancera, People v. Calzada,* and *People v. Ojito.* In such trials, the courts endorsed rap lyrics as proof of crime, criminal intent, and/or criminal mind-set.[7]

By reviewing the influential 1994 case as well as related sentencing, this chapter explores the embedded issues at play in the use of defendant-authored rap lyrics as criminal evidence—issues of race, authenticity, and commercial constraints in the rap industry—as well as the role of the composer in rap music and music more generally. In so doing, I show how issues of race complicate the use of rap lyrics as evidence and how rap lyrics are conditioned by the construction of authenticity in contexts of marketing. These considerations undermine any reading of one-to-one correspondence between composer and composition.

This examination does not focus on rap lyrics involved explicitly in crime. That is to say, I do not analyze cases that admit lyrics addressing victims directly or given to victims, but rather lyrics arguably composed independent of the crime.[8] With this focus, building on the legal writing of Sean-Patrick Wilson and Andrea L. Dennis, this chapter explores how the prosecutions' arguments for lyrics as evidence, the defense lawyers' contestation of this evidence, often based on issues of prejudice, and the resulting judgments reflect and influence attitudes about rap music. Specifically, I argue that the prosecution's use of lyrics as text, devoid of context and even music, ultimately reveals and contributes to society's ambivalence about rap as an art form.

The case of *People v. Olguin* established much of the legal framework on which subsequent cases involving defendant-authored lyrics relied. With the submission of rap lyrics as evidence, the defendants, Cesar Javier Olguin and Francisco Calderon Mora, were convicted of second-degree murder for the killing of John Ramirez, a rival gang member who had defaced their gang-related graffiti. Both defendants appealed the decision. In 1994, the Fourth Appellate District Court of Appeal of California confronted the issue of the rap lyrics' use in prosecution. The defense argued that the lyrics' prejudicial effect substantially outweighed their probative value. However, the appellate court upheld the initial inclusion of the lyrics, found in Mora's home after the killing.[9]

The lyrics, offered as evidence only against Mora, a part-time disc jockey, included, "I keep riming do it by my self I don't need your friendship or your help just give me the mic and Ill rock your world with my visius voice Ill take control of your body and soul. When I walk out my door I have to pack my forty four. R.I.P. there a bunch of punks they will get beat were the South Side Trooper were number 1."[10] The defense contended that these lyrics as well as additional lyric excerpts admitted at trial contained general threats of violence and were thus inflammatory. Despite this possible prejudice, however, they were allowed as evidence to demonstrate the defendant's gang affiliation as well as his knowledge of "gang culture." The appellate court confirmed that decision:

> This was a crime alleged to be gang related. Gang membership was obviously important, and evidence tending to show it was highly relevant . . . The mere fact the lyrics might be interpreted as reflective of a generally violent attitude could not be said "substantially" to outweigh their considerable probative value. It looks to us like the trial court got it right; certainly it has not been shown there was any abuse of discretion.[11]

As precedence, the court cited a case involving defendant-authored newsletters. In this earlier case, the defendants were charged with murdering a police officer and had used newsletters to express their hatred of law enforcement and to encourage violence against the police. The Nebraska Supreme Court held the articles as admissible to "establish the defendants' intent, malice and motive." In Mora's case, the court accepted the lyrics, arguing that they similarly exposed the defendant's opinions concerning gang members and rival gangs.[12]

Olguin, however, also objected to the admission of Mora's rap lyrics, insisting that the lyrics reflected negatively on his character through association and were thus inadmissible character evidence. However, the prosecution had specifically instructed the jury to consider the lyrics only in their discussion of Mora. And thus the appellate court disagreed with the defense's argument on appeal: "There is little risk the jury would find [the rap lyrics] so authoritative as to overwhelm their ability to follow the instruction to consider them only against Mora."[13] In the end, the court affirmed the judgments against the defendants as well as the admission of the rap lyrics.

Following this case, more and more rappers—amateurs as well as burgeoning professionals—have found their work used against them in court. In these cases, the prosecution offers rap music as a written text, reading the lyrics to the jury in even tones or submitting the texts to the jury as paper documents. According to Dennis, judges and jurors thus "apply a basic method of interpreting language: literal interpretation."[14] The Department of Justice has officially sanctioned such a course of action. For example, in the department-sponsored training manual, *Prosecuting Gang Cases: What Local Prosecutors Need to Know* (2004), the authors offer prosecutors tactics that might help the jury see past the defendant's genteel attire at court, arguably a disguise that conceals her or more likely his true character. Rather than the man wearing a suit present in the courtroom, the pamphlet insists, "the real defendant is a criminal wearing a do-rag and throwing a gang sign. Gang evidence can take prosecutors a long way toward introducing that jury to that person. Through photographs, letters, notes, and even music lyrics, prosecutors can invade and exploit the defendant's true personality."[15] Prosecutors in this way use lyrics as evidence of biography and thereby identity. However, while courts admit rap lyrics as confession, intent, or knowledge in respect to the crime, they also consciously or unconsciously use rap lyrics exactly as Olguin and Mora had feared—as a means of general character assassination by linking defendants with a perceived culture of violence. That is, the courts admit rap lyrics with a variety of direct and indirect connections to the crimes at hand.

For example, in *Greene v. Commonwealth* (2006), the court charged Dennis Greene with the murder of his wife, who died after he slit her throat. At trial, the court admitted as evidence a rap video made by the defendant after the crime but before arrest: "My name is Dennis Greene and I ain't got no F—ing wife. I knew I was gonna be givin' it to her . . . when I got home . . . I cut her mother f—in' neck with a sword."[16] Here, the court allowed Greene's lyrics as a confession given the direct connection between the lyric content and the crime. However, in another case, the link between the crime and the rap lyrics, mentioned only by a third party, was less concrete, with no direct description of the specific criminal robbery. In this case, prosecutor Cheri Pham attempted to implicate Joshua Adam Moore, who was charged with two counts of armed robbery in 1999, by interrogating his friend, rapper Gary Johnson (G-Bone):

PHAM: Are you into rap music?
JOHNSON: Yes I am.

PHAM: Do you know if the defendant is into rap music?
JOHNSON: Yes, he is.
PHAM: Has the defendant ever written any lyrics to rap music?
JOHNSON: Yes, he has.
PHAM: Do those lyrics include using guns, robbing people, etc.?
JOHNSON: Uh-huh, yes.
PHAM: I have nothing further.[17]

This sort of testimony, more akin to character evidence, was similar to the prosecution's strategy in Snoop Dogg's case. In both examples, the courts used a more general link between crime and lyrics to reflect negatively on the defendant's identity.

In *State v. Miller* (2002), the prosecution again employed this more casual threshold of probative evidentiary value. In the death of Steve Thomas outside of Club Platinum in Harvey, Louisiana, the prosecution employed rap lyrics as well as the defendant's persona as a rapper to ensure a murder conviction. The prosecuting attorney, Douglas W. Freese, often referred to Miller, the brother of Master P and a successful rapper with several albums, by his professional name, C-Murder, and read aloud inflammatory lyrics depicting general violence.[18] Though no hard evidence was offered that Miller shot Thomas, an avid fan of C-Murder's music, Miller was convicted of second-degree murder, a verdict that was upheld on appeal despite Miller's professional name change from C-Murder to C Miller.[19] This name change reveals Miller's understanding of the role his professional persona played in his conviction.

In *People v. Richardson* (2004), the Court of Appeal of California addressed this type of rap use in prosecution—specifically, the submission of lyrics with no direct description of the crime at hand. The prosecution offered rap lyrics by one of the defendants, Jason Jermell Jake, accused of involvement in an attempted murder, to show "plan, intent, motive."[20] But Jake's counsel argued that the lyrics constituted inadmissible "character evidence, plain and simple." At the earlier trial, the court, referencing a conversation in chambers, conceded that "there is some truth to the argument that the defense is arguing, that it's nothing more than just a rap song, it's not directed at a particular group of people, and that this is the nature of rap songs and it certainly is the nature of rap music."[21] Nonetheless, the lyrics were admitted. On appeal, though recognizing some error in the use of the rap lyrics to imply a defendant's "bad" character, the court did not conclude that the error was prejudicial.[22]

Defense attorneys frequently object to the treatment of lyrics in these ways based on several grounds: relevance, unfair prejudice, and First Amendment protection. However, these objections rarely prove successful.[23] On appeal, filed on October 17, 2007, the defendant in *United States v. Stuckey,* Thelmon F. Stuckey, objected to the introduction of his handwritten rap lyrics in his conviction for the murder of a police officer and an informant. His counsel argued that his lyrics, which referred to killing "snitches," were irrelevant and that their admission was more prejudicial than probative. However, the appellate court did not reverse the initial decision to admit the lyrics: "You can certainly not say when somebody writes about killing snitches that it doesn't make the fact that they may have killed a snitch more probable."[24] Given this probative value, the appellate court dismissed the issue of prejudice: "Rap is no longer an underground phenomenon and is a mainstream music genre. Reasonable jurors would be unlikely to reason that a rapper is violent simply because he raps about violence."[25] However, even when courts do admit some error in accepting lyrics with flimsy ties to the crimes, such as in the Richardson case, courts rarely reverse initial verdicts, citing any repercussions as minimal or inconsequential and thus sidestepping the issue of music, as in *People v. Kelly.*

Yet others have argued that the repercussions of lyrics as evidence are far from harmless. Indeed, even in cases with strong links between the lyrical content and the crime, the perception of the rap genre itself may have the greater negative impact on the jury, unfairly casting the defendant in a generally violent light. In *State v. Rollings* (1992), the court admitted lyrics to implicate the defendants, charged with murder. The defense called the psychologist Stuart Fischoff, who argued that based on "Implicit Personality Theory," which recognizes the basis of judgment in inference, a jury would be more likely to offer a guilty verdict after hearing rap lyrics based on "the negative personality trait associations conjured up by the inflammatory lyrics" rather than lyric content that linked the defendant to the crime.[26] In 1999, Fischoff published the findings of a study that tested the basis of his theory. According to his study of people responding to a fictitious man on trial for murder, a rapper not on trial, a nonrapper not on trial, and a male rapper on trial for murder, he concluded, "The target male rap lyricist received more negative evaluations than did the target male nonlyricist on all trait dimensions." In addition, he concluded, "Clearly, participants were more put off by the rap lyrics than by the murder charges."[27] Along these lines, Cynthia Moore, the mother of Joshua Adam Moore, may have been right when she remarked after her son's conviction, "My son is in jail because . . . he listened to rap music . . . That's what put him in prison for 12 years."[28]

This weighty issue of prejudice, however, in some ways obscures the fundamental wrong in the admission of rap lyrics as evidence against their authors. Responding to the lyrics as texts akin to newsletters ignores the traditions and contexts of gangsta rap. As Dennis recognizes, the courts "treat rap music lyrics not as art but as ordinary speech and allow jurors to do the same."[29] In so doing, the courts ignore various facets of rap in performance (authenticity, commerce, boasting, and voice) that undermine and invalidate the idea and use of rap as confessional. This misguided application of rap as speech or text alone rather than music further exposes a general valuation of rap as nonart.

To prove these claims, let us begin with the role of authenticity in rap. Various authenticities are central to popular music in general. Authenticity, for example, has been fundamental to the genre of country music, which relies on accessible performers and "constructed rural settings" as well as live performance.[30] In rap, authenticity is similarly significant, though dependent on different concerns: honesty and sincerity in self-representation, local alliances and identity, and connections to established and accepted rappers.[31] Despite the significance of authenticity defined accordingly, rap lyrics are hardly authentic or honest confessions. In general, as an evaluative term, authenticity is "ascribed, not inscribed" as a "fabrication" and "invention."[32] In other words, authenticity is a fluid ideal, constructed within an ever-shifting social context.[33] "Keeping it real" in rap is thus far from simple.[34]

Graphically violent lyrics, packaged as authentic, also are a response to commercial demands. A 2004 study revealed that increasing sales of rap music, especially among white middle-class consumers, corresponded to increasingly violent lyrics.[35] The violent content of gangsta rap, therefore, does not necessarily relate directly to the composer's authentic experience but is often a collaborative response to commercial concerns that involves a producer or label. In this vein, the sociologist Edward Armstrong, discussing the violence of rapper Eminem's lyrics, surmises, "It would seem reasonable that Eminem and Dre, his producer, would design his lyrics to appeal to his projected audience."[36] In other cases, there is direct testimony that record labels recommend and to a certain extent determine the production of violent rap content. During the 1990s, Carmen Ashhurst-Watson, president of Def Jam in 1990, wrote of the label, "Right now gangsta rappers are the big thing. If [a hypothetical rap group] look like the kind of group that has the capacity to do that, then [our label] might suggest they do some gangsta-style songs."[37]

Death Row records took this marketing strategy a step further by capitalizing on the profitable image of the rapper as violent in the production of *Murder Was the Case: The Movie*. Recalling the movie, produced by Suge Knight, Snoop Dogg explained, "I got the feeling that Suge had taken the whole publicity angle one step too far by trying to hook my situation into another opportunity to move some product."[38] Robert J. Brym, a professor of sociology, even wonders if labels and artists stage the crimes on which they capitalize: "One way of maintaining street cred is by staging fake gun battles."[39] Brym believes, in fact, that the 2005 gunfight between the entourages of rappers the Game and 50 Cent may have been staged. With many rounds fired, he finds it suspicious that only one man was shot in the leg. He concludes, "The shootouts are properly seen as low-risk investments by savvy businesspeople."[40] Whether or not Brym is correct, it is clear that, though authenticity is significant to rap, as Clarke argues, "hard-core rap is closely and paradoxically intertwined with capitalism."[41]

The commercially accepted and even commanded brutality in rap, however, is not necessarily interpreted or intended as a simple glorification of gore. Eminem addresses a fan's problematic literal reading of his violent lyrics in the song "Stan": "I say that shit, just clownin' dogg, Come on, how fucked up is you? You got some issues, Stan, I think you need some counseling."[42] Instead, the violence depicted in gangsta rap lyrics often signifies power, courage, or skill, building on raps' use of metaphor, play on words, and braggadocio.[43] Cultural historian Robin D. G. Kelley argues, "Many of the violent lyrics are not intended literally. Rather, they are boasting raps in which the imagery of gang bangin' is used metaphorically to challenge competitors on the mic."[44]

Within an often powerless context, rappers also appropriate negative images of the drug dealer and thug as a source of strength by investing these images with positive values.[45] That is to say, rather than mourning an inferior societal status, some artists celebrate it as outlaws. The fear generated by this outlaw positioning becomes in part power for artists and audiences. That is, some derive power from the fear associated with rap. Graphic lyric content for these individuals is thus positive, even life-affirming. This thinking resembles Tani Graham Shaffer's conclusion in her study of the psychology of rap: "What is deemed to be harmful to one may be helpful to another."[46] In other words, audiences may respond to rap in contradictory ways, and rap can serve multiple ends. As the linguistics professor Michael Newman argues, "Critique can identify interpretations, but it cannot determine what meanings people actually take from texts."[47] An informed listener attends to these potential multiple meanings and uses.[48]

Along these lines, explicit content in gangsta rap represents a reaction to market forces, a response built on rap's tradition of boasting and aggressive masculinity, offering power and even hope to some who may feel or are perceived as powerless. This metadiscourse of power, authenticity, and commerce functions as a larger layer of voice in rap. But the music itself represents another configuration of layering in rap, further confounding the courts' direct correlation between lyric content and the composer's voice.

Rap music is built around the layering of multiple voices or looped tracks.[49] Accordingly, as David Clarke argues in his work on Eminem, rap is akin to philosopher Mikhail Bakhtin's "concept of the polyphonic novel, where each voice in the narrative retains independence from that of the narrator or author."[50] This independence, for Bakhtin, can further retain competition and contradiction, a function of his concept of heteroglossia, or the multiple social voices present in any utterance.[51] The rapper Eminem's music is a special case of such constructed union, given his projection of multiple characters and alter egos, such as Slim Shady, Marshall Mathers, and Eminem—personas that mix in his first three major-label solo albums. These albums also blend short skits involving a host of auxiliary characters based in reality and fiction.[52] Such a cultivation of character, though extended by Eminem, is a characteristic element of rap, an aspect of the tradition of styling.[53] As the music scholar Simon Frith recognizes, this projection of persona involves multiple metaphorical masks: "Rap is part of a shared subculture of dressing up and strutting free, of house calls and designer charms. This is the performance of identity in which the face behind the mask (all those masks) is just another mask."[54] The rapper Daniel Dumile (Metal Face Doom or MF Doom) underscores the role of disguise in rap by literally wearing a mask.[55] Further playing with the contested place of identity in rap, Dumile often has colleagues assume his identity by lip syncing his shows in his Doom costume. Reporting in the *New Yorker,* Ta-Nehisi Coates elaborates, "If Dumile had his way, he would take it further. He jokes that he'd like to dart backstage after a performance, take off the mask, and then wade into the crowd—beer in hand—and applaud his own work."[56]

The musical setting and its performance condition the projection of these multiple voices and identities in rap. In other words, text and music are inextricably bound. Specifically, the music functions as a constitutive determining voice by dictating the text to some extent. In the context of song, Frith argues that composers and artists choose their words based on sound, "their sound in a particular voice," and especially in rap according to rhythmic schemes, rhyme, and syllabic count rather than specific meaning.[57] For example, in the 1980s, music scholar Cheryl Keyes recognized in rap regular rhymed couplets and a two-bar melodic bass line,[58] effectively necessitating "a more condensed way of saying something"[59] in addition to words that rhyme. Artists may alter certain words to facilitate the rhyme pattern. For example, in MC Lyte's "I Am Woman," *pretected* replaces *protected* to match *respected.*[60] Rappers also often favor assonance, juxtaposing words with similar vowel sounds to create a more musical quality.[61] With these methods, words are chosen for reasons beyond dictionary meaning. The words in their musical setting (rendered in performance) further determine the interpretation of this text and therefore meaning. Frith clarifies, "The point is that as speakers we create meaning through stress; music creates stress; therefore music creates meaning."[62] These compositional decisions in rap are often ascribed to the rapper/performer despite the involvement of ghostwriters in production. In this way, the focus in rap, as in popular music in general, is on the performer as a conflation of public persona and composer, despite the production team involved.

The context of performance also plays a significant role in determining the music and text of rap. Of early hip-hop, Greg Dimitriadis writes, "Like many African musics and popular dance music, early hip hop cannot be understood as aural text alone but must be approached and appreciated as multi-tiered event, in particular contexts of consumption and production."[63] This idea of rap as event is apparent in early rap singles (1979–82), such as "Rapper's Delight," which feature "floating" phrases that circulated in New York City parties.[64] The setting of rap's performance thereby marked the recorded product. Similarly West Coast rap, which was played often in cars, incorporated heavy bass, catering to the site of the music's sounding.[65]

With this in mind, the reading of rap lyrics as literal texts or autobiographies denies the nuances of voice in the musical performance of rap. As Frith argues more generally, song is theater, with an implied character and narrative.[66] That is, "the issue in lyrical analysis is not words, but words in performance."[67] The musicologist Carolyn Abbate similarly argues, "The text of music is a performance. Thus music is fundamentally different from the written texts that have for the most part shaped critical theory."[68] In the context of opera, she recognizes "multiple, decentered voices localized in several invisible bodies"—voices dependent on performance.[69]

In making such arguments, both Abbate and Frith attempt to rectify a wrong: the tradition of equating the composer's monological voice with her or more often his work, a convention that endures from the Romantic era with its conception of high art as reflective of the composer's innermost being. The prosecution's use of lyrics as evidence grows from this fallacious tradition, a tradition that can no longer validate such a strategy. Here, I contend, we have a peculiar paradox. While courts deny rap's traditions as a performance art by presenting it as literal text—stripping it of its cultural significance—they in some ways rely on rap as reflective of its composers' actions and thoughts in keeping with Romantic ideas of music as high art. The rap industry invites this treatment through its promotion of rap as authentic, a redeployment in some ways of Romantic thinking within popular music.[70] This treatment of rap in court as well as the promotion of rap's authenticity represents a surprising moment of flux in the legacy of late eighteenth- and nineteenth-century music aesthetics. While Romantic notions expanded beyond classical music in chapter 2, they arguably did so within a process designed in part to exclude and even antagonize rap and those associated with this music. Yet Romantic notions here seem to extend to rap from within the industry as well as in court. Indeed, by interpreting rap as an authentic extension of the composer's identity and ignoring the multiple determining and determined voices involved, courts in this example respond to rap's own ascriptions of authenticity by tapping into the Romantic tradition of equating high art—in this case, rap—with the soul of its maker. This association and the problems of simplistic one-dimensional readings both in the past and in our example cast further doubt on the use of rap lyrics as evidence as well as thinking, past and present, that supports notions of music's ability to penetrate and thus reflect one's soul.

During the Romantic era, this idea of music grew from the elevation of music as the expression of a higher realm and thus autonomous—valuable thinking that lent music a new respectability among the arts.[71] However, in early Romantic aesthetics, this valuation corresponded to a similar elevation of the composer, the music's creator. This simultaneous focus on the composer and disconnected work may seem contradictory: Romantic aesthetics celebrated music as divorced from context while honoring music's point of origin in the composer and thus a degree of context. But, for early Romantic theorists, art could be conceived of as divine if the artist was similarly elevated as deity. With this approach, music and its composer could remain both distinct and interconnected, "separated" yet "bound to one another."[72] This idealization of the composer and his work was a response to the new economic plight of the artist. Such a response was apparent in the cult of the composer surrounding Beethoven. In the writing of E. T. A. Hoffman, Beethoven was pronounced a genius.[73] No longer a servant, Beethoven was embraced by writers as messenger—a messenger, like music, from a spiritual plane. Richard Taruskin ties this early elevation of the composer to Beethoven's deafness, which "turned the composer's biography into a drama of struggle and victory" and "effectively removed him from this world—that is, the world of daily musical business in which composers functioned visibly as performers."[74] This valuation, which Beethoven consciously and unconsciously encouraged, was also evident in early Romantic performance practice—specifically, the dictum that the singer or player perform "as if from the soul of the composer."[75]

This elevation gave way to theories that tied expression in music directly to the spirit of the composer. In his *A History of Western Musical Aesthetics,* Edward Lippman credits the German philosopher Georg Wilhelm Friedrich Hegel (1770–1831) with the impulse to make this connection.[76] Related to the privileging of music in the Romantic era, Hegel in lectures during the 1820s proclaimed music "the art of the soul," a subjective art "directly addressed to the soul."[77] But earlier, in 1771, Johann Georg Sulzer tied expression in music directly to the personality of its composer:

> The extent to which personality affects art is illustrated in the work of two much-admired German composers—Graun and Hasse. Nature endowed Graun with a tender, gentle, complaisant soul; though he may have mastered all the skills of his craft, he was at home only in the gentle, the pleasant, and the charming emotions; and more than once he ran into problems when he had to express boldness, pride, or resolution. Nature endowed Hasse, on the other hand, with loftier courage, bolder emotions, and stronger desires, and he was most at home with the emotions that were consistent with his character rather than with those that were gentle and pleasant.[78]

Likewise, Hoffmann, in his 1813 essay on Beethoven, described Haydn's and Beethoven's music as reflective of the composers' respective personalities. For example, he observed, "In Haydn's writing there prevails the expression of a serene and childlike personality."[79]

Such thinking has continued in the influential work of the music scholar Edward T. Cone. In *The Composer's Voice* (1974), Cone admits various layers of meaning in song: verbal, vocal, and instrumental. However, he traces these voices back to the composer or at least to the persona of the composer.[80] This gives way to the "expression theory," which credits expression in art to the artist's expression of his or her emotions or feelings in art.[81] In 2006, the scholar of philosophy Stephen Davies wrote, "We know that musical composition can be an intensely involving experience revealing of the personality of the composer."[82]

Notions of the authentic have worked similarly in popular music. Popular music has been besieged with various attacks during its history—the most common of which must be the charge that the music is merely entertainment or commercial. In the post–World War II era, writers in the United States revived mass-culture theory to counter Soviet communism and the promised rising "masses." Within a powerful group of New York intellectuals, Dwight Macdonald wrote effectively in the 1950s and 1960s about this threat. He defined mass culture as a fabrication created by "technicians" rather than artists and marketed by businessmen. This "masscult," in his terminology, offered mere distraction with no value beyond the monetary. Rock music, an example of the masscult, was in this way a cultural medium with no set standards and thus no cultural value.[83] But with claims of authenticity, rock music, in the case of influential albums, can overcome such criticism and, ironically, generate a guaranteed "payout."[84] Related to the idea of the Romantic artist as outsider who reflects his truth in art, discourses regarding the great works of rock have focused to this end on "perceived truth" and the connection between that sincerity and the "author/genius." In great rock music, the album is heralded as an authentic extension of the artist. Carys Wyn Jones explains, "Again and again albums are regarded as direct expressions of the artists who made them, cast in the role of the troubled Romantic genius, and perceived truths and honesty of expression become markers of value."[85] This trope is particularly evident in the reception of Bob Dylan, who, with his rough vocals and expressive form and lyric, is regarded as "the ultimate example of the authentic, autonomous singer-songwriter in rock."[86]

Despite the endurance of this evolving notion of expression in art, this thinking contains clear contradictions. As previously discussed, authenticity is an invented means to elevate popular music, both rock and rap. Moreover, authenticity works within the commercial processes it hides.[87] Davies, who admits the possibility of personal revelation in art, also challenges the notion that artists inevitably express themselves in their work: "Composers have not been inhibited in writing sad requiems by their glee at receiving the commission for the work."[88] Similarly, he writes, "It is not common for most composers to work creatively under the duress of emotion. Strong emotions would disrupt and distract them from the concentration and toil involved in composition."[89] A composer may, however, choose to write a piece evocative of emotions that correspond to his or her current mood. However, the resulting piece would not be a direct expression of the composer's emotional state but a mask manipulated to imitate the corresponding emotion.[90] The composer Philip Glass doubts even this constructed correspondence: "When an artist says that he expresses himself, I don't believe it because in order to express oneself consciously one will probably generate a lie, will create a falsehood."[91]

In a practical sense, our analysis of rap as evidence refutes this tradition of equating the composer's music with his or her soul, personality, or emotions. The complications involved in this practice—denial of context, voice, commercial constraints—cannot support the Romantic ideal of the composer's relationship to his music, just as this contested ideal cannot justify the use of rap as evidence. Though each rap has its own set of voices, in way of illustration, let us examine the complexities of a specific example by returning to Snoop Dogg's "Murder Was the Case."

At trial in 1995, Snoop Dogg appeared in "a smart blue suit" in an attempt to play "down his image as a bad boy."[92] For the prosecution, his music could subvert this performance by providing a more "realistic" image of the defendant. Yet "Murder Was the Case" is difficult to take seriously as an honest confession of autobiography. In the song, multiple voices participate: Snoop Dogg, Dat Nigga Daz, female voices, and male voices. The song opens as a conversation between the fictional characters Jaycee and Aron, who are looking for Snoop. When they find him, gunshots ring out over the percussive track that unifies the song. From the ground, so the story goes, Snoop Dogg raps of his predicament in the first verse over a recurring two-bar chromatic ostinato, a motive that marks phrases and downbeats, at times embellished two octaves higher by a kind of electronically mediated whistle and punctuated by a funeral bell. Snoop's voice is generally languid and lithe, with roots in his early experience in the Golgona Trinity Baptist youth choir.[93] Though confronting in his role the possibility of death, after the line, "Dear God, I wonder can ya save me," Snoop raps in a higher-pitched, lighter style: "I can't die, my Boo-Boo's bout to have my baby." With such a nickname and vocal inflection, the effect is comedic, given the incongruity of such a line within a "serious" context. This humorous statement completes the rhymed couplet and through such coupling heightens the mood disparity between the two lines.

As the verse continues, Snoop bargains for his life with an otherworldly voice. If he agrees to the terms, Snoop asks, "Will I be the G that I was?" Again, the tone is light, even humorous. In the chorus, a female choir sings "Murder," letting the pitch slide down on the last beat of the measure as yet another male voice raps, "Murder was the case that they gave me," all layered over the percussive track, ostinato (with embellishment), and funeral bell. (See figure 2 for the juxtaposition of voice and ostinato.) After a repetition of this passage, Snoop awakens in the next verse with all that he desires. Rather than repentant, however, he still wants more. At the close of the second verse, a male chorus intones a portion of the Lord's Prayer, setting the stage for the serious ramifications of Snoop's lavish lifestyle. As punishment, in the last verse, Snoop finds himself in prison.

In this complicated song, Snoop and his production team enact in minutes multiple characters, conversations, and dramatic events, relying on Faustian and even Dickensian scenarios of the relationship between life and death. Furthermore, the tone is often fantastic or humorous. Many rappers include humor in their music, especially the humor of boundary transgression. In fact, Russell Simmons calls much gangsta rap "grown-up comedy."[94] And Ralph M. Rosen and Donald R. Marks single out *Doggystyle* as one of the most prominent examples of the comedic voice in rap: "This recording attempts to sustain a comedic tone throughout by exploring the humorous shock value of obscenity offering lyrics that traduce classic popular songs and explicit parodies of earlier musical styles."[95] Snoop announced this aspect of the album in a graphic accompanying cartoon of various sexualized dogs involved in illegal activity, an explicit comic strip that oversteps the bounds of sex and violence that traditional cartoons observe. Snoop Dogg also later highlights this characteristic of his art in film roles and cameos in comedy films such as *Half Baked, Old School,* and *Starsky and Hutch,* in which he plays the informant Huggy Bear.

From this perspective, Snoop Dogg's "Murder Was the Case" is hardly a sincere reflection of his relationship to criminal activity. By citing Snoop Dogg's lyrics at his trial, the prosecution denied the complexities of voice inherent in rap more generally and specifically in "Murder Was the Case," including a humorous voice, while perpetuating the flawed Romantic thinking that ties music, which always implies a set of contradictory contexts and traditions, directly to the composer's soul. Though this strategy failed in Snoop Dogg's trial—the jury accepted the defense's claim that the rapper acted in self-defense—admission of rap lyrics as evidence has proven successful in other cases. These cases treat rap as both art and nonart, reflecting and contributing to social anxiety about rap. That is to say, by treating rap as text

Figure 2. Excerpt from "Murder Was the Case"

and denying its complexities in performance, the courts treat rap as nonart. But by attaching such significance to rap as a reflection of the composer's identity, the courts in some ways accept rap as art in accordance with evolving Romantic valuations of music as well as the rap industry's promotion of rap's authenticity. In practical terms, by allowing rap as evidence, courts often unfairly prosecute rap artists, implying guilt through disingenuous means—that is, through the treatment of music as text alone.

So how should courts approach rap lyrics, if at all? Dennis, for one, does not argue for the wholesale abandonment of the use of lyrics as evidence. However, she insists, "Courts should interpret the meaning and import of defendant-authored rap music lyrics from the perspective of the defendant and in light of the factors derived from the social constraints and artistic conventions governing the composition of rap music lyrics." To do so, according to Dennis, courts should allow expert testimony about the art form.[96] Without such caution, Dennis worries that the courts will endanger the creativity of rap as art: "I suggest that society must be mindful and wary of the negative impact this effort will have on the production and quality of art when individuals must worry that their artistic sensibilities and creative expressions might later be used against them in a criminal prosecution." Wilson similarly argues that fear of prosecution and the use of rap as evidence of crime may dull rap, affecting the production of the art form and thus implicitly censoring and possibly silencing the music.[97] This notion is in keeping with Martin Cloonan's broad idea of censorship as the result of processes that are not always overtly concerned with restricting material. Rather, censorship can be the by-product of varied acts, including the regulation of sampling in rap, for example.[98]

Legal scholar Helen A. Anderson inadvertently offers another applicable course of action in her discussion of the use of listening habits to implicate consumers in court. In this related tactic, prosecutors offer listening habits as evidence of motive, intent, or state of mind. Such a strategy relies on the idea that culture is connected to identity. While that may be true, the motives for identification with a given musical composition can vary based on personal associations and valuation. Moreover, a person's musical collection can reflect a projected or willed identity. That is, as a symbolic good, music "signals how one perceives oneself and wants to be perceived."[99] To circumvent the complications inherent in reading any relationship between music and its consumer, Anderson suggests a higher threshold of relevance and even some sort of criteria evidence must meet for admittance: "There must be some clear evidence that the defendant viewed, listened to, or read the work for inspiration, encouragement, or as a source of ideas."[100]

This suggestion could also prove worthwhile in the introduction of lyrics as evidence against their composer. For admittance, the courts could require that the lyrics have a direct link to the crime, with proof that the composer authored the work in reaction to or preparation for the crime. In this way, lyrics could still be used in cases with direct application (with implications beyond evidence of supposed identity). To illustrate, in *Jones v. State* (2002), the allowance of lyrics proved appropriate. In 2001, Blake Jones was a fifteen-year-old student with a prior criminal record. Angered by a friend and classmate, Allison Arnold, at school, Jones handed her violent rap lyrics he had written:

> You gonna keep being a bitch, and I'm gonna click
> You better run, bitch, cuz I can't control what I do.
> I'll murder you before you can think twice, cut you up and use you
>   for decoration
> to look nice.
> I've had it up to here, bitch, there's gonna be a 187 on your whole
>   family, trick.
> Then you'll be just like me, with no home, no friends, no money.
> You'll be six feet under, beside your sister, father and mother.

After receiving this text, Arnold contacted the school's principal, who alerted the police. At court, the lyrics were not treated as protected speech based on the "true threat" exception. Arnold's genuine fear as well as the direct communication and suggestion that the text had been directed at Arnold justified the admittance of the lyrics.[101]

This reevaluation of evidentiary relevance could also help those involved avoid charges of racial bias. After all, the use of rap lyrics as evidence could be seen as one more means of targeting rap within the legal community. There are many similarities between the lyric content of gangsta rap and country music, which has, as Armstrong recognizes, "a highly consonant underclass rhetoric of violence."[102] But country music is not used in the some way in court. Why? The social psychologist Carrie B. Fried conducted a study in which certain respondents were given a folk song about the murder of a police officer and others received rap lyrics of the same graphic nature. Rap lyrics were judged more harshly, according to the study, perhaps because of associations with rap and stereotypes of African Americans.[103] Accordingly, the use of rap lyrics as evidence against their authors at court may reveal societal values about rap as well as those associated with the creation of rap. To circumvent such dangerous assessments, the courts must carefully consider the handling of rap lyrics as evidence.

While the future of this practice seems to me unclear, the admittance of rap lyrics as evidence in the present offers a unique test case for enduring, though evolving, Romantic thinking surrounding the role of the composer. Trials with such evidence present rap lyrics as an authentic extension of the composer's identity, a strategy that ignores the multiple determining and determined voices involved. In this way, the courts treat rap as art in theoretical application while negating such treatment and, by extension, the reimagining of Romantic thinking surrounding the role of the composer in the interpretation of rap as one-dimensional text. This use of lyric represents a danger in court, introducing grounds for bias and skewed perceptions of identity that could taint the trials of those involved in rap.

Despite the potential danger, the courts push this connection between music and identity further with charges that music incites violence. In this way, the courts consider how rap might determine identity and even action. This focus shifts attention from those involved in the crime to the music and its composers despite a complete disconnect between the musicians and the crimes. In so doing, the question of music's incitement offers more direct insight into contemporary appraisals of rap than do consideration of lyrics as evidence.

4 ✦ "The Music Made Me Do It"

Obscenity and Incitement in
Legal Valuations of Music

The court's treatment of rap as art and nonart in the use of lyrics as evidence is in keeping with other legal confrontations with the art form as well as past societal valuations of rap. The humanities professor Richard Shusterman summarized early appraisals of rap in "The Fine Art of Rap" (1991), which responds to ideas that rap is not art. Rap employs "neither live musicians nor original music; the sound track is instead composed from various cuts (or 'samples') of records already made and often well known. Finally, the lyrics seem to be crude and simple-minded, the diction substandard, the rhymes raucous, repetitive, and frequently raunchy."[1] To legitimate the art form, Shusterman recast as positive these seemingly negative attributes associated with rap.[2] His case relied on a new idea of art as postmodern—an art that reconciles art and traditional ideas of nonart in a form that is hardly timeless, monumental, or autonomous. For the music scholar Jonathan Kramer, this idea of postmodern art invokes an attitude rather than a distinct time period—an attitude that acknowledges the diversity of music in various contexts of place and time.[3] Such a conception of art, for some, uniquely conforms to practices of rap. As Shusterman explained, postmodern traits in rap include "recycling appropriation rather than unique originative creation, the eclectic mixing of styles, the enthusiastic embracing of new technology and mass culture, the challenging of modernist notions of aesthetic autonomy and artistic purity, and an emphasis on the localized and temporal rather than the putatively universal and eternal."[4]

Shusterman's need to justify or elevate rap clearly reflects the status of rap in the early 1990s. Its inferior position was similarly apparent in 1995, in the music scholar Robert Walser's exploration of society's uncertainty about rap. Like Shusterman, Walser reviewed negative opinions that distinguish rap from art, adding to the earlier list rap's perceived lack of virtuosity and use of technology.[5] In his subsequent elevation of the art form, he argued for examination of the music in conjunction with the lyrics and offered a reading of Public Enemy's "Fight the Power" in musical notation. He explained, "Transcription is particularly useful in this case because coherence and complexity are precisely what have been denied to hip hop, and those are the qualities that notation is best at illuminating."[6] Walser's article is thus similarly a product of the time—a time that witnessed rap's simultaneous rapid rise in mass popularity and increasing controversy in the media. Thus, his "justification" of the music—argument that the music is music—is understandable.

Fifteen years later, much has changed in the reception of rap. The year 2009 witnessed the creation of the first accredited program in hip-hop at McNally Smith College of Music in St. Paul, Minnesota; in 2010, the rapper and music producer Swizz Beatz was named "producer-in-residence" at New York University.[7] This inclusion of rap in academic settings represents an important step in rap's formation of a canon and general acceptance.[8] Therapists have also recently employed rap in work with at-risk youth, including youth ordered into treatment by the courts. Though some practitioners have misgivings about rap, this "rap therapy" or "hip-hop therapy" generally uses discussion of preexisting popular rap songs as a means to establish trust and as a starting point for exploration of a youth's related troubles.[9] Despite this institutionalization of rap, the courts still, with the treatment of rap as text in evidence, reflect and contribute to the same sort of ambivalence about rap as art to which Walser and Shusterman responded. After all, part of rap's devaluation in 1995, according to Walser, was consideration of rap detached from the music—that is, treatment, as we saw in chapter 3, only of rap's lyrics.[10] And this handling of rap in court is not the only instance of the legal realm's current grappling with rap and its standing as art.

In this chapter, I explore an explicit example of legal engagement with the question of whether rap qualifies as art: the prosecution of music as a means of incitement to violence. Specifically, I examine the high-profile civil suit filed by the family of police officer Bill Davidson, who blamed rapper Tupac Shakur for inspiring the officer's murder. In this case, the court reiterated music's First Amendment protection: "First Amendment protection extends to rap music." The court thus confronted the definition of music as it applies to rap. But the court's apprehension about rap and its status as music, evident in the preceding chapter, was most apparent in its focus on the possibility of rap's incitement to violence. There was no question about who physically killed Davidson; nor was there interest in the tangible perpetrator, as in the previous example. The case instead directly concerned the role of rap in that crime. With this concentration, the court offers overt insight into rap's contemporary reception.

Yet this prosecution, despite the seemingly clear commitment to evaluating rap, clouded the issue and the possibility of such revelation about rap's status by entangling charges of rap's violent instigation with the issue of obscenity. The blending of obscenity and incitement charges further muddles a second musical debate that goes beyond controversies implicated in cases involving the use of rap lyrics as evidence: the contested idea of music's negative potential. Indeed, unlike previous examples, the charge of musical incitement seems an admission that music is not solely positive, that music can even be dangerous. Do the courts here reflect a general understanding of the multiplicity of music, acknowledging its darker potential? If so, how do we reconcile such recognition with the enduring legacy of Romantic aesthetics? The confusion of incitement and obscenity, which implies judgment about art's societal standing, is key to both queries. With the blending of incitement and obscenity, it is my contention that this prosecution ultimately offers evidence of the courts' conflicted attitudes about the possibility of music's negative use while further revealing the law's role in the creation of new hierarchies of music. Indeed, the courts here render a rather definitive negative verdict on the status of rap in our postclassical era and its relationship to new canons and thus conceptions of music's supposed elevation.

On April 11, 1992, eighteen-year-old Rodney Ray Howard sped south of Houston in a stolen truck while listening to a cassette tape of Tupac Shakur's *2Pacalypse Now*. He eventually pulled to the side of the road in response to state trooper Bill Davidson, who pursued Howard for a missing headlight. When Davidson approached, Howard shot and killed the officer. At his trial, Howard's attorney, Allen Tanner, blamed the music for inciting Howard's violent reaction as a way of arguing for the defendant's diminished capacity. He thus made a case for leniency in punishment. To this end, Tanner played for the jury the music of Shakur as well as other examples of arguably provocative rap music, including excerpts by the Geto Boys, Ice Cube, and Ganksta N-I-P, among others. Howard himself testified that Shakur's music inspired in him "a fight-back attitude."[11] But the jury still convicted Howard and recommended the sentence of death.

In 1992, Davidson's family filed a civil suit, which requires a lower threshold of proof than criminal prosecution.[12] Exploiting Howard's argument at trial, the case charged Shakur, Interscope Records, and its parent company, Time-Warner, with liability in Davidson's death. The Davidsons did not know to which song Howard was listening at the moment he shot the officer with a 9 mm Glock handgun, but one song, "Crooked Ass Nigga," was cited in the court transcript as especially relevant:

> Now I could be a crooked nigga too
> When I'm rollin with my crew
> Watch what crooked niggas do
> I got a nine millimeter Glock pistol
> I'm ready to get with you at the trip of the whistle
> So make our move and act like you wanna flip
> I fired 13 shots and popped another clip
> My brain locks, my Glock's like a f—kin mop
> The more I shot, the more mothaf—ka's dropped
> And even cops got shot when they rolled up.[13]

Offering no disagreement about the facts of the case, the defense moved for summary judgment, hoping to win the suit based on law alone. The judge would have to respond to the plaintiff's main arguments: that Shakur's album "tends to incite imminent illegal conduct on the part of individuals like Howard" and thus that the defendants are "liable for producing violent music that proximately caused the death of Officer Davidson."[14]

The judge, John D. Rainey, did not argue that *2Pacalypse Now* is harmless and in fact cited it as "tasteless, violent music" that "entreats others to act on Shakur's violent message."[15] However, the judge insisted that the probability that a listener would act on this message was not so great as to deny it First Amendment protection. Indeed, the judge noted, Howard was a rap fan and had listened to rap, including the music of Shakur, without previously acting out violently. According to this logic, the album did not qualify as a potential cause of imminent violence under the court's *Brandenburg* incitement standard—a standard designed with speech in mind, not music. Responding to a Ku Klux Klan gathering and a Klansman's suggestion there that the group take lawless action against African Americans, the U.S. Supreme Court in *Brandenburg v. Ohio* (1969) disqualified from First Amendment protection speech that is "directed to inciting or producing imminent lawless action and is likely to incite or produce such actions."[16]

In this way, the courts can punish speech that meets a three-part test based on violent intent, the imminence of the violent act, and the likelihood of subsequent violence.[17] As the judge ruled, Shakur's music did not meet such a standard. And thus, Rainey ruled in favor of the defendants, insisting that they were not liable "under a negligence theory because they did not have a duty to prevent the distribution of the music when they could not reasonably see that distributing the music would lead to violence."[18]

As this case demonstrates, the *Brandenburg* test proves a difficult threshold for those who target music in cases of incitement at court. And, in fact, two other high-profile suits citing music's power to incite similarly failed. On October 27, 1984, John McCollum, a nineteen-year-old with emotional problems and a history of alcohol abuse, responded to Ozzy Osbourne's album *Speaking of the Devil* by pointing a .22 caliber handgun at his head and pulling the trigger. The subsequent lawsuit blamed the macabre persona of Osbourne and the intimacy of his lyrics for McCollum's death. In the song "Suicide Solution," the suit claimed, the lyrics—"Make your bed, rest your head / But you lie there and moan / Where to hide, suicide is the only way out"—spoke directly to the decedent in part through the use of first person. Despite the song's actual denunciation of alcoholism, depicted as a means of suicide, the prosecution contended that this intimacy made suicide a likely listener response. The case also included the charge of masked, subliminal messages that encouraged McCollum to act. In December 1986, the judge ruled against the plaintiffs, citing the First Amendment. On appeal, the court confirmed in July 1988 "that, under the First Amendment, Osbourne would have had to engage in an immediate incitement to violence to lose his free speech right."[19]

Likewise, in the summer of 1990, the courts considered the heavy metal artist Judas Priest's legal liability in a case of suicide. Two youths in Reno, eighteen-year-old Raymond Belknap and twenty-year-old James Vance, listened to Priest's album *Stained Class* on December 23, 1985, and subsequently each attempted suicide with a shotgun. Belknap was successful, and Vance died shortly after the incident from complications related to the blast. The album contained such songs as "Beyond the Realms of Death" and "Heroes End."[20] The prosecution again blamed subliminal messages in the music for the violent act as well as the character of the music itself: According to the case, "the suggestive lyrics combined with the continuous beat and rhythmic non changing intonation of the music combined to induce, encourage, aid, abet, and otherwise mesmerize [the deceased] into believing the answer to life was death."[21]

With this focus on the music's potential to "mesmerize," the prosecution invoked music's connection to trance, defined as "a state of mind characterized by intense focus, the loss of the strong sense of self and access to types of knowledge and experience that are inaccessible in non-trance states."[22] Partly credited to the rhythmic element of music, such trances enmesh one in the music, or, in neurological terms, "one is held within the relative constancy of the continual activation of a particular complex or neuronal groupings."[23] This complex power could have been further explored in court and might even have offered the prosecution a significant means of support. However, the court did not address this potential in music or general line of argument. And again, the judge ruled in favor of the defense.[24]

While it is difficult to prove that music meets the *Brandenburg* criteria, in some ways any utterance could be argued to be incitement. In 1925, Justice Oliver Wendell Holmes wrote in *Gitlow v. New York* that "every idea is an incitement. It offers itself for belief, and if believed, it is acted on unless some other belief outweighs it, or some failure of energy stifles the movement at birth."[25] At a legal symposium addressing "Potential Liability Arising from the Dissemination of Violent Music," the lawyer and law professor Rod Smolla similarly explained, "You put out a television show, you write this book, you put out this hip-hop CD, and there is some residual risk that somebody might respond to it in some crazy way and engage in some terrible act."[26] Within this symposium, a frank discussion among colleagues, Smolla thus admitted the impossibility of such cases that charge musicians with liability. There, panelist Zazi Pope further cited the unpredictability of violent inspirations: for example, the Branch Davidians recognized the Book of Revelations as inspiration, while Charles Manson looked to the Beatles.

And of course, works with violent connotations do not necessarily incite violence. In *McCollum v. CBS Inc.* (1988), the court recognized this line of thinking, first argued by the defense, identifying suicide as a common theme in great literature and music—works that do not inevitably result in violence: Hamlet's "To Be or Not to Be" soliloquy as well as works by Puccini, Menotti, Massenet, and Verdi.[27] The same is true of works that glorify violence against police. In response to Dennis R. Martin's *The Music of Murder*, which cites Ice-T's "Cop Killer" as "an affront" to officers killed in the line of duty, Mark S. Hamm and Jeff Ferrell enumerate less controversial songs that arguably advocate or at least glorify similar action without response, such as fiddler Tommy Jarrell's "Policeman" and Bob Marley's "I Shot the Sheriff."[28] Based on this logic, a reaction to music or any artistic medium is dependent on the individual rather than the specific artwork in question. Indeed, academics have not proven that art alone can incite violence. Researchers Peter Christenson and Donald Roberts explain, "It is not so much a case of 'you are what you hear' as 'you hear what you are.'"[29] Individuals do not fall under the sway of music that extols a message contrary to their belief systems and in fact to some extent create the meaning of the music to which they do listen. That is, listeners either reject a piece of music based on its message or "create their own definition of the song's meaning."[30] Listeners therefore have agency in their negotiation of identity through music and the construction of music's message.

In a legal counterargument, the attorney Peter Alan Block further negates the possibility of immediate action in conjunction with music and literature based on the idea that if a subject were held by the power of art, the voice of the author or performer then "controls the time, place, and manner of presentation."[31] According to this logic, under the influence of an artistic work, a reader or listener would be unable to act instantaneously. But such thinking, according to the legal scholar David R. Dow, negates free will. According to Dow, this is the clear error in cases arguing that music incites violence. To him, words cannot "overcome human will."[32] Words, he further claims, are never dangerous enough to warrant punishment and cannot undermine democracy: "There has never in the history of the modern state been a democracy that collapsed due to the presence of too much speech."[33] Thus, words must be separated from action in legislation and should not be punished as such.[34] Dow offers an example, however, of one possible exception: "Suppose that Shakur kidnapped Ronald Howard, hypnotized him, and during the hypnosis implanted the instruction that Howard do exactly what Shakur commanded. Under such a scenario, Howard would be permitted to argue that the rap lyrics he was listening to constituted a command from Shakur that Howard was incapable of ignoring. . . . Under this scenario, Howard is just a robot, an extension of Shakur; Shakur is the actor."[35] Here Dow relies on the absurdity of this scenario to strengthen his case against this prosecution of musicians.

More useful for our purposes, however, the musicologist Judith Becker offers testimony that music, even in Dow's ridiculous example, is not deterministic and has no inherent ability to ensure action. In her discussion of trance, she argues, "One can go into trance without music; one can listen to music and not go into trance."[36] After all, trance is partly a skill, and to enter such a state requires practice. There is no one-to-one relationship between music and mesmerization. Though music may arouse, music cannot inspire with this arousal a single inevitable response.[37]

Despite these arguments that undermine cases of musical incitement, the legal community seems to assume the possibility of music's negative use in past and present prosecution. In such cases, no scholar or judge negated the charge that music could incite violence based on Romantic notions that music is wholly positive. In fact, the appellate court judge in the Shakur case readily admitted that the music is potentially destructive. The fact that such cases are allowed at all, put to the test by the *Brandenburg* standard, seems to reveal further legal recognition that music can act toward good and bad— music is dialectic. In this way, the legal community implicitly supports early Greek understandings of music, most notably recorded in the work of Aristotle and his teacher, Plato.

In a Senate subcommittee, Virginia senator Paul Tribe stated that "more than 2,300 years ago Plato recognized that music is a powerful force in our lives that forms character and therefore plays an important part in determining social and political issues. In Plato's words, 'When modes [or styles, types] of music change, the fundamental laws of the state change with them.'"[38] Indeed, Plato promoted in his *Republic* education in music as essential given music's powerful hold on the "inmost soul," a hold that imparts "grace, if one is rightly trained, and otherwise the contrary."[39] A fundamental determining factor to this end was the modes (defined here broadly as ways of organizing music theoretically). Each was thought to imitate a different temperament, which, based on the doctrine of imitation, would elicit that temperament within the listener or performing musician. Accordingly, music was the image of character and as such was the vehicle of ethos (character or disposition), with the power to influence behavior or deportment.[40] Aristotle held a similar belief. In *Politics,* he wrote, "Rhythm and melody supply imitations of anger and gentleness, and also of courage and temperance, and of all the qualities contrary to these. . . . [I]n listening to such strains our souls undergo a change."[41]

The modes, according to both Plato and Aristotle, were decisive in this respect, and both writers cited constructive and destructive modes in their writing. For Plato, the Dorian and Phrygian modes were proper, given their imitation of bravery and temperance, respectively.[42] However, Aristotle disagreed with these ascriptions, especially Plato's positive characterization of the Phrygian.[43] Aristotle further complicated the matter by admitting that each mode affects each listener differently.[44] He also labeled different modes as proper based on context: "In education the most ethical modes are to be preferred, but in listening to the performances of others we may admit the modes of action and passion also."[45]

Both men, however, recognized the danger of the *aulos,* an early wood-wind instrument, and favored the string instruments associated with the cult of Apollo, the lyre and kithara.[46] This position was a reflection of common gendered associations with the aulos as the instrument of the cult of Diony-sus and thus ecstasy and unreason as well as the "aulos girls," the lowest class of musical performers in ancient Greece.[47]

Despite the complications involved in these specific constructs of the positive and negative in music, the ancient Greeks clearly accepted music as a powerful force of good and bad. Greek literature corroborates: "Amph-ion's music brought down the walls of Thebes. Antigenidas, a flute player, was performing martial melodies at an important banquet when Alexander the Great flew into such a rapture that he jumped from his table, grabbed his weapon, and almost bludgeoned the guests."[48] This thinking influenced subsequent philosophers. In ancient Rome, which relied on many of the musical philosophies and theories of ancient Greece, Quintilian offered the practicing orator a fictitious case concerning a flute player who had been held legally responsible for the death of a priest. The musician had played a melody in the Phrygian mode that prompted the priest to descend into madness and throw himself over a cliff.[49]

Early and enduring thoughts about music in writings connected to the world's major religions similarly recognize the destructive potential of music given its dual nature. As Maria Korpe, Ole Reitov, and Martin Cloonan observe, "A common idea that pervades Jewish, Christian, and Muslim writings on the topic is that music causes sensual feelings of pleasure and that such feelings lead unerringly to debauchery and thoughtlessness."[50] In much of this writing, music intended to promote worship, especially sacred song, is positive, while music in secular settings, especially instrumental music, is characterized as dangerous. Rabbinical scholars credit the ban on instruments in the synagogue to the mourning surrounding the destruction of the Second Temple in 70 C.E. However, given the history of negative attitudes toward instrumental music within the world's religions, Korpe, Reitov, and Cloonan wonder if this explanation of the ban is a bit disingenuous: "But can we perhaps imagine that this prohibition was simply a convenient means of eliminating what may have been the sensual consequences of instrument playing in the temple."[51]

Such sacred distrust of music can be traced to later religious movements in the United States. In the 1600s, the Puritan settlers in the American colonies did not allow instrumental music in worship and were generally apprehensive about music, forbidding the playing of most instruments by women, except the drum, trumpet, and "jew's harp." In the nineteenth century, writers in the southern United States similarly connected the fiddle to the devil.[52] With the advent of jazz in New Orleans, however, fears of music in the United States became important within the secular realm, coalescing around the notion that music could threaten racial purity and unleash the passions, thereby making whites as "uninhibited as blacks were said to be." Such criticism extended to ragtime, which was opposed as sexually provocative and crude. But jazz further inspired condemnation based on its perceived threat to the social order. With its "fugitive sounds"—blue notes of inexact pitch, for example—jazz defied musical conventions. Critics of jazz linked this defiance with breakdown on a larger level, the encouragement of unruly behavior, and the loss of social regulation.[53] In the 1950s, many adults in the United States similarly reacted to rock music, which they feared could inflame the libido—a fear aggravated, for racist whites, by the music's relationship to the blues heritage and thus African Americans.[54]

Though the nineteenth century generally avoided such negative formulations of classical music in the secular realm, in 1928 the English composer Cyril Scott offered "a vindication of Plato" by recognizing music as a force with both constructive and deconstructive potential: "We propose, in fact, to show that each specific type of music has exercised a pronounced effect on history, on morals and on culture; that music—however horrifying this statement may appear to the orthodox—is a more potent force in the moulding of character than religious creeds, precepts or moral philosophies."[55] In one representative example, he argued that Handel's music inspired "awe and reverence" but also indirectly "some of the less agreeable characteristics of the Victorian age," including prudishness and even "priggishness."[56]

In this way, thinkers in both secular and sacred contexts have accepted constructive and destructive musical ramifications. The history of this thought gives firm foundation to U.S. cases that charge music with incitement. Yet the issue of obscenity, I maintain, complicates any reading of seeming overlap between treatments of music's oppositional potential historically and cases of musical incitement.

The charge of obscenity often finds its way into legal discussions of incitement despite the latter's very different implications. But in the end, both charges have similar goals. The legal scholar Tracy Reilly recognizes charges of obscenity and incitement as ways to legally prosecute what she views as "music gone extreme," death metal and gangsta rap.[57] Given the common purpose, courts often confuse cases of musical incitement, which similarly involve these genres (the two most disliked musics in 1993) with charges of obscenity. In the *Davidson* case, the prosecution argued that the defendants produced music legally constitutive of "obscenity," which thus did not warrant First Amendment protection. The court transcript continued, "Because the recording lacks constitutional protection," the Davidsons maintain that the defendants were responsible for Officer Davidson's murder. In so doing, the prosecution muddied the issue of incitement with obscenity in the hopes of breaking down First Amendment protection of Shakur's music and increasing the probability of a favorable ruling. But such conflation of incitement and obscenity charges entails judgment about the standing of Shakur's music. That is, by allowing such a line of attack, the courts suggested that only obscene music, or nonart, could be destructive. With this insinuation, the courts negated the idea that music has negative potential, an idea inherent in incitement charges, by granting only music deemed nonart this power. This contradiction destabilizes charges of incitement while subverting general acceptance of the notion that music can be dangerous.

The problematic standard of obscenity within legal thinking invites such negation. The law deems speech obscene based on the 1973 *Miller* decision, which requires speech to meet three criteria to lose First Amendment protection. This test asks "whether the average person, applying contemporary community standards would find that the work, taken as a whole, appeals to the prurient interest," "whether the work depicts in a patently offensive way sexual conduct, specifically defined by applicable state law," and "whether the work, taken as a whole, lacks serious literary, artistic, political, or scientific value."[58] Accordingly, the test as a whole explicitly evaluates art based on the accepted incompatibility of art and "negative" conduct or interest. This legal ruling is unique in its attempt to engage with art, a presumed subjective arena beyond the law.[59] Its genesis further sets it apart from traditional legislation.

In 1967, the Supreme Court justices had all but given up their attempt to define obscenity. In *Redrup v. New York,* they held that obscenity was to be determined by a vote. Based on a majority count, the Supreme Court could reverse a lower court decision regarding obscenity without an opinion or oral explanation.[60] Under *Redrup,* the justices therefore spent countless hours reviewing material offered as obscene, which could hardly be argued an efficient use of time. Justice William Brennan is quoted as saying, "I'm sick and tired of seeing this goddamn shit."[61] But this approach to obscenity was consistent with earlier standards.

In *Jacobellis v. Ohio* (1964), Justice Potter Stewart avoided defining obscenity, acknowledging the subjective nature of such a venture. He wrote instead, "But I know it when I see it."[62] Justice William O. Douglas argued in a 1969 case (*Stanley v. Georgia*) that any definition of obscenity was simply unconstitutional: "If the First Amendment means anything, it means that a state has no business telling a man, sitting alone in his own house, what books he may read or what films he must watch."[63] Yet without a standard of obscenity, the Supreme Court was bombarded with cases alleging obscenity, and thus year after year, justices and clerks were forced to view together in one of the larger conference rooms of a basement storeroom feature films that were exhibits in obscenity trials. The case of *Miller v. California* (1971) finally forced a move toward definition.

On May 19, 1971, Chief Justice Warren Burger circulated a memo setting out definitions of obscenity. He reasoned, "In the long run this Court cannot act as an efficient Super Censor, and the sooner we leave the problem to the states the better off we and the public will be."[64] In the memo, Burger attempted to redefine the idea of "redeeming social value." In a 1957 case, *Roth v. United States,* Brennan had endeavored to protect serious literature, such as James Joyce's *Ulysses* and William Faulkner's *Sanctuary,* from obscenity prosecution by defining material as obscene if, to "the average person, applying contemporary community standards, the dominant theme of the material taken as a whole appeals to the prurient interest."[65] As artistic work continued to appear in court, Brennan attempted to clarify this formulation in a 1966 opinion, explaining that the material should be "utterly without redeeming social value."[66] In this way, Burger, in his memo, refined this criterion, protecting from obscenity prosecution works with "literary, artistic, political, or social value."[67] This memo gave way to the *Miller* standard.

But at the time there were skeptics. Justice Brennan wondered if the standard was actually more hurtful than helpful since it was highly subjective and vague.[68] Current scholars are similarly skeptical. Law professor Kathleen M. Sullivan has recently argued that the *Miller* terms are incoherent. For example, the *Miller* test requires an audience to be both offended by an obscene work and simultaneously "turned on" by it.[69] Of the latter criterion regarding artistic value, she writes, "In an age where university literature departments teach 'trash-lit' courses and where Madonna is a heading subject for doctoral dissertations, surely the serious/non-serious boundary in art is at risk."[70] In *Pope v. Illinois* (1987), Justice Antonin Scalia addressed this problem when he reasoned that "just as there is no use arguing about taste, there is no use litigating about it."[71] The consideration of "artistic merit" is especially contested, according to legal scholar Anne Clark, in regard to music: "Music leaves more room for interpretation than photographs in the average pornographic magazine. Furthermore, due to the distractions of the music and beat, many people may not even be aware of the message of the lyrics. There is also the question of how to treat the music accompanying the lyrics."[72]

In the seminal obscenity case concerning the rap group 2 Live Crew, the courts confronted these concerns in practice. On March 9, 1990, Judge Mell Grossman ruled in favor of Florida sheriff Nick Navarro, who opposed as obscene the 2 Live Crew album *As Nasty as They Wanna Be* based on a statement in the *Miami Herald* held as reflective of community standards. The paper wrote on February 28, 1990, "Many of 2 Live Crew's lyrics are so filled with hard-core sexual, sadistic, and masochistic material that they could not be printed here, even in censored form."[73] 2 Live Crew and its distributor fought back by filing suit against the sheriff. The trial began on May 14, 1990. The lawyer John Jolly defended the initial obscenity ruling by attacking the artistic merit of 2 Live Crew's music. He played the album *As Nasty as They Wanna Be* in its entirety and pointed out its use of sampling while characterizing the music as simply a conglomeration of drumbeats, obscene words, and previously popularized music by composers such as Jimi Hendrix and Van Halen. When Jolly questioned band member David Hobbs, the attorney even asked about permission—did the group have the right to exercise such musical borrowing?

This attack furthered the case for obscenity by introducing the notion that the album's subject matter was not redeemed by its social or artistic value: The album was not art. Providing a foundation for Jolly's strategy, this line of thinking draws on legal confrontation with rap in copyright litigation. Indeed, many copyright cases have brought the issue of rap—specifically rap's dependence on borrowing—to the forefront of courts' considerations of artistic boundaries. The results have been less than ideal. Rap historically relies on sampling and borrowing as well as related affronts to property law—bootlegs, demo tapes, and mix tapes. The legal scholar Andre L. Smith therefore rightly recognizes rap's "inherent clashes with property law."[74] Rap artists may choose to pay a fee to the sound recording owner for use of a sample track or other borrowed material. They may also re-create or modify a small enough portion of the "original" work to evade legal infraction based on the nebulous justification of "fair use." But for the professor of law Olufunmilayo B. Arewa, this system is unacceptable: "Current copyright doctrine does not adequately reflect the reality of musical borrowing."[75] In his recent book *Parodies of Ownership,* Richard L. Schur further argues that the courts' legal regulation of rap is unjust. He contends that copyright legislation ignores the artistic merit of borrowing and unfairly sanctions African American culture systems dependent on borrowing or sampling, such as rap, "without any apparent knowledge of its operation."[76] In so doing, the courts deny the legitimacy of rap as art and consciously or unconsciously privilege a Romantic ideal associated with artistic creativity—that of the autonomous Romantic artist and original art object, which endure today in the reception of popular music.[77]

This correspondence between property law and Romantic thought is no coincidence: Conceptions of copyright evolved alongside Romantic thinking about individual originality. The idea that an artist could possess ownership of an artistic creation was not discussed until the late eighteenth and nineteenth centuries in Italy and Germany. Though England and France had adopted viable copyright protection in the early and latter parts of the eighteenth century, respectively, Germany did not regulate copyright with official strictures until Prussia's 1837 statute.[78] This move again relates to the necessary elevation of music and the composer. However, its endurance today generally ignores traditions of borrowing in the accepted repertoire of classical music before the Romantic period as well as during and after it.

Composers during the Middle Ages and Renaissance depended on the use of existing material, but this use did not diminish their accomplishments. Musicologists Suzannah Clark and Elizabeth Eva Leach characterize Guillaume de Machaut's and Philippe de Vitry's "use of citation" as borrowing "at an artistic height." This use of existing material was not mere copying but was central to the creative process, especially in the composition of the motet (a genre marked by allusion and intertextuality).[79] Borrowing endured in the Baroque period: J. S. Bach alone borrowed from Vivaldi, Corelli, Albinoni, Benedetto Marcello, Torelli, Telemann, Rosenmüller, Buxtehude, as well as J. C. Bach, among others.[80] And again, there was creativity in such reworkings. In *Der volkommene Capellmeister* (1739), Johann Mattheson advised, "Borrowing is permissible; but one must return the object borrowed with interest, i.e., one must so construct and develop imitations that they are prettier and better than the pieces from which they are derived."[81] Though the conception of creativity transformed in the nineteenth century, adaptation of existing material continued in variation, in paraphrase, as model, and as programmatic device, among other techniques—so much so that musicologist J. Peter Burkholder argued in 1994 for consideration of the uses of existing music as a field.[82] Lydia Goehr explains, "Though it remained admissible after 1800 to 'recompose' music, that activity was now understood in terms of producing versions or variants of works. It was no longer allowable for someone to complete or recompose an original work of a given composer."[83] Despite this history, Arewa observes, "Although courts and legal commentators sometimes acknowledge the existence of borrowing and collaboration in 'original works,' the full implications of such borrowing and collaboration rarely filter through in the application of copyright doctrine."[84] Andre L. Smith notes the specific victim of this stance as "African-based genres," such as rap and jazz, which similarly has a significant tradition of borrowing.[85]

In the 2 Live Crew case, opposing counsel recognized the prejudice and baggage involved in Jolly's questioning regarding originality and therefore objected. The judge, Gonzales, sustained: "You're saying that something borrowed from something else can't be art and that's not the issue here."[86] Though he did not counter the basic premise, he dismissed the argument as irrelevant. Still, to combat such thinking, Greg Baker, a music critic for the Miami newspaper *New Times,* offered expert testimony about the history of rap and its traditions. He also introduced to the court consideration of the role of humor in explicit rap.[87] And yet, on June 6, 1990, the judge found the album obscene, holding, "It cannot be reasonably argued that the violence, perversion, abuse of women, graphic description of all forms of sexual conduct . . . are comedic art."[88]

In May 1992, the Eleventh Circuit overturned the 1990 decision. First, the court noted that the initial idea of the album's obscenity was based on lyrics alone, once again evaluating rap without consideration of the music. As Anne Clark concludes, this partitioning of rap put the music "on a different artistic plane than more melodic music" and unfairly rejected the "possibility of finding musical value in rhythmic music."[89] The appellate court thus rightly insisted that the *Miller* test should be applied to the work as a whole—music and lyrics. Further noting the unaddressed expert testimony on rap, the appellate court said, "We reject the argument that simply by listening to this musical work, the judge could determine that it had no artistic value."[90] This case therefore failed in part based on the subjectivity of the *Miller* standard. However, the case again exposes a reluctance to evaluate music in the legal realm, despite the power *Miller* accords the law to do so.

We can also see this reluctance in the *Davidson* case, when the judge sidestepped testimony from Dr. Clarence Joseph Stuessy Jr., a musicologist. The judge wrote, "Dr. Stuessy suggests that rap music may become 'almost hypnotic' in its effect to the listener." The judge did not engage with this statement but focused on the latter aspect of Stuessy's testimony, which admitted the importance of context in determining Howard's violent reaction: his background, experience, and presence in a stolen vehicle. The judge further upheld the First Amendment protection of Shakur's music as rap music, citing as precedent *Betts v. McCaughtry* (1993), which had previously acknowledged rap music's constitutional protection. The court accordingly found the issue of obscenity irrelevant. In other words, the judge defended the music based on free speech—avoiding definitions of obscenity, music, or high art.

Yet by linking the issue of obscenity with incitement, the prosecution offered as significant the argument that Shakur's album was not artistically valuable and implied a connection between nonart and violence while implicitly negating the potential relationship between high art and violence. In this case, the issue of obscenity thereby undermined the courts' recognition of music's potential use toward negative ends and reflected once again an enduring belief that music is solely elevated and elevating. Accordingly, we see here additional evidence that the legacy of Romantic aesthetics extends in contemporary examples to thinking about multiple musics but remains contested in its application to rap.

While the criminal-legal process has exploited as lofty classical music and even popular music of the 1950s, this case assigned rap a position below these accepted musics. My reading of the *Davidson* incitement trial therefore further exposes a musical hierarchy, though hardly fixed, within crime prevention and punishment. Such a hierarchy is also implied in the types of music subjected to incitement prosecution—inferior or supposed nonmusic seen as capable of eliciting negative repercussions. Along these lines, as Robert Walser points out, the courts treat rap differently than classical music of the past. For example, the public at large accepts Berlioz's *Symphonie Fantastique* as high art—the inclusion of his music in the music history classroom does not prompt prosecution—though the symphony's program, influenced by the composer's use of opium, includes a murder and the hero's explicit decapitation.[91] How does the legal system reconcile this contradiction? Walser writes, "The solution is simply to assume that the meanings of classical music are essentially benign because they are art."[92] But such artistic appraisal does not concern a simple divide between classical and popular music. Canonical works of rock and jazz, despite histories of controversy, are today accepted as harmless, regardless of the subject matter. The litigation of rap, as well as heavy metal, reflects the music's low contemporary status in society at large. Though the music is widely popular and there are efforts to canonize it in academic writing and study, accolades, and the promotion of its authenticity, rap has not yet become culturally authoritative. Along these lines, rap's place in cultural reception is not the result of simple elitism but rather contemporary taste and complex new status hierarchies.

The trials examined in this chapter do not just reflect this rather low societal positioning of rap but also contribute to its poor standing—sanctioning fear of the music and general panic to explain away the monstrous acts of "ordinary citizens." With this reaction, as Johnson and Cloonan argue, society can "isolate the perpetrators by demonization but the offending music as well," thus leaving the music open to censorship.[93] Accordingly, the legal scholar Block recognizes the possibility of indirect censorship in the courts' practice of permitting cases charging music with incitement: "Yet by allowing a plaintiff to bring an action against the disseminator of allegedly injury-causing rock music, the musician/producer/distributor's expression is somewhat restrained, but the question remains whether this restraint is, nonetheless, constitutionally allowable."[94] Judge Rainey similarly acknowledged potential negative repercussions within the music industry: "To create a duty requiring Defendants to police their recordings would be enormously expensive and would result in the sale of only the most bland, least controversial music."[95]

Beyond this issue of censorship, a similar concern in the previous chapter, cases that charge music with violent incitement offer fascinating examples of the courts' grappling with music's potential negative powers. The legal system ultimately allows only inferior or arguably obscene music this power, in this way revealing a general assignment of music to categories of high and low or even art and nonart. This system of cultural authority can further affect those connected to specific genres of music. Valuations of music evident in legal responses to crime often unfairly skew perceptions of those associated with the music in question. In this way, the criminal-legal process exploits and responds to music as an unmediated signal of identity. However, in cases of incitement, the connection between music and identity goes deeper by purporting not only affinity but music's potential negative influence on who we are and what we do. This complicated relationship between music and personhood—identity and action—is further explored in chapter 5. In the context of prison, a relationship between music and identity is similarly at work. However, in this case study, such connection is not on trial, debated as harmful or harmless. Instead, it works toward more practical or neutral ends. Music in prison therefore offers evidence of a musical middle ground. Between good and bad, high and low, music can function toward rather ordinary ends in the maintenance of discipline in incarceration.

5 ✦ Music in Prison

In previous chapters, we discussed engagement with various musics toward seemingly negative ends within crime prevention and punishment: music in crime deterrence, music to punish, music as evidence of crime, and the charge that music is responsible for crime. In so doing, our examination has gradually progressed through the criminal justice system, from music's roles in crime mitigation to sentencing, and from evidence to direct prosecution. According to this succession, in this chapter I focus on music's place in the next stage of the criminal-legal process: incarceration. In so doing, I focus on music in general, rather than a specific genre. By way of explanation, multiple genres of music thrive in prison. Moreover, discussion of music in prison often concerns general ideas of music or Music, a category beyond fragmented and flexible notions and valuations of specific genres of music. Often this discussion of Music replaces classical music, the previous focus of cultural valorization in the nineteenth century, as the subject of contemporary aesthetic debate. In this way, ideas from the past that music is elevated open up in our contemporary examples to include not only specific genres of music in complicated ways but also, on another level, a more conceptual notion of music in the abstract.

To investigate the role and ramifications of music in prison—in both a practical sense as well as such theoretical abstraction—this chapter focuses on the controversy generated by VH1's series *Music behind Bars* (2002). This series roused outrage and ultimately condemnation and litigation, including the provocative case of *Young v. Beard* (2008). I use *Music behind Bars,* the reactions it triggered, and the experience of its producer, Arnold Shapiro, who spoke to me to "set the record straight,"[1] as a lens through which to view the changing goals of imprisonment and perceptions of music's role therein. By further investigating various functions of music and arts education in prison, I insist that music, regardless of type, is in some ways the perfect complement to conflicted ideals of incarceration as rehabilitation and retribution. With a more balanced view of music's potential in prison (and in general), music programs in prison could appeal to both current advocates and opponents of such programs.

Music behind Bars premiered with an episode devoted to bands at Pennsylvania's Graterford Prison. The program began with an official disclaimer: "*Music behind Bars* is a documentary that examines music programs from across the nation. The inmates profiled in this documentary have been convicted of serious crimes. This is what their life is like behind bars." After an introduction by the host Dylan McDermott, the initial episode introduced the heavy metal band Dark Mischief, which included lead singer Troy Spencer, convicted of armed robbery, and Christopher Bissey, who was serving a life sentence for two murders. According to the opening line of an article in the *Philadelphia Inquirer,* one of Bissey's victims, a fifteen-year-old girl, "loved music and hoped to be a professional dancer someday." Instead, the article continued, "it is her killer who is making his mark in the music world."[2] The girl's mother, Mary Orlando, recognized her daughter's killer in a commercial for the first episode of *Music behind Bars* and, in an interview, exclaimed, "I couldn't believe it. . . . It was like slapping me in the face."[3] Orlando went public with her outrage before the series' official premiere in an interview with Bill O'Reilly on his Fox program, *The O'Reilly Factor.* There, she explained, "In my opinion, watching this makes you want to be this person, because you're able to go ahead and, you know, be a rock star in prison if you do these kinds of crimes."[4] O'Reilly similarly charged the series with giving a killer national exposure and glorifying him as a rock performer.[5] O'Reilly, however, was not content with this single charge. He railed against the series on three consecutive nights, urged viewers to address formal complaints to VH1, and characterized VH1's president, Christina Norman, as "morally bankrupt."[6] He even pledged to support a class-action suit against VH1 on behalf of victims' families.[7] Eventually, in March 2003, after the completion of the series, the family of the murdered Michael Hart did pursue a suit against VH1's parent network in response to an episode of *Music behind Bars* that featured Hart's killer, Jason Henthorne. Representing the Hart family, the attorney Cy Weiner explained, "A criminal who has harassed this family is being celebrated as someone of merit and it's causing the family to feel more harassed."[8]

VH1 and the executive producer of *Music behind Bars,* Arnold Shapiro, would have to respond. An Oscar and Emmy Award–winning producer, Shapiro was an entertainment industry veteran who had had previous success with *Scared Straight!* In this 1978 documentary, Shapiro had already visited the theme of criminality and incarceration: Juvenile delinquents are filmed confronting criminals, who berate and terrify them. Facing their possible future behind bars, the youth, it is hoped, will change their ways. The reception of this documentary differed markedly from *Music behind Bars.* *Scared Straight!* earned Shapiro accolades, won him an Emmy and an Oscar, and inspired law enforcement to institute similar programs that force juvenile delinquents to experience the harsh realities that await them if they remain on their current path.[9] With such initial success, Shapiro produced *Scared Straight! Another Story* (1980), *Scared Straight! 10 Years Later* (1987), and *Scared Straight! 20 Years Later* (1999). Such longevity earned the concept a place in mainstream American culture in popular parody, including *Saturday Night Live* sketches featuring Kenan Thompson as ex-convict Lorenzo MacIntosh. In contrast, *Music behind Bars* existed for only one season, a total of eight episodes. While amazon.com offers a DVD collection of *Scared Straight!,* in 2010 *Music behind Bars* was almost impossible to obtain. (After repeated calls to VH1, I was able to obtain only informal DVDs of episodes three, five, and eight.) Given the controversy, it is only logical that all those involved would abandon *Music behind Bars* and even efface evidence of its existence through omission. As VH1 insisted in a 2003 statement to Fox regarding the Hart lawsuit, "The episode in question aired once and has not been aired since. Series completed its run. We have no plan to run the series again."[10]

Arnold Shapiro offers a fuller explanation of the series' disappearance.[11] No one orders a television show hoping it will last only one cycle; that would be, in Shapiro's words, "like hoping a marriage lasts only two years." Moreover, although VH1 ran all eight episodes of the initial order, Shapiro recalls that episodes three, four, five and six ran unannounced during the night. This decision was VH1's practical response to the growing controversy. But faced with O'Reilly's early denunciation, VH1 could not simply ignore *Music behind Bars* by letting it run its course without ceremony or promotion. Shapiro recalls a conversation with Rob Weiss, the VH1 representative responsible for the series, about the next step: a possible on-air explanation of the show and its goals. However, Weiss thought Shapiro could act as spokesman and defend the series in broadcast interviews. As Shapiro points out, he had not chosen the initial location or participants in Pennsylvania and had even balked at an initial proposal that the show culminate in a music competition among various profiled prisons (he called this early idea "unethical" and "frivolous"). Yet Shapiro remembers himself alone at the center of a media firestorm. In separate interviews with Connie Chung and Katie Couric, he attempted to promote and exonerate the show but was "caught off guard" when both personalities challenged him, questioning the series' goals. Though O'Reilly launched what he terms a "crusade," Shapiro avoided another public attack by refusing to agree to O'Reilly's interview (a refusal O'Reilly regularly noted on his show). Shapiro calls this series of events his "absolute unhappiest" postproduction experience and, though his career has continued (with *Beyond Scared Straight*, among other highly regarded endeavors), he has never again worked with VH1.[12]

At the time, Shapiro defended the series by explaining that it sought not to celebrate prisoners as artists but rather "to turn the spotlight on something positive in a negative environment."[13] Shapiro also cited the show's focus on the "redemptive powers of music" and music's role in the reduction of recidivism in prison and influence on inmates' behavior.[14] He insisted, "One of the main points . . . was that in showing the redemptive aspect of music in prisons, we would be showing how these music programs take some of the most violent prisoners and makes [*sic*] good prisoners out of them."[15] This latter goal, as Shapiro stressed, is good not only for the prisoners but also (as the public might forget) for those who work in prisons, including civilians—nurses, doctors, and teachers, among others. When inmates engage in something "constructive," they are less likely to be "destructive," Shapiro maintains.[16] And music's role as constructive in prison corresponded with VH1's initial concept for the show. "We have been noodling around with lots of different ways to show how music plays an important role in all our lives," explained Weiss at the time. "What really struck us here is that one way it can be powerful is in a redemptive way, and in prison, music can have a profoundly positive impact."[17] With this goal, *Music behind Bars* premiered on October 18, 2002. In a statement issued that day, VH1 insisted, "The inmates profiled in this documentary have been convicted of serious crimes. We think that once the first episode of the series has aired, people will see for themselves that it in no way glorifies prison life or these programs."[18]

But for critics in 2002, an insurmountable wrong outweighed any purported benefits; the proposed glorification of music rather than criminals was hardly justification. Orlando insisted, "When you murder someone, you should lose all your rights. And that includes being able to sing and dance in bands."[19] Others agreed. VH1 received a few thousand messages objecting to the series.[20] The Cincinnati group Parents of Murdered Children further contributed to the public outcry. By complaining to VH1 sponsors, the group's executive director, Nancy Ruhe-Munch, sought to prevent the continued airing of the show: "I have no doubt we'll stop it. We've stopped many others before."[21] The Pennsylvania legislature discussed additional measures: the donation of proceeds from the show to a survivors' fund as well as the notification of victims and their families before their victimizers appeared on air. On O'Reilly's show, Pennsylvania governor Mark Schweiker announced the cancellation of the music program in all of the state's prisons. Schweiker explained to O'Reilly, "Today we're making sure that in all of our prisons, no more music programs or opportunities of this kind again will be afforded to murderers."[22]

But these "murderers" had recourse in the court system. In the 2008 case *Young v. Beard,* Richard Glenn Young, an inmate at Graterford featured in the controversial first episode of *Music behind Bars,* alleged that the elimination of the music band program "violated his right to freedom of expression." The band program at Graterford supported independent bands that regularly rehearsed and were required to perform at least three times a year. In 2002, approximately ten such bands existed, organized by inmate leaders. Staff members made periodic rounds to supervise activity. After the negative reactions to the premiere of *Music behind Bars,* the program was suspended. The secretary of the Pennsylvania Department of Corrections, Jeffrey A. Beard, established a committee to evaluate the future of the prison music programs. Based on committee findings, Beard supported the continuation of most music programs but concluded that the support of independent band programs "undermined prison security."[23] Young filed several complaints in 2004 and 2006. The courts reviewed the rights of inmates and in the 2008 case recognized that "inmates' rights may be more restricted than those of non-inmates," as long as those regulations have "legitimate penological interest." In so doing, they cited *Turner v. Safley* (1987), which upheld for this reason Missouri's almost complete ban on inmate marriage and correspondence. And indeed, the court insisted that the elimination of the independent band program had a reasonable basis in the interest of prison security: "The poor supervision of the program itself created an unsafe inmate environment." The impetus for the program's suspension was therefore irrelevant. Although Beard "initially suspended the performance of music at Graterford in reaction to the VH-1 controversy," the court insisted that his subsequent changes were the result of his opinion that the program "was not safe."[24]

This concern for safety had provided the courts an out before. In *Herlein v. Higgins* (1999), a former inmate had filed suit against officials at the Mount Pleasant Correctional Facility (MPCF). Michael Jon Herlein alleged the prison's ban on the inmates' possession of music cassettes displaying the warning "Parental advisory—explicit lyrics" constituted a violation of the First Amendment. Prison officials insisted, according to the court transcript, that a security threat "can arise from exposing the gang members and sex offenders detained at MPCF to music with explicit lyrics." The trial court ruled in favor of Herlein, concluding that the prison officials had failed to demonstrate a "rational connection between banning tapes with warning labels and maintaining security." On appeal, the court reversed this decision. In so doing, judges avoided a seemingly inevitable confrontation with the impossible task of somehow objectively verifying music's potential for incitement. Instead, taking shelter in *Turner v. Safley,* the appellate court insisted that the case did not require "actual proof" or evidence that music had previously created difficulties in prison—such a connection was simply logical. To further side with the prison, the court cited the time involved in reviewing tapes, which "would significantly affect guards and resources."[25] Nine years before the *Young* case, the Pennsylvania Department of Corrections had thus found a way around the controversy of music's role in prison by claiming that the time involved, if not the music itself, was a risk to security.

This recourse circumvented the real issue in both cases. In the 2008 case, the fundamental concern was not one of safety but rather the controversy surrounding *Music behind Bars.* In other words, whether or not it posed a genuine safety risk, the independent band program became an issue of contention within the legislature in direct response to the first episode of *Music behind Bars.* The debate of interest was not one of security but rather focused on the role of music in prison, inmates' rights as prisoners, and society's conception of imprisonment. In this way, this case functions as an overlooked lens through which to examine recent attitudes toward incarceration. More specifically, the negative reaction to the series' premiere suggests a changing conception of incarceration's aims and of programs of music and arts education in prison. While seen in public outcry as incompatible, music and imprisonment actually have a long history of entanglement, and *Music behind Bars*'s focus on what Shapiro terms "the redemptive powers of music" corresponds to historical images of prison and goals of rehabilitation. To examine the negative response, we must first understand its departure from positive conceptions—past and present—of this overlap between prison and art.

The primary early goal of punishment was the demonstration of power through retribution. Within a "ceremony of power," authorities enacted the public spectacle of physical torture, which often resulted in death. This performance of punishment included decapitation, hanging, the stake and the wheel, and quartering, among other techniques.[26] The Catholic Church was one of the first institutions to punish through imprisonment. The goal of this confinement was partly to effect change through contemplation and ultimately penitence. Enlightened thinkers embraced similar aims and, in the eighteenth century, Europe witnessed the beginnings of imprisonment's use as a perceived means to elicit positive change—displacing the cruel objective of vengeance accepted in previous eras of punishment. Notable early examples include the Hospice di San Michelle (1704) in Rome, the Milan House of Correction (late 1750s), and the House of Correction in Ghent, Austria (1772), all of which required inmates to work—to develop "habits of industry"—as a means of rehabilitation. Colonial settlers brought to the United States these varied traditions of penal justice based on ideas of rehabilitation in addition to older aims of retribution through torture and public shaming. Pennsylvania, however, was at the forefront of penal reform. The founder of the Province of Pennsylvania, William Penn, replaced physical injury with labor as punishment, a provision that endured from 1682 to 1717.[27] In 1829, legislation established solitary confinement as Pennsylvania's official means of punishment. But early reform in the United States was ambiguous to this end: the prison walls were oppressive but imagined as "mirrored surfaces," allowing convicts "to reckon with themselves" and in so doing to achieve liberation.[28] Such tension, according to the American culture scholar Caleb Smith, was at the heart of the American condition, shaped by the American history of captivity—imprisonment of Native Americans and then the slave population—and related fascination with freedom.[29] The contradiction in early American prison reform represented in some ways a microcosm of the American dream in context.

Despite the ultimate goal of rehabilitation and reform, French historian Alexis de Tocqueville and his travel companion, Gustave de Beaumont, recognized a similar paradox in the unintended violence within American penal reform—specifically, systems of isolation. They deemed such solitary confinement "beyond the strength of man" and wrote, "It destroys the criminal without intermission and without pity. It does not reform. It kills."[30] New York's Auburn System represented a possible compromise, with its maintenance of enforced silence but sanction of inmate congregation and communion while working and eating. The inclusion of labor in this system, widespread in U.S. prisons in the nineteenth century and early twentieth century, was effective economically. However, it also arguably played a role in the barbarous breaking down of the prisoner—a precondition of supposed liberation. Still, the immediate work had justification morally in the idea that labor provided the prisoner with skills useful after release. With the increase of such examples of rehabilitation and reform, by the end of the nineteenth century, the primary goal of imprisonment in the United States had become reformation rather than retribution. Despite the enduring inclusion of violence—a breaking down to build up—the ultimate aim had changed.[31] To encourage the inmates' transformation, prison administrators implemented a system of probation and parole in the early twentieth century.[32]

The push to reform in Europe and then the United States, especially through solitary confinement, was inspired and reinforced by Romantic artistic evocations of the prison, including the idea of *felix carcer,* or "happy prison." This tradition "represents confinement as a fortunate fall, in which solitude is the generative circumstance for heightened self-awareness, even transcendence."[33] The scholar Victor Brombert writes of this imagining of prison in French Romantic literature. In *The Romantic Prison,* he explains that the utopian vision of the prison cell indexes the monastic model as a place of noble contemplation and even enlightenment. This link is made explicit in Alexandre Dumas's novel, *Le Comte de Monte-Cristo* (The Count of Monte Cristo, 1844). In this work, the hero, Edmond Dantès, is liberated in his cell through his interaction with his cellmate, Father Faria, the monk-prisoner.[34]

Crucial to this Romantic depiction of prison, however, was the victimization of the prisoner. Dantès is just, unfairly persecuted by a host of auxiliary characters. As a result, the reader identifies with the central prisoner as victim and roots for his liberation. As Suzanne Keen argues in *Empathy and the Novel,* "Spontaneous empathy for a fictional character's feelings opens the way for character identification." The character's "negative affective states," induced by victimization through persecution, grieving, or the experience of pain, increases the likelihood of a reader's empathy.[35] Examining the "rescue opera," Stephen Meyer recognizes a similar pattern in musical representations of prison—specifically, in operatic prison scenes from 1790 to 1815. In many of these works, terror is sublime as the persecuted and virtuous prisoner, the focus of the audience's interest and empathy, sings in the harsh present of a better future.[36] The attraction to such idealization of the prison and identification with the prisoner, for French Romantic writers such as Victor Hugo, corresponded to general Romantic themes: according to Brombert, the "tragic beauty of solitude, glorification of the individual and concern for the problem of identity, existential anguish [and] exaltation of the rebellious outlaw."[37] In this way, the Romantic image of prison and its relationship to the nineteenth-century goal of prison reform depended on the elevation of the righteous prisoner, the noble and empathetic Romantic outsider.

Meyer links such positive images of the prisoner and prison specifically to the philosophy of musical idealism.[38] In other words, the depiction of the elevated prisoner and transformative prison in music corresponds to the Romantic ideal that music is elevated and transformative. Both prison and music represent a means of inner if not outer freedom. In his *Letters on the Aesthetic Education of Man,* Friedrich Schiller, "the poet of freedom," extended this connection to art's potential inspiration and thus the arts in general: "It is only through beauty that man makes his way to freedom."[39] However, Romantic-era music was afforded a special connection to this freedom—with music's supposed power of moral transformation or inner liberation as well as historical connections between music and political freedom. As Hegel wrote in *Vorlesung über die Äesthetik,* "If we are in a general way permitted to regard human activity in the realm of the beautiful as a liberation of the soul, as a release from constraint and restriction . . . it is the art of music which conducts us to the final summit of that ascent to freedom."[40] Various political leaders have perpetuated and responded to this link between freedom and music, specifically in the appropriation of the music of Beethoven. Beethoven is connected to the French Revolution, the wars of liberation, and Schiller with his use in the Ninth Symphony of the poet's "An die Freude" (Ode to Joy), originally titled, according to early German nationalist Friedrich Ludwig Jahn, "An die Freiheit" (Ode to Freedom).[41] With this foundation, Beethoven's music was included, for example, in the Berlin Philharmonic's three appearances at Carnegie Hall following the 9/11 terrorist attacks. In a statement, the orchestra explained that management "felt that the works of Beethoven, a composer who was motivated by great ideals and believed strongly in liberty and freedom, are an appropriate musical statement in light of the tragic events of Sept. 11."[42]

This link between music and freedom also endures in the reception of popular music, most noticeably in the elevation of jazz in the early 1960s. In 1962, the jazz saxophonist John Coltrane explained, "We all know that this word which so many seem to fear today, 'Freedom'[,] has a hell of a lot to do with this music."[43]And this freedom, a contested political ideal at the time, was reflected in jazz lyrics, song titles, album titles, and the music itself (with the improvised solo, for example). Members of the "free jazz" movement pushed this musical freedom further, breaking with traditions of harmony, meter, and form.[44]

In Romantic thinking, this evolving attention to freedom was central to a link between prison and the creative process. Brombert writes, "The link between enclosure and inner freedom is at the heart of the Romantic sensibility."[45] By way of explanation, Brombert recognizes the prison cell's depiction as a means of freedom for the poet—an opportunity for "withdrawal into the self" and thus to access the unrestricted creativity of the mind. The artist was free from worldly demands, a goal similar to that of the Romantic composer.[46] According to this logic, the prison cell becomes a refuge. This idea of confinement has natural overlap with Romantic notions of authentic creativity, dependent on the valuation of autonomous creation. Perceived as separate from the outside world, artistic creation in isolation has been seen as pure and truly original.

This connection between artistic creativity and prison fueled efforts to collect prison work songs in the first half of the twentieth century. In 1933, John Lomax and his son, Alan, recorded work songs at the Louisiana State Penitentiary at Angola. For inmate-workers and prison guards, these work songs were practical: a distraction from work and a means to maintain speed of labor, similar in some ways to the purpose of Muzak's use in office and factory settings.[47] But, for the Lomaxes, the prison walls represented a process of authentication beyond concrete function. Indeed, ethnomusicologist Benjamin Harbert recognizes their mission as genealogical: "They hoped to find music untouched by popular influence and preserved behind prison walls."[48] This music would be pure, authentic, and original, specific to the prison environment.[49]

This notion of music's authenticity in prison has been invoked more recently in rather nostalgic terms. In *Wake Up Dead Man* (1999), Bruce Jackson introduces his collection of work songs from southern prisons with the words, "The song tradition documented in this book no longer exists." He blames the demise of the tradition on the end of segregation in the prisons: "Once blacks and whites and Hispanics worked in the same squads, the group songs became a physical impossibility: you cannot synchronize body movements if half the people cannot or do not want to follow the beat."[50] Of course, the end was also hastened by the termination of convict leasing in the early twentieth century and chain gangs generally in the mid–twentieth century. In this way, for Jackson, his presentation of songs, akin to salvage anthropology, is bittersweet. He detests the penal system that gave rise to these songs, but "there is also a beauty to them, the songs, and it is always sad to see things of beauty becoming anachronisms or curiosities."[51]

His conflicted languor resembles other current claims that music in prison is on the decline today. The criminal justice scholar Marianne Fisher-Giorlando blames in part "the availability of commercial music played and performed on radio, tapes, and television" since 1972 for the absence of music making in prison.[52] While limiting the need for live performance or original composition in some ways, the incursion of the outside has also undermined the possibility of the authentic, even negating the existence of the pure, isolated artistic environment of prison.[53] However, music does indeed continue, as the VH1 series endeavored to capture. According to Mikael Elsila, who has worked with inmate/songwriters in Michigan prisons, "Structurally, music in prison today sounds the same as music in the free world."[54] The difference, according to Elsila, is function. Beyond its role as accompaniment to penal labor, music's purpose in prison has evolved with the rise of prison arts and education programs. Music's historical connection to prison and ideas of prison thereby endures but is directed toward new ends in more recent contexts. However, past notions persist of the prisoner as victim or Romantic outsider and the prison as a utopian site of transformation.

The prison education movement began under the leadership of Austin MacCormick, who established the Correctional Education Association in 1930. MacCormick strove to address not only vocational and literary skills but cultural and moral matters as well.[55] Today, resources for prison education and arts programs vary widely across the United States.[56] Without federal organization, "the arts in prison have no originator, no one agenda, and are ethically profoundly complex."[57] Still, in *Arts in Other Places,* William Cleveland, who directed California's prison arts program for eight years, identifies in the early 1970s the beginnings of a significant rise in artistic instruction in prison. With the sponsorship of state senator Henry Mello, a great lover of music, these efforts led to the eventual formation of California's Arts in Corrections program after the success of a 1977 pilot project directed by Elouise Smith.[58] In 1994, Arts in Corrections was responsible for programming at twenty-seven facilities in California.[59]

The website of the National Endowment for the Arts features a link to a "Arts in Corrections Resource List," which cites other examples of arts programs in correctional settings, including the Southwest Correctional Art Network, Shakespeare behind Bars, and the work of the William James

Association, which attempts to continue the vision of the Arts in Corrections program, disbanded by the California government in 2003.[60] There are also countless smaller musical operations organized within individual prisons. For example, the choral conductor Elvera Voth, "tired of providing dinner music for people who are not very hungry," established the East Hill Singers in the fall of 1995 at Kansas's Lansing Correctional Facility. Her efforts, in addition to a benefit sing-along conducted by Robert Shaw, resulted in the foundation of Arts in Prison in 1998.[61] Catherine Roma, a music professor at Wilmington College, similarly organized a choir at the Warren Correctional Institution in Lebanon, Ohio. In 2004, the group released its second CD, *Do It for the Children*.[62] The work of individual inmates has also generated artistic innovation on a more local level. In 2004, Brian Wong and nine other inmates in the Kulani Correctional Facility in Hawaii worked to record original songs, composed by Wong, reflective of a prisoner's plight. Proceeds from the album were donated to the Crime Victim Compensation Commission.[63]

Practitioners in recent and current arts programs in prison continue to index positive Romantic thinking about the prison. Various authors, for example, cite the role of transformation and inner freedom in the function of arts in prison, both of which are conditions fundamental to the Romantic conception of incarceration and music. In her guide to *Teaching the Arts behind Bars*, Rachel Marie-Crane Williams writes, "In prison, art functions as recreation and stress relief, and it is a way for inmates to transform and move beyond their current reality. Inmates use art to overcome deprivation."[64] Fundamental to such conceptions of art in prison for many of these author/practitioners is the belief that the prisoner's plight warrants such release from deprivation. Williams, for example, writes, "Fewer than half of all state prison inmates are sentenced to prison for committing a violent crime. . . . This means that our society is locking up individuals who easily could be sentenced to community alternatives."[65] With such qualification, William seems first to exonerate the criminals she intends to transform through arts education.

This process of seeming justification, for some, is related to self-identification with the prisoner. In *The Land Where the Blues Began*, Alan Lomax describes a Romantic conception of the African American prisoners with whom he interacted in the 1930s while collecting songs in prison with his father. He viewed the prisoners then and more recently in recollection as "rebels against the South . . . who refused to endure a black fate mildly and with complacent smiles."[66] Their crimes were acts of warranted political protest. With this idealized image of the courageous inmate, Lomax recalls, "I longed and was unable to talk freely with these newfound brothers of mine whose songs triumphed over their misery."[67] He continued, "I fantasized committing some crime so that I, too, could experience what they were experiencing and thus write about them with real understanding."[68]

There are myriad grounds for such identification. Grady Hillman, a poet who worked in Texas prisons and now serves as president of the Southwest Correctional Art Network, taught like many prison instructors "partly out of curiosity and partly out of economic necessity." However, he also admits an attraction he views as natural between two outsiders, prisoner and artist.[69] In this way, we once again see perceived overlap between the inmate and the artistic outcast. For others, this empathy is more complicated. Judith Tannenbaum describes her early experience in 1985 reciting poems in prison. Like Voth, she recognized a need, comparing it to a hunger for sustenance: "I had no idea what to expect, but I discovered that the prisoners responded as I did to poems: as though they'd received bread, actual matter with the power to nourish."[70] Part of her later work in San Quentin, under the auspices of California's Arts in Corrections program, stemmed from her confinement in a mental hospital and resultant deep distrust of those with the power to deny another's personal freedom.[71] Through this experience, she had a natural affinity for those comparably confined.

Whatever the motivation, identification and related justification allow prisoners to shift from victimizers to victims. This complex positioning informs certain current Romantic ascriptions of music in prison and, despite vastly different contexts, further permits tenuous links between music in prison and artistic activity in other settings: Nazi concentration camps and Japanese internment camps, among other examples. In one example, Susan Goldman Rubin explicitly aligns these disparate environments in the second chapter of her *Art against the Odds*, "Captured," which discusses art in modern prisons, a Japanese internment camp in California during World War II, and the Nazi showplace ghetto Theresienstadt.[72]

The appeal of this positioning is exploited in the movie *The Shawshank Redemption* (1994), based on the Steven King novella *Rita Hayworth and Shawshank Redemption* (1993). In a pivotal scene, the innocent and thus deserving Andy Dufresne (Tim Robbins) commandeers the prison sound system to issue "the letter duet" or "Canzonetta sull' aria" from *The Marriage of Figaro*. As the camera travels over the transfixed inmates, Red (Morgan Freedman) speaks: "I tell you, those voices soared, higher and farther than anyone in a grey place dares to dream. It was like some beautiful bird flapped into our drab little cage and made those walls dissolve away. And for the briefest of moments every last man at Shawshank felt free."[73] Fundamental to this scene is our identification with the incarcerated men—made possible in part through the guards' abuse of individual prisoners earlier in the film.

This film also highlights another utopian musical ascription related to the contested idea that music is a universal language: the inmates' momentary union seemingly created through the music. Just as the duet underscores class connection between the Countess and her maid, Susanna, the film accentuates the common reaction to the music that unites the male prisoners, young and old, black and white.[74] VH1's *Music behind Bars* at times highlights a comparable communion through music. This harmony represents in the series a significant means of transformation in prison. As a narrative device, the documentary also fosters empathetic identification with the prisoner and his plight.

In the fifth episode, at California's Salinas Valley State Prison, Curt sits in his cell and explains his murder of two individuals as well as the wounding of others as he made his getaway. He pauses midsentence, and the camera zooms in as he appears contemplative, adding "and that's a horrible thing." With his remorse clear, the next cut features his explanation of music's role in his life. In this way, his participation in music as an elevating privilege is somewhat justified by his evident suffering. In the same episode, Cole, a guitarist, attributes his prison sentence (twenty-five years to life for repeated robbery) to his heroin addiction, expressing regret that his children must endure hardship on his account. All are tormented by his acknowledged mistake. The two men cope with their sentences at the secure facility, described by the host as one of the most dangerous in the nation, in part through their participation in a band, Uncle Dave's Rusty Banjo. The production team highlights in the prison racial division and segregation, even showing a prisoner with a tattoo of Hitler amid a group of white, skinhead inmates. In Uncle Dave's Rusty Banjo, which performs in the episode, however, music helps those involved transcend race, according to the episode's production. The band is described as multiracial, with four white men and one African American man. While rehearsing, the men speak of the music room as a site beyond race—a place, in the words of the music program facilitator, Leslie Hara, of "no race." Asked about the prospect of seeing the multiracial band, two inmates describe the configuration within the segregated prison as a "miracle" and "beautiful." At the close of the episode, the band performs the American folk song "Man of Constant Sorrow."

Similarly, in the third episode, which takes place at Mount Olive, a maximum-security prison in West Virginia, the music instructor, Valerie, tests inmate Jason Henthorne, the focus of the Hart lawsuit. If he wants to work in the music room, which is a desirable position, Jason, a white man, must first demonstrate his strength of character by working with Tony, an African American, on the performance of Jason's original song, which addresses his crime and his regret. Performing together, the two, in the host Dylan McDermott's words, will seek "common ground" through their work and through their music.

Historical ideas of prison as a means of reform and the perceived overlap between this aim and art therefore endure in modern programs of music in prison. In response to such activity, art teacher Phyllis Kornfeld writes, "At first glance, the term 'Prison Art' seems self-contradictory. If we at all associate artmaking with the unfettered flight of the creative impulse, then it would hardly seem likely to take off behind iron bars."[75] However, with the goal of transformation, art—specifically, music, given its Romantic associations—may seem the perfect complement to prison life and the aim of transformation in prison. So why did *Music behind Bars* generate controversy? This correspondence might be the central problem. While efforts to reform persist, the negative reactions to the VH1 series call attention to a striking change in attitude toward goals of incarceration—attitudes more akin to prereform goals of retribution. Though Romantic notions of music mesh easily with goals of prison reform, positive conceptions of music are at odds with the return of conservative trends to the contrary.

Older models of punishment resurfaced in the 1970s. Conservatives challenged the goal of rehabilitation with the aim of retribution and deterrence, "scaring straight the impressionable," and simply caging the "chronically dangerous."[76] They further "attacked rehabilitation on the grounds that it 'permitted the intolerable victimization of the innocent citizen.'"[77] This change in attitude was evident in "What Works?: Questions and Answers about Prison Reform" (1974), in which Robert Martinson insisted that "the rehabilitative efforts that have been reported so far have had no appreciable effect on recidivism."[78] Since the mid-1990s, resulting regulation has focused on limiting "luxuries." In 1996, federal legislation enacted the No Frills Prison Act. Until that time, prisoners could use their own funds to procure musical instruments. With this legislation, federal inmates were no longer allowed personal musical instruments, or in-cell televisions, coffeepots, hot plates, boxing, weight lifting equipment, and movies rated R, X, or NC-17 (with some exceptions).[79] This ideological change has also fueled stricter sentencing guidelines and "tough-on-crime" initiatives, such as "three strikes" laws, which impose mandatory extended incarceration after three or more serious criminal offenses. In *Hard Time Blues,* Sasha Abramsky explains this regulation: "In part, the toughening up of the criminal justice system was an understandable response to the violence and terror that racked America during the height of the crack-cocaine epidemic during the latter part of the 1980s and the early 1990s."[80] A direct consequence of harsher sanctions was a rapid rise in the prison population.[81] With crime rates approximately the same as they were in the mid-1970s, four times as many people served time in American maximum-security prisons in 2000.[82] The prisons simply could not accommodate such an increase. By 1987, twenty-seven out of fifty states operated prisons responsible for the management of 30–90 percent more inmates than the facilities were built to hold.[83]

Grady Hillman, cofounder of the Southwest Correctional Arts Network, connects the burgeoning prison population to a recent decrease in support for the fine arts in prison: "Fundamentally, I believe we began to incarcerate more people than the system could handle, and all treatment programs— education, job training, drug treatment—suffered with the massive buildup of what has been rightly termed 'the prison industrial complex.'"[84] But cuts in prison programs and larger prison populations are related symptoms of the larger cultural shift. Abramsky writes, "Partly, I believe, the prison boom can be explained by a transformation in the political rhetoric away from language of inclusion and hope and toward one of cynicism and fear."[85] Motivated by fear, many enact a strict divide between citizen and crimi-nal—a criminal who is less than human. Caleb Smith insists, "Today . . . the prison no longer promises to correct criminals or to train citizen-subjects. Instead, it appears as a kind of grotesquely violent warehouse whose inmates have been divested of rights, even of humanity, and condemned to a living death."[86] Michelle Brown connects this state of affairs to the infamous Abu Ghraib scandal by arguing that torture in the name of the war on terror grew from the American penal shift toward retribution and cultural insensi-tivity. As evidence, several of those charged in the Abu Ghraib scandal had experience working in American prisons. In fact, the pictured abuses in Abu Ghraib have been linked to corresponding acts of degradation and dehu-manization in correction facilities in the United States.[87] In the war on terror at home and abroad, we thus see in "the management of populations" and "exercise of sovereignty in the acts that suspend and limit the jurisdiction of law" what philosopher Judith Butler terms "the new war prison."[88]

The public reaction to *Music behind Bars* underscores this change. In the Hart case, the lawyer Weiner explained that prisoners are to be confined primarily as punishment, with reform only a secondary concern. With this ranking, Weiner explained, music programs do not make sense: "There is no constitutional right to play the electric guitar."[89] Moreover, music in prison in some ways challenges the new goals of imprisonment. After all, retribution is desirable in part as deterrence. Music may contest this goal if the prison is not feared but instead is perceived as a place of positive musical expression or if prisoners are at all glorified as musicians. As Orlando reacted to *Music behind Bars,* "In my opinion, watching this makes you want to be this person, because you're able to go ahead and, you know, be a rock star in prison if you do these kinds of crimes."[90] Legal scholar André Douglas Pond Cummings recently voiced an analogous concern but focused on rap's representation of imprisonment "as a rite of passage." Further, given rap's portrayal of an unjust justice system, the prisoner is viewed as Romantic outsider and thus "with respect and admiration." As a result, he opines, "the value of deterrence is diluted and stigma is lost on the hip-hop generation."[91] According to such thinking, prisons should not have music to maintain the possibility of retribution and deterrence. Furthermore, prisoners in this system, perceived as less than human, simply do not deserve music. For many, the virtuous prisoner no longer exists, and criminals hardly merit music. As Orlando explains, "When you murder someone, you should lose all your rights."[92]

This idea that music is a dessert, a privilege for the deserving, was evident in Romantic thinking and even musical performance. In Carl Maria von Weber's *Der Freischütz* (premiered in 1821), the Devil Samiel cannot sing (and only speaks); as other characters choose to collaborate with him, they too lose their musical voices and speak—first Caspar, the corrupt and corrupting ranger, and then the hero, Max. This depiction of the devil and those of a similar caste was present centuries earlier in "Ordo Virtutum" by the medieval abbess Hildegard of Bingen. In these examples, an individual without humanity is incapable of song—not worthy of music. He or she occupies a plane below music, a transcendent art for only the transcended.

Today, this notion lingers in other contexts. The National Association for Music Education sponsored a 2008 discussion under the heading "Music Is a Privilege??" The initial poster, a music educator, described her frustration with a teacher who would not bring her students to music class if the students did not behave: "Today this particular teacher said that she would not bring them to Music at all, that it was a privilege, and she would have them go to the classroom with their heads down for 45 minutes instead if they didn't behave." The music instructor, having encountered such a position before, explained, "As soon as she said 'music is a privilege' I wanted to speak up and say no it's not—it's their right to have music, and their behavior in the classroom shouldn't preclude them coming to me!" Another respondent stressed the importance of educating parents and other teachers about music's benefits—"how participating in music class allows children to be creative, work together, solve problems, etc."—and relative importance in comparison to math, for example.[93] Of course, these educators are fighting a complicated battle, even among fellow musicians. The twentieth-century Italian pianist Arturo Benedetti Michelangeli, for example, wrote, "Music is a right, but only for those who deserve it!"[94]

In the prison environment, this attitude and related responses ignore the complexities of music. Music—of all types—is not simply a pleasure linked to a world above vice. Music can serve practical purposes within the current prison warehouse. In fact, music has served practical aims in prison. Despite the purported aims of rehabilitation or more recently punishment, Michel Foucault argues that the true function of the modern prison is and always has been discipline, or the control of another's body and thus activity. Though obscured by today's Romantic notions of Music, music in prison has furthered and continues to further this aim. In the remainder of this chapter, we will review the use of music toward this more practical end by examining inmates' responses to music as well as music's functioning in prison as a "total institution."

Prisoners cite positive functions of music—connected to Romantic ideals—such as freedom or escape. In the fifth episode of *Music behind Bars,* Curt, a guitar player and murderer, explained that "music gets me through the day": it allows him to "escape" into his "own world." In his study, Elsila asked prisoners, "What purpose do you feel music has for you?"; "Is music liberating to you? How?" Like Curt, Ace responded by highlighting music's role as escape: "Yes the music is very liberating, actually beyond belief to someone that isn't in this particular type of situation."[95] This freedom is often achieved by focusing on life beyond prison rather than reflecting on everyday life in prison through music: "I feel if I were to dwell upon the fact that I am incarcerated, it would be quite easy for me to allow myself to be swallowed up by this system and thus become useless as a human being."[96] This concentration is evident in the reactions of many experiencing loss associated with confinement, whether or not they were responsible for that loss. For example, the composition of Olivier Messiaen's *Quartet for the End of Time* took place in captivity, during the composer's time as a prisoner of war during World War II. For this reason, many have viewed the work as an expression of the composer's response to that experience. But Messiaen himself emphasized the piece's connection to his escape, a world beyond his reality. In a 1958 radio interview, Messiaen explained, "I would instead say that I composed this quartet in order to escape from the snow, the war, captivity, and myself."[97]

In this way, music presents a means through which to regain that which the prisoner lacks: freedom and even humanity or individuality. Given music's relationship to identity, music reminds some prisoners of their personhood outside of incarceration. In music, Ace explained, "You aren't an inmate, you aren't an animal, you are a full fledged musician and you are jamming."[98] Similarly, before the Shaw benefit concert, the inmate Frank Dominguez, in his introduction of Robert Shaw, declared, "Six months ago I was 34036 singing in this Lansing choir. And today I am Frank Dominguez."[99] These inmates thereby recover a sense of their humanity and add to their self-identification the distinction of musician.

For Chet, the self-identity he gained or regained through music was related to his experience of cooperation in music: "Music changed me from a social degenerate into a man who truly feels connected to humankind . . . . Music empowered me, revealed my connection to the universal spirit."[100] Such a response is significant in the act of choral singing, a powerful feat of cooperation in various contexts. Of his participation in a prison choir, one inmate said, "I absolutely hate the behavior that resulted in my incarceration but I have stopped hating myself. It is programs like [name withheld] that can help me in this process of believing in myself."[101] The prisoner felt accepted by the singing group and through this collaboration experienced support that enabled him to begin to accept himself.

This renewed self-esteem can be further accessed through communion with the past, which played an important role in music making among inmates involved in Fisher-Giorlando's sociological study of music composed by inmates serving time in Ohio. One inmate composed music about his hometown of Akron, known historically for its production of tires. Of his song, he explained, "It's about the town I live in, Tire Town, which is Akron. And even though I thought it was the armpit of Ohio at one time, I guess I do like it."

I'm Back in Tire Town
And I'm never feeling down
On my own piece of ground
I'm back in Tire Town.[102]

In his study of music in a Louisiana prison, Ben Harbert also recognized prisoners' response to the comfort of the past in music. The inmate Russel Joe Beyer, for instance, explained that music "reminds me of New Orleans. . . . Everybody here, just about, is from New Orleans. So they all play with a certain feel. When you're doing it, it all clicks in. It brings you back home."[103] According to Harbert, prisoners endeavor to heal through music the fractured worlds of home and institution and may simultaneously experience past and present.[104]

To these ends, music making represents a powerful "niche," in social psychologist Hans Toch's terminology: "A niche is a functional subsetting containing objects, space, resources, people, and relationships between people. A niche is perceived as ameliorative; it is seen as a potential instrument for the relaxation of stress and the realization of required ends."[105] The stress of prison is manifest in noise, threats, humiliation, and even violence. The niche represents for some an important means of survival in an overwhelming environment. But music making is not only positive for prisoners. Ace, thankful for his access to music, explains that music can also be painful: "There is nothing more that you want to do than play, but you hate to play because it's a painful reminder that you are a number and you have no rights."[106] After engagement with music, other prisoners also cite their frustration with their perceived limited musical skills or those of other inmates. They may also react negatively to peer behavior both outside of and within the music-making context (ridicule). Of his experience singing in a prison choir, one inmate commented, "The only criticisms I have are with my own peers . . . coming into practice late . . . not learning material, whining about the amount of work."[107]

Music's function is therefore profoundly complex. This convolution is augmented by music's role in prison operation as a whole. For example, music in a more practical sense represents a productive means of occupying time. Inmate Leotha Brown, interviewed by Harbert, said, "Some people might just sit down and just get into a mood or a spirit of ennui, of nothingness, where they just stare, they just exist. . . . They [feel they don't] have any type of essence in their lives, but you have to create. You have to create within yourself some types of intrinsic value."[108] In Michael Santos's experience behind bars, music has no magical power in this regard, and many mundane activities can have this effect: "playing a musical instrument, attending education courses, painting, or even the obsessive-compulsive cleaning of one's cell."[109] However, Santos realized that this occupation of time, so significant to inmates, is equally important to administrators, who often seek to reduce an inmate's idleness: "Their experience suggests that when prisoners have nothing but time on their hands, they frequently find trouble."[110]

With this reciprocal reliance on music, music's function in prison is again similar to music in office and factory work settings. Studies during and after World War II showed that, with music, workers were more productive for their employers and satisfied on-site: "Music could decrease boredom, conversation, and absenteeism while improving morale."[111] In this way, music can function at the nexus of a contested system of exchange that is particular to the "total institution."

In sociologist Erving Goffman's conception of the term, the "total institution" is "a place of residence and work where a large number of like-situated individuals, cut off from the wider society for an appreciable period of time, together lead an enclosed, formally administered round of life."[112] There is no culture in which to acculturate or assimilate but rather something more limited. Instead, total institutions, such as prisons, "create and sustain a particular kind of tension between the home world and the institutional world," as recognized previously by Harbert, and "use this persistent tension as strategic leverage in the management of men."[113] In the prison as total institution, that is, authorities exploit that which the inmate desires to ensure compliance. Given its associations with home and identity, music can play a powerful role in this system. The authorities exchange the privilege of home and humanity in music for good behavior. This treatment of music as privilege in an arrangement of direct exchange is analogous to music's handling in the school setting. That is, music in prison is often regulated within a system of rewards akin to that within the educational institution.[114] But through this exchange, music can play a direct role in discipline, fundamental to the prison, according to Foucault: "In discipline, punishment is only one element of a double system: gratification-punishment."[115] As in this system, Santos observed that prisoners with an interest, such as music, "are less likely to engage in disruptive behavior because they do not want to lose access to the activity that has been carrying them, like a magic carpet, over the hassles associated with confinement."[116] Accordingly, music actually enhances security, despite the courts' judgment to the contrary in the case of Pennsylvania's independent band program.[117]

Music's role in this maintenance of discipline is significantly illustrated in *Music behind Bars*. Shapiro purported to focus on music's redemptive powers, and the series' production did highlight certain Romantic ideas of prison life. At the same time, opponents perceived an inexcusable glorification of murderers. The two sides, however, I argue, had common ground:

music's role as incentive in the maintenance of discipline or behavior. As the series demonstrated, this function, which Shapiro recognized, could appeal to both opponents and proponents of music in prison.

In the third episode, at Mount Olive, the series focuses on Jason's sentence of life with mercy for a first-degree murder. With "mercy," he has the chance of parole. Jason recognizes a job in the music room as a valuable means of enhancing his possibility of parole. As the warden, Thomas L. McBride, explains during the episode, the parole board takes "a very dim view of an inmate choosing to remain idle." Willingness to work and success in work is perceived as an indicator of attitude. But time in the music room "is a privilege for inmates with good records," as the episode makes clear in bold letters on screen. In the episode, Jason must maintain his good behavior and cooperate with Tony to work in the music room and thereby improve his chance of parole.

This impetus for exchange varies based on sentencing. For inmates without a chance for parole, for instance, music's exchange value differs. In Salinas Valley, the music instructor Ken Arconti explains that music is constructive in the exercise of discipline: Inmates involved are "more likely to watch their behavior" because they look forward to making music in the program. Similarly, the correctional captain M. Collier insists that inmates involved are careful not to lose this "privilege," which he also terms a "luxury." They do not maintain discipline to increase the chance of parole but rather simply to keep the "privilege" of music. As Curt, an inmate with a life sentence and no hope of release, comments in the episode, "Music gets me through the day." Likewise, Dave, a musician in Uncle Dave's Rusty Banjo, insists that playing music is like "sleep," the "only time you can be free."

This use of music as incentive is confirmed in the final episode of the series, set at a maximum-security prison in Pennsylvania. As the episode opens, the host stresses the relationship between participation in music and the reduction of misbehavior. In the episode, the music facilitator, Mike Dohanich, makes it clear that inmates involved in music are less likely to misbehave: "They want their music." One prison infraction can end the music program; the central character in the episode, a rapper named Jibreel, finds his participation in music nearly ended when he does not stand during count. In this way, the warden Jeff Merrill at Maine State Prison in Thomaston, featured in another episode of *Music behind Bars,* comments on the prison music program, "I see it as a win-win all around."[118]

Discipline, inherent in this strategy of incentive, is also built into the act of making music itself. Examining several prison choirs in Kansas, Mary

Cohen recognizes the role of choral singing in positive behavioral change. In group singing, inmates gain group responsibility and must work together toward a common goal.[119] This relates to her theory of interactional choral pedagogy, which suggests "that thoughtful and effective choral musicking leads to assessable growth in desirable personal and social behaviors."[120] Such cooperation is fundamental to discipline, in Foucault's conception of the term, with the goal of constructing "a machine whose effect will be maximized by the concerted articulation of the elementary parts of which it is composed."[121] This process effectively regulates time, another element of discipline, according to Foucault, as those involved in group music making work through stages in time toward the goal of mastery, often in performance.[122]

The performance, therefore, represents a major component of discipline, as the ultimate stage of this progression. But the performance has another purpose. For Foucault, an ideal means of discipline is observation: "The exercise of discipline presupposes a mechanism that coerces by means of observation."[123] A useful means of such observation, according to Foucault, is the examination: "The examination combines the techniques of an observing hierarchy and those of a normalizing judgment. It is a normalizing gaze, a surveillance that makes it possible to qualify, to classify and to punish."[124] The musical performance represents the culmination of artistic activity, a test of rehearsal and collaboration, and, in this way, a chance for authorities to adjudicate and observe work in examination. Indeed, the performance allows authorities total access, inviting judgment of performed discipline. Music in this manner extends the possibilities of the panopticon, a circular architectural design imagined by Jeremy Bentham in 1787 to enhance visibility and the possibility of observation.[125] Foucault writes, "The major effect of the panopticon: to induce in the inmate a state of conscious and permanent visibility that assures the automatic functioning of power."[126]

Music making and especially performance in prison, however, can serve another function for the administration in public performance. Harbert writes, "For the administration, music is part of a system of carceral techniques that regulates inmate behavior and, in the case of Angola, also expresses an image of reform to the public."[127] In other words, the public performance can promote a facade of reform and progress. James Thompson views this public dimension with distrust: "We need to examine how our performances relate to other performances of punishment and check that they do not display prisoners to the further delight and voyeuristic pleasures of the crowd."[128] This darker attraction to artistic output in prison is evident, for example, in the sale of the serial killer John Wayne Gacy's paintings. Public concerts in prison thereby invoke additional complications beyond discipline in exchange: the display of rehabilitation and grotesque curiosity or "spurious glamour"—which is extended by inmate music recordings and CD sales.

Music thus functions within a complex system of exchange—for multiple ends simultaneously. Music can play a role in prisoners' goals by enabling for example self-realization while working at the same time for authorities by ultimately serving the goal of discipline. As Lawrence Brewster, who conducted a 1981 study of the effects of the Arts in Corrections program, concludes, "The best evidence to indicate that the AIC Program does improve the attitude and behavior of inmates is the reduced number of disciplinary reports among those participating in the Program." He cites a reduction of disciplinary actions by 35.9 percent and 65.7 percent, respectively, at two institutions he studied.[129] This claim of successful exchange can also be made on a larger scale, at least in regard to prisoners with the chance of release. In 1994, Henry Mello explained, "When you say this is good for the artist, it's good for everybody, it's also good for the taxpayers who are making a small investment here and they're getting back a tremendous savings by really doing a job of rehabilitating people and not having them return to prison. And then they benefit from their new direction in life and so everyone wins in this situation."[130] Similarly, Brewster insists on a connection between participation in arts programs in prisons and a reduced rate of recidivism: "The assumption is not only that higher self-confidence and self-discipline is an important individual benefit, but also a social and potentially a taxpayer benefit. . . . The social and taxpayer benefits are the result of a decrease in the recidivism rate among inmates."[131]

Despite these manifold benefits, VH1's *Music behind Bars* generated denunciation and litigation and now is banished to obscurity. The 2002 series may be related to the end of the Arts in Corrections program the following year. At the time, the budget cut that ended the program still allowed for a single arts administration position as a means to maintain some arts in California's prisons. As of January 31, 2010, even this minimal support was terminated with the final elimination of the artist facilitator position. Paul Katz responded in the *Huffington Post*, "Many of you may be thinking, 'why should I help prisoners in jail do activities that sound like fun?' You must look at it from a different angle. Reinstating a program like 'Arts In Corrections' is not about rewarding people who have committed varying degrees of crime. It is about having foresight."[132] With a more nuanced understanding of music's potential in prison, perhaps music programs could appeal to current supporters as well as critics of such programs. Music can serve a practical good. Evolving notions of music's positive powers, reflected and reinforced in the criminal-legal process, obscure negative uses of music but may also obfuscate music's more mundane potential for a complicated bureaucratic functioning in the maintenance of discipline.

As chapter 6 shows, authorities have stretched such disciplining through music in extreme cases of detention—in torture and interrogation abroad. This last chapter therefore highlights again the working of music toward contested ends while bringing us back to a recurring concern: the ethics of music's use in darker contexts.

6 ✦ Music as Torture

Ibrohim Nasriddinov and his family fled Tajikistan as civil war
refugees and arrived in Afghanistan in 1992. As a young man, Nasriddinov
was sent to Pakistan to study at a madrasah but ended up in an Al-Qa'idah
school. During the war on terror, he was arrested by the U.S. government
and interned in the detention center at Guantánamo Bay for more than
a year. There, shackled and in solitary confinement, he was subjected to
torture: "I was irritated by loud music, various marches, people's shouts,
animal sounds, and all this put pressure on the mind. I did not feel my own
body, touching myself, I noticed my numb body. This is called civilized
torture. One might endure physical beating, but not everyone can overcome
psychological torture."[1] In this account of his confinement, Nasriddinov
suggests a more sinister means of maintaining discipline through music in
prison. Building on his account, the role of music in incarceration becomes
overtly menacing in this final chapter, which addresses music's controversial
use in the aftermath of 9/11, specifically in U.S. detention centers in Cuba,
Iraq, and Afghanistan. Though music has helped ensure a total control in
detention abroad as well as imprisonment at home, the intent of music's
use in torture was explicitly negative, while music's function for many in
prison has been positive. The case of music in torture, however, has certain
connections with that of music in prison. Indeed, music's use as torture,
like music's operation in prison, has invited diverse reactions, including the
threat of legal action against the U.S. government. This chapter ultimately
considers these responses, including the claim that music cannot function as
torture—or, rather, that music used in this way ceases to be music.

With this concentration, this chapter joins its predecessor in focusing on valuations of music more generally, or Music, rather than conflict surrounding a specific genre. However, as I argue, the contestation of music's use as torture stems from a belief that habitually resurfaces in this study and has affected the place of music in each of our examples, regardless of the specific musical genre involved: the idea that music is positive and should be used accordingly. Critics of music's use in crime deterrence and punishment take such a stand—in both cases, concerned that these contexts will tarnish music's inherent goodness. Though complicated by associations with rap, the discussions in chapters 3 and 4 expose a comparable anxiety about the proper place of music, given its supposed transcendence, in the application of the idea that music offers a window onto the soul (chapter 3) and consideration of music as obscene or nonart in cases alleging musical incitement (chapter 4). In chapter 5, positive notions of music further complicated our inquiry by colliding with recent trends in theories of incarceration. In this chapter, I examine the debate regarding music's functioning as torture to offer a final statement against qualification that music is solely good. This qualification, based on the shifting legacy of Romantic aesthetics, weakens the processes and state institutions that maintain societal safety by diverting attention from certain dangers of music's use while ignoring the realities of music's various operations beyond the concert hall, past and present.

Music has a long history of use in war.[2] Around 400 B.C.E., Greek galley oarsmen developed chants for various activities, including battle. Napoleon's troops prepared for the Battle of Waterloo accompanied by regimental bands. During the Civil War, band music offered soldiers distraction and consolation at camp and motivation on the march. Some regiments even responded to bugle melodies or drum patterns as combat commands.[3] More recently, in the war on terror, soldiers have used music for personal enjoyment, to relieve boredom, and to heighten aggression in confrontation with insurgents. But as Jonathan Pieslak argues in his study of American soldiers' use of music in Iraq, often "the distinction between music that was intended to motivate troops for combat or psychologically threaten an adversary is blurred."[4] In this way, music often performs various tasks simultaneously. For instance, music broadcast from loudspeakers in public areas has served as both motivation and threat. These speakers can offer insurgents instructions for surrender but have also been employed to irritate and frustrate through the programming of seemingly interminable music, often heavy metal or rap, as a means of sensory deprivation. In this context, Pieslak categorizes music as "unwanted sound" within the army's "sonic arsenal."[5]

Along these lines, Ben Abel, spokesman for the U.S. Army's psychological operations (PsyOps) command at Fort Bragg, North Carolina, comments, "It's not so much the music as the sound. It's like throwing a smoke bomb. The aim is to disorient and confuse the enemy to gain a tactical advantage."[6]

In conception, this approach resembles American soldiers' employment of music in detention camps in Cuba, Iraq, and Afghanistan. In these facilities, U.S. officials broadcast music to "harass, discipline, and in some cases 'break'" detainees.[7] Citing the success of heavy metal's use in this context, Sergeant Mark Hadsell, working within PsyOps, explains, "If you play it for twenty-four hours, your brain and body function start to slide, your train of thought slows down and your will is broken. That's when we come in and talk to them."[8] Adam Piore lists specific selections exploited in this regard: "Bodies" from Vin Diesel's *XXX* movie soundtrack, Metallica's "Enter Sandman," as well as children's songs, such as the theme from the television program *Sesame Street*.[9] While exploring allegations of torture in 2004, the Iraqi lawyer Yasir al-Qutaji was arrested by U.S. troops and subjected to precisely the techniques he sought to expose. In addition to hooding and beatings, he was left in a room soldiers called the Disco and subjected to loud music, characterized as "Western." According to reports, in Guantánamo Bay, this torture, termed "torture lite" or "no-touch torture," included the music of Eminem, Britney Spears, Limp Bizkit, Rage against the Machine, Metallica, and Bruce Springsteen—sometimes in stretches of fourteen hours.[10]

At Forward Operating Base Tiger, near al-Qaim, such music was often a part of initial interrogations. One guard recalls,

> So, typical first-time interrogation consisted of some kind of heavy metal music really loud, strobe light, lot of yelled questions and stuff like that, until they finally would break down and say "I don't know anything . . ." He's on his knees, usually with a rifle pointed at him, strobe light going, music going, whatever. Then the guys sitting at the desk asking him questions directly. It was always yelling at that point—you had to, in order to hear [over the music]. They'd ask and ask and ask and ask.[11]

At Guantánamo Bay, however, at least in the case of Muhammad al-Qahtani, accused of involvement in the September 11 attacks, music worked within an ongoing program of torture and interrogation.[12] In addition to loud music, programmed to prevent sleep, from late November 2002 through early January 2003, soldiers appropriated the music of pop star Christina Aguilera.[13]

Soldiers thus used various types of music in different stages of torture and interrogation. However, as in Hadsell's and Pieslak's discussion of music in combat, the role of music in torture has been described as incidental—the music categorized as sound rather than music. That is, the salient aspect of this technique has been theorized as the operation of unwanted sound or loud noise. This distinction was at the center of a debate between the music scholars Jonathan Bellman and Phil Ford in reaction to Suzanne Cusick's work on music's transmission as torture. On Bellman and Ford's musicological blog, *Dial "M" For Musicology*, on August 24, 2007, Bellman wrote of musical torture, "That isn't music; it is sonic torture, or just torture." Bellman may have been trying to fix the debate on the issue of torture, as he had attempted in a previous post. But Ford did not respond to intent, instead reacting to Bellman's apparent circumscription of the roles of music. A day later, Ford wrote, "The rub of my disagreement with Jonathan is this: he believes that when music is used in torture, it is no longer music, but merely torture, and so there's no point in talking about 'music as torture,' because torture-music does not exist as an independent entity." In his subsequent discussion, however, Ford ultimately agreed to disagree, "because, while we can keep going back and forth on whether music used in torture is a special case, it's not the kind of point that anyone can 'prove,' but rather a question of interpretation."[14] In her most recent publication on this topic, "Musicology, Torture, Repair," Cusick displays a similar ambivalence: "It is not at all clear that the music aimed at prisoners in detention camps has functioned *as music*. Rather, it has more often functioned as *sheer sound*."[15]

But according to this idea of music's functioning in programs of torture, why play composed music at all? Why not simply play loud noises, crashes, or cries? And why vary the choice of music in this context? The use of music in interrogation and torture has complicated origins that shed some light on these questions.

The historian Alfred McCoy and the journalists John Conroy, Jane Mayer, and Michael Otterman have linked this strategy to interrogation techniques developed in the 1950s but banned after the Vietnam War.[16] From 1950 to 1962, the U.S. Central Intelligence Agency (CIA) was involved in experiments designed to control and torture through psychological means, including drugs, electric shock, and sensory deprivation and disorientation. To this end, CIA operatives assaulted all senses—cultural, sexual, visual, and auditory. These early psychological techniques of warfare, in some ways developed in response to fears of communist brainwashing, were codified in 1963 in the CIA's KUBARK Counterintelligence Interrogation Handbook and culminated in an infamous mind-control program, MKUltra.[17] There is evidence of some reliance in this work on models from Nazi Germany. For example, Henry K. Beecher, a professor at Harvard University, examined a brochure detailing thirty mescaline experiments on Dachau inmates as he pursued his own research related to psychological torture, which similarly involved drugs designed to overcome a detainee's will.[18] Though some have viewed psychological torture as less severe than physical torture, a British journalist publicly insisted that psychological torture is "the worst form of torture": It "provokes more anxiety" than more traditional means of torture, "leaves no visible scars and, therefore, is harder to prove, and produces longer lasting effects."[19] Indeed, while physical torture induces subject disintegration and submission, studies have shown that psychological torture can produce this disintegration faster and is therefore both more efficient and effective.[20]

But this early work on psychological torture, when it did involve sound, employed constant noise, such as hissing or static, rather than music. Describing it as dull instead of aggressive, Pieslak finds this type of noise less than antagonistic. He interprets its deployment as a means "to dull or entirely block out auditory perception, not to sonically antagonize." He therefore sees such experiments in torture as an unlikely precedent for music's functioning in the war on terror. Instead, he cites as a more apt model the use of noise in addition to forced standing and the deprivation of sleep and food in the interrogation of twelve Irish Republican Army terrorists in Great Britain in 1971.[21] A former detainee reported, "After a while the noise in the background became more prominent. . . . I couldn't concentrate, this noise was in the centre of my head."[22] Though neither of these cases explicitly included music, they surely both relate to the U.S. Army's subsequent treatment of music as torture, which evolved from soldiers' initial use of psychological tactics, including noise.

In an October 11, 2002, memorandum, Lieutenant Colonel Jerald Phifer recommended to the commander of the Joint Task Force 170 (Guantánamo) the employment against detainees of "yelling" and "deprivation of light and auditory stimulus." A month prior to this communication, a SERE (Survival-Evasion-Resistance-Escape) conference took place at Fort Bragg. There, soldiers were taught techniques to resist torture, including the imposition of noise. Based on this timeline, the experiments of the 1950s endured in Special Forces training curriculum and may have inspired subsequent ideas of attack at Guantánamo.[23] Phifer's techniques were expanded in Lieutenant General Ricardo S. Sanchez's September 14, 2003, memo regarding interrogation policy in Iraq, in which Sanchez specifically authorized music: recommendations extended to "yelling, loud music, and light control" as a means of creating "fear, disorient[ing] the detainee, and prolong[ing] capture shock."[24] But why the inclusion of music, a supplement to previously endorsed techniques of psychological warfare through noise?

Auditory attack in the war on terror has been tied to the effort to dislodge Manuel Noriega from Panama in 1989. Ben Abel explains, "Since the Noriega incident, you've been seeing an increased use of loudspeakers."[25] The Noriega offensive did involve music, but the specific motivation for doing so is also unclear. According to reports, U.S. troops may have decided to broadcast music to muffle the sound of negotiations. In another explanation, the technique was a response to complaint by Noriega, an opera fan, about a marine's playing of an AC/DC tape too loud near the compound. According to this latter logic, an unintended nuisance thus became catalyst for an intended offense.[26] In this way, music's operation as a repellent, which relates to the use of music against Noriega (chapter 1) and predates music's functioning as a means of torture, may be precedent for music's deployment in the war on terror. Indeed, like authorities in examples of music in crime deterrence, the military has seized on the symbolic value of music, dependent on issues of identity and context. Music's use in U.S. detention centers abroad therefore may have merged the use of noise in psychological warfare with a growing tradition of music's treatment as a repellent. The goals and functioning of music's use as torture in practice, as well as its links to strategies of crime deterrence through music, highlight the operation of music in this new context as music, rather than just noise, despite speculation to the contrary. In other words, aspects unique to music—its organization and melodic contour as well as associations, traditions, and theatrical performance—played significant roles in the operation of sound in interrogation and torture.

This process in U.S. detention centers in Islamic lands is both dependent on and complicated by the place of music in Muslim societies. Though music is generally controversial, historically there has been no consensus in sacred texts on music's handling. Theologian and jurist Ibn Abī'l-Dunyā (823–94) wrote one of the earliest treatises that called for music's ban. In *The Book of the Censure of Instruments of Diversion* (Dhamm al-malāhī), he labeled music a diversion from devotion. However, a religious reformer, Abū Hāmid al-Ghazzālī (1058–1111), accepted music as a means to access one's innermost being and thus self.[27] The Koran itself does not explicitly offer a verdict either way on the place of music. Nevertheless, a number of suras

(Koranic verses) have been interpreted to support music's condemnation, while others have been interpreted to sanction it. In Afghanistan, when the Taliban took control of Kabul in 1996, the new leaders thus justified a complete prohibition on the making, owning, and playing of musical instruments with the exception of the frame drum. A local newspaper described the destruction of a number of instruments under this policy in December 1998, citing a hadith (one of the sayings and actions of the Prophet Muhammad according to his companions): "Those who listen to music and songs in this world will on the Day of Judgment have molten lead poured into their ears."[28] When the Taliban was displaced, music reappeared on the radio and acted for some people as a symbol of freedom. However, in 2003, the state reinstated strong censorship, including a complete ban on the singing of women on radio, television, and stage.[29] This proscription accorded with a prohibition on the music of women, who, in the words of the early twelfth-century teacher Majd al-Dīn al-Ṭūsī al-Ghazālī, would become "an object of the carnal appetite that is lust."[30]

In Iran, there has been comparable attention to music. Instruments have been similarly prohibited on television, and the singing of women is taboo on television and in public more generally. With the election of President Mahmoud Ahmadinejad in 2005, state-run television and radio also enforced a ban on music considered Western. Despite such repression, in his travels in the Middle East, Mark Levine has documented the powerful underground popularity of heavy metal and rap. As the lead singer of Iraq's only metal band, Acrassicauda, explained in a documentary, *Heavy Metal Baghdad*—while pointing to the album cover of Iron Maiden's *Death on the Road,* an apocalyptic vision of the Grim Reaper in motion, ferried by two otherworldly stallions—"This is what life looks like here" (see figure 3).[31]

Given the contestation surrounding the role of women in music, genres associated with the West, and music generally, American soldiers had ample foundations for a psychological offensive through music in the interrogation of Muslim detainees. There were no regulating standards for repertoire choice to this end—musical selections instead were left to the creativity of individual PsyOps soldiers, which Cusick points to as evidence that the use of music was indeed incidental.[32] But the use of specific music in practice was hardly insignificant; it often relied on conflict surrounding certain genres and types of music.

The U.S. sonic offensive had physical repercussions, such as auditory pain, hearing loss, and the prevention of sleep. It also had psychological effects that can be traced to the use of sound generally, such as the creation

Figure 3. The album cover
of *Death on the Road*. c 2005
Iron Maiden Holdings Ltd.
(Picture by Melvyn Grant)

of fear.[33] However, interrogators selected specific music to meet psychological aims beyond those achieved through noise or loud sound—in this way, as in the use of music to repel, taking advantage of associations with music dependent on identity in various contexts. For example, in the interrogation of al-Qahtani at Guantánamo, according to a leaked detention log, interrogators broadcast the music of Christina Aguilera to offend al-Qahtani as a "good Muslim man." In addition to interruptions of his prayer, Aguilera's music was an affront to Muslim proscriptions against sensual or frivolous music as well as bans on the music of women.[34] Related to "gender coercion," al-Qahtani was further subjected to a procedure termed "Invasion of Space by a Female," the close physical invasion of a woman, which especially agitated the detainee, as well as the hanging of pictures of nearly naked women around his neck.[35] This strategy targeted cultural beliefs as a kind of internal attack on personhood.

To augment this affront, al-Qahtani's Islamic devotion and understanding of that devotion were called into question. For example, according to his interrogation log, when al-Qahtani protested his interrogators' use of music on December 7, 2002, an interrogator, apparently aware of the contestation surrounding music in the Koran, challenged al-Qahtani to find the verse in his holy book that prohibits such sound. On December 14, al-Qahtani's detention log similarly attests, "Topic of music was run with Koranic verses that support that music is not forbidden. Detainee was given . . . Koran to read along with the interrogators to see the verses for himself." After continued discussion along these lines, al-Qahtani began to cry and asked God for forgiveness. At this moment of breakdown, the torturers began their interrogation, realizing that their prisoner was powerless to resist.[36]

American soldiers similarly employed music associated with the West. Within "Western music," Pieslak explains, "if music is employed, soldiers often play hard rock/metal and rap because these genres are thought to be the most immediately irritating to insurgents in Iraq."[37] Abel further claims that "Western music" is unwelcome and thus appropriate in torture: "Western music is not the Iraqi's thing."[38] To be sure, given proscriptions against instruments and Western music, the playing of American vocal music with accompaniment could have targeted cultural identity and beliefs, as in al-Qahtani's case. However, based on the preceding discussion, Western music would not have functioned consistently in the negative, despite Abel's unilateral conclusion about Iraqi musical taste. Though Western music has been subject to censorship in various Islamic countries and may be effective as torture, it has also enjoyed popularity, especially in the underground among Muslim youth. Accordingly, the effects of Western music were not inevitably negative. At times, people in the region have heralded Western music as a symbol of freedom or, in the case of heavy metal, linked it directly to life in the Middle East. C. J. Grisham, who claims to have used music in interrogation, attests to the multiple potential reactions to music associated with America: "Mudgrave worked really well and really any kind of American music, except the popular stuff. I didn't know this but walking down the street when we first get into Baghdad and all the kids, all they know is, Michael Jackson."[39]

At the same time, when imposed as torture, even popular music in the region, like that of Michael Jackson, could have assumed menacing overtones, especially given the detention centers' power structure. In this context, the transmission of Western music and its global dominance may have been seen as an insulting demonstration of control, even by people with heavy metal or rap sympathies. As Bruce Johnson and Martin Cloonan hypothesize, the use of music in detention centers was "an attempt to assert U.S. cultural hegemony at a time when its military was showing its might."[40] This subjugation and domination is evident in the titles of specific musical choices so employed: Britney Spears's "Hit Me Baby One More Time," Queen's "We Are the Champions," Bruce Springsteen's "Born in the USA," and even Eminem's "White America," though the latter two songs are in fact critical of American politics.[41]

The varied potential responses to specific choices of music—whether gendered and thus associated with Muslim proscriptions against sexual depravity, instrumental, or perceived Western and therefore similarly wounding as illegal or an extension of military power—point to the diverse roles of music and attendant associations at work in torture. The specific choice of music was therefore important and added additional layers of impact to American soldiers' psychological and physical assault in interrogation and torture. These layers aided interrogators' general goals in this context.

Torture is a profound violation. The torturer takes control of the tortured—his voice and body. Yet through torture, the prisoner's body, no longer under his or her own control, and pain became "overwhelmingly present," as the scholar Elaine Scarry has argued. The body in pain thereby obliterates the detainees' self and subjectivity. The torturer—his or her voice and subjectivity—becomes "overwhelmingly present" instead.[42] At the same time, as the professor of philosophy David Sussman insists, the torturer turns the victim inside out. His or her will becomes that of the torturer. The omniscience of the torturer overpowers the tortured, who experiences his or her torture as a result of self-betrayal, "something I do to myself."[43] This process destroys the prisoner's internal dialogue—a means of connection with the self integral to survival. There remains only the torturer; the tortured has no one on whom to rely. In despair, faced with such extreme lonesomeness, the victim, having lost the ability to communicate with others, begins to lose contact with the self. As Dori Laub has argued based on his work with Holocaust survivors, the "processes that promote the shutdown of the mental registering processes, the cessation of the dialogue with the internal 'Thou' (and, ultimately, of symbolization and of thought), lead to a certain absence, or rather erasure, of memory." Extreme trauma may consequently stop internal dialogue even after torture, obliterating memory and self-awareness for years subsequently, if not permanently.[44]

In the war on terror, music—as sound and music or as organized sound—has generally augmented this exercise of power. Music, connected to identity, functions as an extension of the torturer's voice and thus self. In this example, the use of music associated with the West is especially effective to this end as a means of suggesting the torturer's identity. This suggested identity or voice, manifest in music, helps position the torturer as ever-present—there is no one else. In the interrogation of al-Qahtani, loud music (or the volume of music as sound) was used in this way to establish control and underscore the futility of resistance. His December 10, 2002, detention log states, "Lead established control over detainee by instructing him not to speak and enforcing by playing loud music and yelling. Detainee tried to regain control several times by starting to talk about his cover story. Detainee was not listened to."[45] But specific music as music further served this goal. As we saw, the use of Aguilera's music, for example, worked to break al-Qahtani's communion with himself by challenging his self-identification as an observant Muslim.

The military also used loud music to replace or literally drown out the detainee's thoughts. Donald Vance, a U.S. Navy veteran, had been working with the Federal Bureau of Investigation to gather evidence against his employer, the Iraqi-owned Shield Group Security Company. However, in 2006, he was arrested by U.S. forces and subjected to interrogation and torture at Camp Cropper, a detention center at Baghdad International Airport. There he recalls the blaring of continuous music, such as Nine Inch Nails's "Mr. Self-Destruct" and "March of the Pigs." Though he remembers his struggle to endure in interrogation, he could rely somewhat on his Dyn-Corp's Crucible training course by former Special Forces officers, which had taught him several means of survival. With this experience, he understood the goals of torture and the intent of music's use therein as a way to prevent detainees "from having their own thoughts." He also knew a method of resistance: "The counteracting thing was to try to talk to yourself out loud, animatedly; I'd talk with my hands. Telling stories about me to me, telling myself jokes even though I knew the punchline. I understood that I needed to do something with my mind."[46]

But the intended suppression of thought was not sought only through overpowering sound. The deployment of songs from American television series, such as the children's shows *Sesame Street* and *Barney and Friends,* disrupted thought through natural internal repetition. As an "ear worm," a memorable tune can enter and undermine part of the brain, as physician Oliver Sacks explains, "forcing it to fire repetitively and autonomously (as may happen with a tic or a seizure)."[47] According to James Kellaris, ear worms, which cause what he terms "stuck tune syndrome," thus work like a mosquito bite. The more the mind scratches (plays) the tune, the worse the need to scratch (play) it becomes.[48] Songs from children's television programming lend themselves to such a process given their reliance on repetition—a means to facilitate learning among young audiences, but also a part of the commercial experience of music in general in our consumer society.[49] A particularly illustrative example is "I Love You" from *Barney and Friends,* a confirmed part of the military's arsenal. In addition to repeated sounding within the series, the song also relies on repetition on other levels. That is to say, though with new lyrics by Lee Bernstein, the song is recycled: it appropriates the music of "This Old Man," which uses repetition to help teach children to count to ten. The first verse is as follows:

This old man, he played one
He played knick-knack on my thumb
With a knick-knack patty-whack, give a dog a bone
This old man came rolling home.

After "this old man" plays ten in the tenth verse, to the same music as he played one through nine in the first nine verses, the song finally ends. Though "I Love You" only has two verses, again both set to the same music, the second verse reuses all but two lines of text from the first. Particularly jarring, given the clash between the over-the-top tenderness of the text and the context of its playing in torture, the first verse is as follows:

I love you
You love me
We're a happy family
With a great big hug
And a kiss from me to you
Won't you say you love me too?

The music also contains repetitive musical motives. It begins, for example, by sounding the same motive twice, a simple minor third, which results in six notes and yet only two different pitches (see figure 4). The tune as a whole ranges only a sixth and is dominated by simple stepwise motion. This simplicity and wide-ranging replication gave the military a particularly effective tune on which to capitalize, according to Sacks's and Kellaris's descriptions of music's potential turn as tic, which Sacks further characterizes as a "coercive process."[50] The military also built on this promise by playing "I Love You," and similar tunes over and over again, further mimicking and inducing such a subversion of thought.

When repeated, various musics can also stop regular thought by inducing a trance state. Music is not deterministic to this end, but with a repeated rhythm, continuous music has the potential to entrain. There are various trance states, including "the mild trance of the listener whose whole attention becomes focused on the music" as well as possession trance, "in which one's self appears to be displaced and one's body is taken over by a deity or a spirit."[51] These states produce a kind of focus, with areas of the brain shut-

Figure 4. Opening bars of "I Love You," aka "This Old Man"

ting down, including some areas that keep us in contact with the "normal, wide-awake, non-metaphysical world we normally inhabit." A human can thus "lose oneself in the music," as regular thought ceases.[52] In these ways, music could interrupt or even replace internal dialogue. Laub has demonstrated that art "may serve as a container for the traumatic experience." For example, by writing poetry or singing a song in captivity, art can be a means to maintain some internal dialogue.[53] However, when music operates as torture, the potential of art as savior is denied the prisoner and even turned against him.[54]

Intensifying this process, noise more generally can obscure external sounds that could have acted as a means of orientation or even comfort. In his account of detention in Guantánamo, Bagram, and Kandahar, Moazzam Begg records his awareness of sound in his attempt to make sense of his imprisonment. At Kandahar, he writes, "the noise was deafening: barking dogs, relentless verbal abuse, plane engines, electricity generations, and screams of pain from the other prisoners. Maybe I screamed too."[55] Subsequently transferred while denied the power of sight, he once again turned to sound to decode his surroundings: "I could feel wind on my face, and a deep whir of fans, very noisy and blowing in all directions, and I could hear voices in the distance, too far to make out language. I knew this must be Camp Delta, the main camp."[56] There, he recalls the comfort of sound: "First it came over the camp loudspeakers, but then I heard prayer calls from different detainees. It was so beautiful, after so long."[57] The use of noise—musical or otherwise—could conceal such auditory cues associated with place and solace. But music that is not familiar or foreign to the detainee would have further removed the victim from a sense of reality—or at least a reality he had previously known. As Daniel Levitin, a psychology professor at McGill, has surmised, "These were tonal structures the detainees' brains can't figure out. They kept trying, and they kept failing. Just as if I made you listen to Chinese opera, it'd probably drive you crazy."[58] Accordingly, music, at least for some unfamiliar with music popular in the United States, would have aided in the creation of dread in a place apart. As an American interrogator yelled through an interpreter, according to the recollection of the former detainee Laid Saidi, "You are in a place that is out of the world. No one knows where you are, no one is going to defend you."[59]

With this in mind, the imposition of music, through volume and specific aspects of the music selected as music, obscured both internal and external dialogue by obliterating any point of reference or connection between the world and self, any hope of self-control. The only option became submission. As in American correctional facilities, music therefore worked in the maintenance of a total discipline of the body. That is, music augmented the captor's control of those in captivity—even at times through a system of exchange similar to that in prison. While music can function as a reward for good behavior in prisons in the United States, in al-Qahtani's example, the inverse—the absence of music—functioned as an incentive for cooperation in torture abroad. Al-Qahtani's December 15, 2002, detention log states, "Detainee complained about music being played. Detainee stated that interrogator was an intelligent, understanding man and should know that music was inappropriate. Music was stopped as long as detainee kept talking."[60] Similarly, Nasriddinov, explained, "If you voluntarily make contact with them and answer their questions, the conditions improve. The metal chains on the hands and the feet are loosened, the food gets better, a soft mattress, a pillow and bedding are provided. The loud music is turned off, a list of books and sports news are supplied and one can borrow a DVD to watch."[61] The cessation of music was in this way exchanged for "good behavior" as well as some means of comfort in detention. As in prison, this use of music in the disciplining of detainees further extended the performance of this control. In this example, such a link relates to the theatricality of torture more generally.

The site of torture often includes special lighting and a certain backdrop, all crafted "with a perverse stagecraft to evoke an aura of fear."[62] Scarry thus writes of the involved "acts of display" in torture as "a grotesque piece of compensatory drama" designed to produce "a fantastic illusion of power."[63] In keeping with tradition, music helped produce this drama as a soundtrack of torture while suggesting the interrogators' power. After all, throughout history, those who control music and the means of broadcasting music control power and the means of demonstrating power.[64] Music in these ways worked in the performance of power in torture—a supposed strategy to combat terrorism, which similarly depends on theater, that is the creation of a mood of terror through acts performed before an audience.[65]

In all of these ways, the choice of music in torture, rather than merely loud noise—unmediated yelling or hissing—mattered. The military used music's connections to identity through association, potential in the repetitive and rhythmic makeup of specific musical compositions, contestations regarding the status of music in the Middle East, and music's ties to discipline and power. So why has controversy arisen surrounding the distinction between sound and music in torture? Why the question of music's functioning as music in torture? The debate about music's relationship to torture is one of several controversies sparked by revelations regarding music's roles in the war on terror. These controversies point to greater concerns and motivations, including reactions more generally to the idea that music can be negative.

News of music's involvement in torture inspired a host of responses. As in previous examples, there have been reactions of humor and dismissal. Writing for *The Nation,* Moustafa Bayoumi sums up the sentiment: "Finally, dangerous terrorists—like everyone else—will be tortured by Britney Spears's music!"[66] However, others have responded with outrage. On October 22, 2009, a group of artists, including Trent Reznor of Nine Inch Nails, Roseanne Cash, and members of R.E.M. and Pearl Jam, demanded that the U.S. government disclose a list of music used in torture since 2002. In so doing, they supported a Freedom of Information Act request filed by the National Security Archive, an independent research institute at George Washington University. The National Security Archive sought the declassification of all records involving music in this context. Within *Law Blog,* Jess Bravin, a Supreme Court reporter, wondered if lawsuits might follow this high-profile outcry. Does the government have the right to program copyrighted material as torture without the permission of the associated artists? One poster responded online, "Copyright law has developed something called the first sale doctrine which says that you can do basically whatever you want with the copyright material once you pay for it. So once you buy a cd or dvd you can burn it, lock it in a safe, read/play it a million times, sell it, use it as a sex toy, whatever." Another commentator disagreed: "The government uses copyrighted work without the artist [*sic*] permission, that is a breach of copyright laws."[67] A Canadian lawyer, Howard Kopf, may have been the first to raise this issue when he suggested that the U.S. government might owe performance royalties: "Certain collectives are quick to collect money from those in nursing homes, hospitals, prisons etc, on the basis that these are 'public' places."[68] Following this logic, on March 5, 2006, the United Kingdom's *Sunday Star* reported that the rapper Eminem was set to sue the U.S. government for failing to obtain permission to use his music against inmates at Camp Delta.[69]

Rather than copyright, however, for outraged musicians, the main point of contention has been the issue of torture and the role of their creations therein. As Tom Morello, the guitarist in Rage against the Machine, explains, "The fact that the music I helped create was used in crimes against humanity sickens me."[70] Along these lines, Reznor stated in 2008, "It's difficult for me to imagine anything more profoundly insulting, demeaning and enraging than discovering music you've put your heart and soul into creating has been used for purposes of torture."[71] With such reasoning, these musicians officially issued a protest against torture. The White House countered by insisting that music no longer plays a role within torture—a shift in policy President Barack Obama instituted on his second full day in office.[72] Musicians' protests and subsequent presidential action, however, disclose two related but separate issues: moral outrage against torture and offense related to a perceived misappropriation of music. These two issues are similarly entangled in scholarly response.

In 2008, the American Musicological Society (AMS) issued a condemnation of music's use as torture, referring to this practice as a "misappropriation" of music and "contamination of our cultures."[73] In contrast, the Society for Ethnomusicology (SEM) focused on the effects of such a technique on people: "The SEM is committed to the ethical uses of music to further human understanding and to uphold the highest standards of human rights. The Society is equally committed to drawing critical attention to the abuse of such standards through the unethical uses of music to harm individuals and the societies in which they live."[74] Addressing the AMS statement, Richard Taruskin writes, "I'm afraid I don't agree about the value of the resolution. It's torture, not the use of music per se therein, that decent people oppose, musicologists among. All we accomplish by passing such a resolution is saying, 'We're decent people, and aren't we wonderful!' How much courage does that require? Self-congratulation is not effective social action."[75] This conflict regarding focus was similarly apparent in Ford and Bellman's online debate. In it, Ford focused on interpretation of music and its role in torture, while on August 21, 2007, Bellman insisted, "The problem is the torture, not the music." According to Bellman, the discussion should focus on the morality of torture, not the role of music in torture. For American courts, the former has indeed been the point of concern.

International and U.S. law has traditionally banned torture as unjustifiable, whether in war or peace.[76] Yet within American law in the last decade, torture, physical and psychological, has been arguably sanctioned in the questioning of suspects "so long as the purpose of the investigation is to deter or detect the next terrorist attack."[77] With such latitude, the courts have even offered a rather flexible definition of torture to avoid moral and ethical issues as well as international law associated with torture. In a memorandum to Alberto R. Gonzales, counsel to the president, dated August 1, 2002, the Office of Legal Counsel within the U.S. Department of Justice insisted: "For purely mental pain or suffering to amount to torture under Section 2340, it must result in significant psychological harm of significant duration, e.g., lasting for months or even years."[78] This memorandum further cites the controversy of sound's use in U.K. interrogation in 1971. Though the European Court of Human Rights later ruled it "inhuman and degrading," such a tactic was not judged of "sufficient intensity or cruelty to amount to torture" in the United States.[79]

But given this important question of torture, its parameters, and the consequences for detainees rather than related aesthetic implications for music, why are musicians even involved in this controversy? Along these lines, Cusick recalls with surprise how often she has been asked of her work on torture, "Yes, but is this musicology?"[80] Of course, music's involvement in torture is relatively new and thus has inevitably caught the attention of those involved in music. Furthermore, music scholars are uniquely positioned to decode music's functioning as music in torture and the repercussions of this technique on those so subjected. Yet musicians' and musicologists' discussions of music's role in torture have unfortunately sidelined the salient ethical question of torture and its effects in favor of general denunciation, semantic debate, and concern about music. With such stagnation, it is perhaps not surprising that the philosophy professor and DJ Steve Goodman, in his recent work *Sonic Warfare,* chooses to avoid altogether "critic-aesthetic statement on the use of sonic warfare," instead discussing sound as force rather than sound as text. While he therefore ignores music's associations and operation as music beyond sound, he at the very least moves the discussion forward by analyzing examples of the effects of sound on the ground.[81] But this seemingly calculated move solves only part of the problem. To push beyond current debate regarding music as torture, as I have modeled, we need to respect music's roles as music in torture and seek to understand how sound works with sound perceived as music in this context. Moreover, we need to dismantle the debate that has somehow overshadowed these more practical considerations. This debate has been paralyzed by musicians' and musicologists' concerns about self-identity and their fundamental attention to music.

And this brings us back to Ford's initial post concerning torture, in which he quoted Cusick. In 2006, she wrote, "As press reports conflating music's

use on the battlefield with its use in interrogations proliferated, I began des-
ultory research on a phenomenon of the current 'global war on terror' that
particularly wounds me as a musician—wounds me in that part of my sensibility that remains residually invested in the notion that music is beautiful,
even transcendent."[82] Pieslak recognized this concern in musical discussions
of torture. Music's involvement in war, he wrote, "makes us uncomfortable
because we like to hold on to the romanticized notion that music is something that delights our senses; it doesn't inflict harm on others."[83] Two years
later, Cusick explained her involvement in the issue of musical torture: "We
feel directly involved because something we have chosen to make part of
our selves—music—has been weaponised, used to harm others." Like the
torture victim, she maintained, we are therefore harmed: "Both 'music' and
the part of us that has been made out of our relationship with 'music' shat-
ters like glass."[84] According to this logic, music is good and should be good
to protect those involved in it—their sense of worth and related goodness.
A recent discussion addressing the musicologists' and ethnomusicologists'
"bleak job market" within the online "Musicology/Ethnomusicology" wiki
also suggests economic motivations for such justification of music: If we
protect music by heralding its transcendence, we may ensure employment
in music and thus the financial and psychological support and survival of
music scholars. Wrote one commentator, "Rather than specifically fighting
contingent hiring, I would like to see our organizations become more willing to challenge the status quo at the institutional and disciplinary level by
finding ways to articulate and demonstrate all the reasons (and there are
plenty!) that music/the arts should be an integral part of every student's
training. More demand for the arts = more jobs."[85] Romantic aesthetics,
though shifting in contemporary contexts, provide firm foundation for these
strategies. Romantic musical ascriptions may therefore endure because we
want them to: They are attractive and significant in our own personal construction of identity and meaning. Like Romantic composers confronting
the demise of the patronage system, trained musicians and music scholars
also may elevate music out of necessity: to promote the possibility of future
monetary support.

Thinking about music that privileges it as positive and the motivations
behind such thinking help explain high-profile musicians' public protest.
Rosanne Cash, for example, maintained, "It seems so obvious. Music should
never be used as torture. It's beyond the pale. It's hard to even think about."[86]
And this belief is widespread among the general public as well. One response
to Cash's comment in *The Vibe*, reads, "What kind of sicko could use an

art-form so beautiful as music to TORTURE someone?! It's sick!" Qualifying what music can do, another writer posted, "Music is suppose [*sic*] to be an outlet not a punishment." This outcry explicitly links music's operation as torture with other cases of music's use within crime prevention. Though distinct, music in crime deterrence has invited similar objection. As the British music columnist Norman Lebrecht writes, "Music is a vast psychological mystery, and playing it to police railways is culturally reckless, profoundly demeaning to one of the greater glories of civilization."[87] Likewise, Daniel Ferreira has decried music's employment as punishment: "It's a blow below the belt to all musicians to say their lives' work can be categorized as punishment."[88]

With such concerns about music's sublime status, related positive conceptions of individuals engaged with music, and economic incentive, the proposed distinction between sound and music in torture seems convenient. Whether or not doing so is a warranted act, categorizing music in torture as sonic weaponry or merely torture allows those so inclined to preserve music's supposed sanctity and their own related positive and even lofty sense of self and career trajectory. This response to music's negative potential similarly affects discussions of music in other darker contexts.

At the 2009 American Musicological Society's national conference, musicologist Benita Wolters-Fredlund presented a paper, "Playing the Part: Dehumanizing Music in Concentration Camps." In it, she reviewed music's use by the Nazis to humiliate, torment, deceive, control, and even kill. She concluded that "the history of concentration camp music should persuade us to reject definitions of music as an essentially sublime art, and to recognize that in addition to providing pleasure, encouragement and distraction it can also be an instrument of pain, exclusion and hatred." The ensuing discussion replicated the debate about music as torture. Was music during the Holocaust in this way no longer music but rather unmusic? This distinction was first suggested by Szymon Laks in his memoir about life in the camps: "This is not a book about *music*. It is a book about *music in a Nazi concentration camp*. One could also say: about *music in a distorting mirror*."[89] Even work on music in less overtly dangerous settings, in everyday situations, has invited qualification along these lines. In his work on Muzak, Stephen H. Barnes opines, "Muzak goes beyond a prostitution of one of life's great pleasures, i.e., *listening* to music; Muzak manipulates."[90] Accordingly, Muzak, as Barnes maintains, is "the ultimate perversion of this art form."[91] The composer Ned Rorem likewise seeks to protect his art: "The more an artwork succeeds as politics, the more it fails as art." Elsewhere, he imposed a similar circumscription of music beyond the concert hall: "Music that does impel action tends to be not even music per se, but a hypnotic beat inciting us to battle."[92]

Such qualification and outcry is related to Theodor W. Adorno and Max Horkheimer's idea of autonomous art—art created outside the culture industry—as a precondition of authentic art. Art in violation of this construct, in Adorno and Horkheimer's formulation, ceases to be authentic art. With such logic, these prominent representatives of the Frankfurt School drew a line in the sand: There exists art as autonomous, in keeping with Romantic aesthetics, and works for entertainment or commerce, a nonart for use.[93] This demarcation of cultural offsides was effectively championed in the United States in the writings of Dwight Macdonald, who insisted that the masscult was not really culture at all.[94] Such a black-white boundary, which represents a tidy remedy to seemingly problematic uses of music, implicates the role of genre in this conditioning of music. Along these lines, contested valuations of popular music, especially rap and heavy metal, may in some ways have shaped the musical torture debate. In other words, would music scholars deny the role of music as music in torture if the military employed only classical music in this context or even canonic works of rock or jazz, rather than controversial genres of popular music—heavy metal and rap? How would the use of culturally authoritative music have changed the debate?

Whether or not genre and evolving notions of the solely positive powers of specific musics played a prominent role, it is clear that we are here generally dealing with a broader notion of Music and its elevation, a redeployment of Romantic aesthetics in a wider context. With this thinking, some respond to perceived negative uses of this generalized notion of music with qualifications of music. That is, some insist that music is positive and thus, if music functions toward negative ends, surely the music involved is no longer music. But this circumscription of music according to shifting notions of its supposed transcendence hardly addresses the competing realities behind the production, dissemination, and exploitation of music generally today. Furthermore, such a dichotomy and the related uproar focus on the setting's effects on music rather than music's effects within the setting. This discussion of musical semantics—the debate about when music is music based on context and use—thereby clouds the issue and obscures certain dangers of music of all types in practice. Several scholars would agree. As Jacques Attali writes, "With music is born power and its opposite: subversion."[95] Johnson and Cloonan similarly explain, "We cannot point to any piece of music and say that it must generate violence, but nor can we say that it cannot under any circumstances."[96] French philosophers Gilles Deleuze and Félix Guattari go even further: "Music has a thirst for destruction, every kind of destruction, extinction, breakage, dislocation. Is that not its potential 'fascism'?"[97] Along these lines, Taruskin provocatively writes, "Art is not blameless. Art can inflict harm. The Taliban know that. It's about time we learned."[98]

Throughout this study, we have seen the effects of the chasm between thinking about music in terms of the Romantic sublime and music's practical functioning. In chapter 1, the notion that music is a moralizing force shifted criticism of music in crime deterrence away from the potential danger of this strategy and its effects on people: the creation of hierarchies in society. Likewise, the sentence of music in the punishment of noise violators and Judge Paul Sacco's thinking about the measure as a means to enlighten may disguise issues of racial privileging and even the cruel and ineffective nature of the sentence. In chapter 3, the notion of music's inherent connection to the higher realm of the soul similarly gave way to bias and prejudice, while, in chapter 5, the belief in music's innate goodness prevented many from recognizing music's practical role in the defense of discipline. Privileging the legacy of Romantic aesthetics has faulty foundations and serious ramifications: This thinking ignores philosophical explanations of music from before 1800 that denied otherworldly Romantic constructions[99] while discounting the potential dangers, realities, and significance of music's ubiquitous use today. Moreover, those who seek to protect the sanctity of music may be too late (if they ever had a chance): The growing record shows that the exploitation of music's darker potential is not an aberration but is instead rather commonplace.[100] Although unsettling for some, accepting music's potential toward negative ends—but not the negative ends themselves or their harmful effects on people—seems inevitable.

In this way, our conception of music may need to change. Since the Romantic era, music has been theorized as object, an object of value. But music exists in context, a context that conditions its use and meaning. While a few recent scholars thus view music as process or a constant becoming,[101] if viewed as an object, music must be assigned multiple lives. As Philip Fisher writes, "The life of Things is in reality many lives."[102] Once a sign of battle, a sword can be plundered after a warrior's death as an object of wealth. In a museum, however, that sword is studied "as an example of a style, a moment, a level of technical knowledge, a temperament and culture."[103] This museum stage can obliterate the sword's use in the past. The museum thus further suppresses the "the practices within which any object becomes . . . a tool."[104]

The nineteenth century's elevation of music as object—the creation, as Lydia Goehr writes, "of music's imaginary museum"—and its endurance today has similarly destroyed the multiple lives and uses of music as a tool in the past and present. But despite our lack of vision, music will continue to function as a tool, and its uses as such have consequences for people that require attention. The motivations behind conceptions of music that deny music's involvement in torture are understandable in some ways. However, to care about music is to understand its functioning in all contexts.

For some, music's roles as a tool—even a tool of destruction—may be revelatory. In one exception to the general protest, James Hetfield, the lead singer of Metallica, viewed the use of his music in torture positively: "I take it as an honor to think that perhaps our song could be used to quell another 9/11 attack or something like that." There is a note not only of patriotism in his comment but also of pride in the power of his work: "We've been punishing our parents, our wives, our loved ones with this music forever. Why should the Iraqis be any different. . . . Part of me is proud because they chose Metallica!"[105] Assigned as art, beyond use, art may be assumed harmless and even powerless. The philosopher Arthur Danto argues that "this leads to the nightmare of impotency" that explains in part what he recognizes as the relief some artists have experienced when political leaders in the past have censored art as dangerous.[106] While a musician might enjoy the force of music designated harmful and revel in this chapter, celebration is not my point. I do not seek to replace one valuation that elevates music with another of sorts. In this chapter and in this book as a whole, I have attempted to parse music's operation today, whether as art, weapon, or tool. All three play critical if controversial roles in the lives of people, the organizing of society, and the enforcement of law and order.

Epilogue

This book surveys the use of music in escalating stages of the criminal-legal process. Chapters 1 and 2 explore how authorities fight the activities and sounds of youth through music. Chapter 3 discusses the prosecutions' appropriation of rap lyrics as evidence in criminal cases against rap artists and aspiring rappers. Chapter 4 focuses on the courts' direct confrontation with rap in cases alleging that the music incites unlawful action. Chapter 5 examines public opposition to music in prison. And finally, chapter 6 considers the military's use of music in torture. Vast differences exist between these case studies—in the specific types of music involved and the implications of music's roles in each. However, significant links also exist, and they might aid the legal community in assessing future operations of music in crime prevention and punishment. More broadly, these connections can expose the complicated place of music within the law, as illustrated by the introduction's initial case, *People v. Kelly* (2007).

In *People v. Kelly*, the defense argued on appeal that the music of the Irish musician Enya unfairly swayed the jury to recommend that Douglas Oliver Kelly receive the sentence of death for the murder of Sara Weir. During sentencing, the prosecution presented to the jury a victim impact testimony video consisting of a montage of photos of Weir set to Enya's music, with the narrator, Weir's mother, explaining that her daughter had especially enjoyed Enya's songs. According to the defense, however, the victim's taste in music hardly justified the playing of music in court. The defense argued that Enya's work created excess emotion in the courtroom, thereby improperly influencing the jury's recommendation in sentencing. The judge, however, ultimately affirmed the jury's verdict, concluding that the use of music was inconsequential.

Taken together, this book's six chapters examine the ways in which Romantic aesthetics can conceal the full power and function of music. We have seen how many of the individuals involved in these case studies approached music in solely positive terms—terms that have evolved from the Romantic era. Within the context of crime deterrence (chapter 1), punishment (chapter 2), and evidence (chapter 3), authorities have demonstrated a firm belief in the power of music to effect moral change, to enlighten, and to reveal a composer's innermost being. However, as this book shows, these Romantic notions do not correspond to the way music functions in practice. Furthermore, such notions have a tendency to obscure some of the more destructive ways in which music has been deployed. For example, in chapter 2, Judge Paul Sacco expressed a hope that his musical punishment would enlighten noise violators and even educate them about music. But Daniel Sher, dean of the College of Music at the University of Colorado at Boulder, for one, feared that noise offenders might forge negative associations with the music to which they are subjected as punishment.[1] Once a noise violator hears classical music in sessions of punishment, the violator might always associate classical music with punishment. How likely would he or she then be to attend a classical music concert? Instead of expanding interest in music, Sacco's program could do the opposite.

To get a complete picture of the way music functions in the law, we must look beyond Romantic notions of music and consider several important factors: first, the centrality of the role of the listener rather than that of the composer. We have seen that a composer's intentions have no bearing on the function of music in crime prevention (chapter 1), music in punishment (chapter 2), and cases of musical incitement (chapter 4). In the programming of music to repel (chapter 1), authorities select music they expect teens to loathe so that they will move to avoid hearing it. For that strategy to work, teens need to respond to the selected music as the authorities anticipate. This response depends in part on the teen's biography—experience with music—as a listener as well as the listening context. The use of music in punishment operates similarly: For this approach to succeed, noise violators must react to the music appropriately—listen to the music and perceive the sound as punishment. The role of the listener is also central to cases claiming musical incitement. But here, the role of the listener confounds any potential proof that a piece of music could definitively be incitement. As we discussed in chapter 4, the listener's agency doomed the civil suit that charged Tupac Shakur, Interscope Records, and its parent company, Time-Warner, with liability for the death of police officer Bill Davidson. In this case, Davidson's family attempted to blame Rodney Howard's killing of Davidson on the music to which Howard was listening at the time of the shooting. However, the judge noted that Howard had previously listened to Shakur's music without reacting violently. Why should the music have created a different reaction this time? This inconsistency reveals that no composition can inherently and unequivocally incite action.

As we saw in chapter 3, the admittance of lyrics as evidence in the courtroom relies on the premise that music reveals a composer's identity or biography. In the trial of Joshua Adam Moore, for example, the prosecution sought to bolster its argument that Moore had committed robbery by citing rap lyrics Moore had previously written about robbery. In so doing, however, the prosecution ignored the fact that writers of rap lyrics often choose words for reasons beyond dictionary meaning—rhyme, a tradition of boasting, and so forth. The musical setting of the words further determines their meaning by, for example, creating emphasis or stress. By detaching the lyrics from the music, the prosecution attempted to draw a clear connection between rapping about robbery and committing robbery, thereby encouraging the judge and jury to view a song as a confession. As the Moore case showed, despite perpetuating Romantic assumptions about the role of the composer in the reception of his or her music, the criminal-legal process tends to hide the degree to which such assumptions within the courtroom rely on the subjective interpretation of a specific listener.

In the nineteenth century, musicians were expected to act in some ways as servants to the intentions, real and imagined, of the composer and his or her composition.[2] The work was therefore fixed and transcendent, in keeping with the notion of *Werktreue,* defined by Lydia Goehr as the "ideal of fidelity or authenticity."[3] In the reception of popular music, consumers have treated the album, at least in rock, similarly. The "canonical" album "demands repeated listening"—exact reproduction for the listener—and is "complete in itself, forming an object of endless study and value."[4] Music's functioning in crime prevention and punishment drastically differs from this ideal of faithfulness to the work or to the autonomy of the album. Rather, in this book's case studies, the musical work is fluid. The listener in some ways "recomposes" the music by interpreting it according to a context that is divorced from the composer's intent. Consequently, music's function in crime prevention and punishment is difficult to quantify or predict. Instead, music's operation is the result of a host of contextual considerations specific to the individuals involved in each situation, based on varying biographies, associations, and reactions to the setting. If the judge in *People v. Kelly* had decided to consider the influence of Enya's music on the jury, the court might well have found itself frustrated by the impossibility of reaching a firm ruling, particularly given the fact that for each individual juror, the music might have had a different effect. As attorney Erica Schroeder recognizes, without an ability to quantify music's effect, the best recourse would seem to be a ban on music from victim impact testimony.[5] And this proposal is certainly a viable option. Nevertheless, as the introduction argues, this is not the only way in which the law is permeated with emotion; it is merely an example of one way in which music lays this emotion bare. As the legal scholar Christine Haight Farley writes of visual art, art "creates conflict for law because it has the tendency to expose law's certainty as masking necessary ambiguities."[6]

And yet, while it is true that music influences different listeners in different ways, associations with music that implicate identity can offer a general idea of possible individual response. Individuals identify with a complex of musical associations—associations with genre, with a specific piece's reception history or composer's biography, as well as with the music's structure or sound itself, among other factors; these associations work in concert with an individual's biography and situation to determine influence and reaction. Far from morally elevating teens, classical music generally wards them off. Because classical music is associated with an elite and substantially older class, it tends to clash with a typical teen's projected identity. Teens may therefore leave an area marked by classical music to avoid being identified with it. We have similarly seen the importance of identity and association in rap lyrics used as evidence (chapter 3), in trials involving claims that music incites destructive action (chapter 4), in music in prison (chapter 5), and in music used as a form of torture (chapter 6). In the case of prison, inmates have been known to cooperate with prison officials to gain access to the music with which they identify and which reminds them of home. This sense of self-identification with music was turned against prisoners in detention centers abroad. There, the military employed music to attack a detainee's identity—for example, by programming music proscribed by a torture victim's faith.

The links between music, association, and identity are not, however, always exploited to negative or neutral ends. In rap or hip-hop therapy (referenced in chapter 4), practitioners in most cases play rap to stimulate discussion to reach a clientele associated with rap—often at-risk African-

American youth. In his 2003 study, Edgar H. Tyson observes hip-hop therapy as a means to work with "African-American and Latino youth." In a similar circumscription, Adia McClellan Winfrey's hip-hop therapy manual, *Healing Young People thru Empowerment (H.Y.P.E.)*, is described as "A Hip-Hop Therapy Program for Black Teenage Boys." In his master's thesis in psychology, "Hip Hop Wisdom for White Therapists," Kevin Klinger makes the racial exchange even more explicit by "specifically targeting White therapists as the audience" for his research and "focusing exclusively on African American clients."[7] In this way, rap or hip-hop therapy relies on music's complicated connections to identity, much like the use of classical music to repel youth: through music, authorities can challenge identity and repel or create empathy and thus a therapeutic bond.

With this relationship between music, association, and identity in mind, let us again consider *People v. Kelly*. What if the video montage had featured not the music of Enya but "6 Feet Deep" by the rap group Geto Boys? Though I cannot hope to know the jury's reaction to this hypothetical scenario, this question leads me to reflect on certain associations with the work of Enya that may have conditioned individual members' response. Since the victim's mother explained in the video that her daughter was especially fond of Enya's music, associations with Enya would have reflected on the character of the deceased in much the same way that prosecutors have used rap lyrics to draw negative characterizations. In *Bailey v. State* (2000), a Mississippi case, the defendant appealed his murder conviction on the grounds that a cassette tape found in his car should not have been admitted as evidence. The tape was *Another Mississippi Murder* by the rap group Mississippi Mafia, and the prosecutor had argued in closing, "Ladies and gentlemen, in going through the evidence of the case and looking at something that was in this defendant's possession, it speaks true as to this defendant's attitude. This isn't nothing but another Mississippi murder."[8] While in this case, the prosecution had introduced the tape to cast the defendant in a negative light, in *Kelly* the music would likely have worked in the reverse.

Enya enjoys widespread popularity, especially among adult contemporary audiences in the United States.[9] But this music also has particular appeal for funeral and memorial services.[10] In one prominent example, CNN showed scenes of the collapse of the World Trade Center on 9/11 to the accompaniment of Enya's "Only Time."[11] The song, which embraces life's unanswered questions ("Who can say / where the road goes / where the day flows / only time"), has also featured prominently in subsequent tributes marking the anniversary of this date, including tenth anniversary remembrances.[12] But

"Only Time" is not the only candidate for such appropriation. Enya's music generally lends itself to commemoration, given the music's connection to spirituality and Celtic culture, which is imbued with mystic overtones. The music itself has ethereal qualities that derive from its repeated, legato melodies—the backbone of Enya's craft—and from the use of synthesizers, keyboards, and voice, including simple layered vocal effects that emanate from Enya's lone voice. In addition to the unearthly dimension of this sound augmentation, the liberal application of reverb makes the music sound as if it plays in a vast open site, such as a hall or church.[13] As the ethnomusicologist Anna Maria Dore argues, Enya's music also has ties to an idealized femininity, invoked musically by the use of the female voice as well as by keyboard instruments, viewed historically as feminine.[14] With these musical signs and associations, Enya's music in *People v. Kelly* could have linked Sara Weir to a higher plane—as both a woman and a heavenly entity. Even to the average jury member unfamiliar with Enya, Enya's music, given its connection to high-profile commemoration of 9/11, could have subconsciously acted to summon feelings associated with great tragedy. In these various ways, Weir's taste in music may have operated in part to enhance her image or intensify reactions to her slaying. With the introduction of this evidence, the jury could therefore have judged her murderer a criminal deserving of the strongest possible punishment.

Enya's Celtic-influenced music also carries racial implications. As James McCarthy and Euan Hague argue, Celtic identity in Europe as well as America is predominantly a Caucasian identity.[15] In *Kelly*, the defense contended on appeal that the prosecutor unfairly challenged a prospective alternate juror because she was African American. The defendant, too, was African American. But the court countered this accusation with the racial descent of the victim, Weir, who, to justify the defense's argument, would have to be "a member of the group to which a majority of the remaining jurors belong." This condition, according to the court, was "debatable" since "her biological mother was a Blackfoot Indian."[16] The playing of Enya's music, however, would have linked Weir to Enya and to Celtic traditions and thus associated her with whiteness. The music therefore complicated the court's confrontation with prejudice by ascribing to Weir a racial identity beyond her actual ancestry.

With these factors of musical identity and association in mind, the defense in *Kelly* could have argued more forcefully on appeal that Enya's music influenced the jury. Specifically, the defense could have made a case that the music swayed the jury to view Weir in an especially positive light or to connect her death to great tragedy. The music would then potentially have strengthened negative reactions to her killer, made manifest in sentencing. Furthermore, the defense could have cited Enya's relationship to Celtic culture to further the claim of bias in the dismissal of the alternate juror. At the very least, the defense could have insisted that the music, given its associations, prejudiced the proceedings. Justice is supposed to be blind. The political scientist Austin Sarat and the legal scholar Thomas R. Kearns clarify, "Law promises to treat all persons equally, to honor us by ignoring what marks us as different. Law, in theory, knows no culture and recognizes no identity."[17] Lady Justice signifies this legal ideal: With scale and sword in hand, she appears blindfolded in fidelity to this goal of fairness and equality.[18] However, the presence of music and thus identity in *Kelly* undermines this ideal. And as we have seen in this book's various examples, music in every instance entails such subversion of fairness and impartiality.

In the end, the role of music in the prevention and punishment of crime undercuts enduring ideas of music's sanctity and inherent goodness while offering evidence of the ways in which Romantic aesthetics have shifted in contemporary uses and valuations of music. At the same time, the role of listener interpretation and response as well as the complex function of personal identification and musical association position music as a threat to the law's false polarization of reason and emotion. These factors also in some ways confound the law's belief in unqualified right and wrong, its need for concrete resolution in judgment, and its promise of blindness. Consideration of music is to a certain extent a veritable Pandora's box the courts cannot afford to open. Yet confronting the role of music in crime prevention and punishment offers a fuller understanding of the operation of law, including its uncertainties and its embedded prejudices. The criminal-legal process does not and cannot function in terms of absolutes, despite efforts to depict its workings as such. But with insight into the system's muddiness, we stand a better chance of approaching this ideal.

Notes

INTRODUCTION

1. *People v. Kelly,* 2007, LEXIS 13795, S049973, Supreme Court of California, 763. See also Alicia N. Harden, "Drawing the Line at Pushing 'Play': Barring Video Montages as Victim Impact Evidence at Capital Sentencing Trials," *Kentucky Law Journal* (2010/2011), *LexisNexis Academic,* 2 September 2011, http://www.lexisnexis .com.

2. *Salazar v. State,* 2002, LEXIS 230, No. 2180–1, Court of Criminal Appeals of Texas.

3. *People v. Prince,* 2007, LEXIS 4272, Supreme Court of California.

4. Similar premises affect visual art. Christine Haight Farley summarizes conventional ideas about art and law: "First, art and law belong in separate cognitive and intellectual spheres. Second, art and law exist in polarity where law is objective and art is subjective." Christine Haight Farley, "Imagining the Law," in *Law and the Humanities: An Introduction,* ed. Austin Sarat, Matthew Anderson, and Catherine O. Frank (Cambridge: Cambridge University Press, 2010), 36.

5. Erica Schroeder, "Sounds of Prejudice: Background Music During Victim Impact Statements," *The University of Kansas Law Review* (January 2010), *LexisNexis Academic,* 12 March 2010, http://www.lexisnexis.com.

6. Susan A. Bandes, "Exploring the Interaction between Emotions and Legal Institutions: Repellent Crimes and Rational Deliberation: Emotion and the Death Penalty," *Vermont Law Review* (Spring 2009), *LexisNexis Academic,* 5 February 2010, http://www.lexisnexis.com.

7. *F.W. Woolworth Co. v. Wilson* (5th Cir. 1934), quoted in John Leubsdorf, "Presuppositions of Evidence Law," *Iowa Law Review* (May 2006), *LexisNexis Academic,* 5 February 2010, http://www.lexisnexis.com.

8. Jeremy A. Blumenthal, "A Moody View of the Law: Looking Back and Look-

ing Ahead at Law and the Emotions," in *Emotion and the Law: Psychological Perspectives,* ed. Brian Bronstein and Richard Wiener (New York: Springer, 2010), 185.

9. Leubsdorf.

10. For more information, see Bandes.

11. Blumenthal, 186, 198, 200.

12. See Roy F. Baumeister, C. Nathan DeWall, and Liqing Zhang, "Do Emotions Improve or Hinder the Decision Making Process?" in *Do Emotions Help or Hurt Decision Making? A Hedgefoxian Perspective,* ed. Kathleen D. Vohs, Roy F. Baumeister, and George Loewenstein (New York: Sage, 2007), 11–34.

13. Leubsdorf. See also Brian Bornstein and Richard Wiener, "Emotion and the Law: A Field Whose Time Has Come," in *Emotion and the Law: Psychological Perspectives,* ed. Brian Bronstein and Richard Wiener (New York: Springer, 2010), 2. Bornstein and Wiener wrote, ". . . Emotion has both crept into law through the back door and entered directly through the front door. Indeed, some would still try to argue along with Aristotle that law is reason free from emotion."

14. More than that, emotions constantly interact with our context, our experience of a given situation, and are not stable and fixed or states of mind with an off-and-on switch. Based on Gadamer, Hans Lindhal admits, ". . . Subjectivity and objectivity in the law cannot be understood independently of the mediated character of the human relation to reality. The very possibility of both objectivity and subjectivity in the law is anchored in the fact that human beings can only experience reality by interpreting it." Hans Lindahl, "Dialectic and Revolution: Confronting Kelsen and Gadamer on Legal Interpretation," *Cardozo Law Review, Yeshiva University* (January 2003), *LexisNexis Academic,* 5 February 2010, http://www.lexisnexis.com.

15. With the emotion inevitable in victim impact statements, perhaps it is no surprise, given the recent controversy over the emotional impact of music, that Alicia N. Harden goes even further than Schroeder by recommending a complete ban on victim impact testimony. She writes, "Recent scholarship has advocated for a bright-line rule barring musical accompaniment to victim impact videos as the music is 'irrelevant and highly prejudicial' and results in prejudiced decision-making and a fundamentally unfair trial. While this argument is well taken, it does not go far enough. Removing the music may remove some of the video's emotional impact, but the emotional impact factor of individual components is not quantifiable; barring the video altogether ensures rational and even-handed decision-making." Harden.

16. Bandes.

17. See I. Bennett Capers, "Crime Music," *Ohio State Journal of Criminal Law* (forthcoming).

18. Robin L. West, "Adjudication Is Not Interpretation: Some Reservations About the Law-As-Literature Movement," *Tennessee Law Review* (Fall 1986), *LexisNexis Academic,* 5 February 2010, http://www.lexisnexis.com. This resistance is similar to that within American law schools, which generally treat the study of law in conjunction with the humanities as "useless" in practical application. See Austin Sarat, Matthew Anderson, and Catherine O. Frank, ed., *Law and the Humanities: An Introduction* (Cambridge: Cambridge University Press, 2010), 11–12.

19. See Schroeder.

20. Richard L. Schur, *Parodies of Ownership: Hip-hop Aesthetics and Intellectual Property Law* (Ann Arbor: University of Michigan Press, 2009); and Joanna Demers, *Steal This Music: How Intellectual Property Law Affects Musical Creativity* (Athens: University of Georgia Press, 2006).

21. For a concise definition of intellectual property law, crime and criminal law, see James E. Clapp, *Webster's Pocket Legal Dictionary* (New York: Random House, 2007), 66 and 209.

22. Carol Weisbrod, "Fusion Folk: A Comment on Law and Music," *Cardozo Law Review, Yeshiva University* (May/July 1999), *LexisNexis Academic*, 7 February 2010, http://www.lexisnexis.com.

23. Alex B. Long, "[Insert Song Lyrics Here]: The Uses and Misuses of Popular Music Lyrics in Legal Writing," *Washington & Lee Law Review* (Spring 2007), *Lexis-Nexis Academic*, 7 February 2010, http://www.lexisnexis.com.

24. Peter M. Mansfield, "Terrorism and a Civil Cause of Action: Boim, Ungar, and Joint Torts," *Journal of International and Comparative Law* (Spring 2003), *Lexis-Nexis Academic*, 26 May 2010, http://www.lexisnexis.com.

25. See Carys Wyn Jones, *The Rock Canon: Canonical Values in the Reception of Rock Albums* (Aldershot: Ashgate, 2008).

26. See Victoria S. Salzmann, "Honey, You're No June Cleaver: The Power of 'Dropping Pop' to Persuade," *Maine Law Review* (2010), *LexisNexis Academic*, 26 May 2010, http://www.lexisnexis.com.

27. Long.

28. Weisbrod.

29. See Desmond Manderson, *Songs without Music: Aesthtic Dimensions of Law and Justice* (New York: Palgrave Macmillan, 2009).

30. Desmond Manderson and David Caudill, "Symposium: Modes of Law: Music and Legal Theory—An Interdisciplinary Workshop Introduction," *Cardozo Law Review, Yeshiva University* (May/July 1999), *LexisNexis Academic*, 11 January 2010, http://www.lexisnexis.com.

31. Sanford Levinson and J. M. Balkin, "Essay/Book Review: Maw, Music, and Other Performing Arts," *University of Pennsylvania Law Review* (June 1991), *Lexis-Nexis Academic*, 12 March 2010, http://www.lexisnexis.com.

32. Robert H. Bork, *The Tempting of America: The Political Seduction of the Law* (New York: The Free Press, 1990), 143. See also Richard A. Posner, *Overcoming Law* (Cambridge: Harvard University Press, 1995).

33. Jerome Frank explained, "The legislature is like a composer. It cannot help itself: It must leave interpretation to others principally to the courts." Quoted in Levinson and Balkin. In 1947, Jerome Frank opened the door to such considerations when he insisted that a musician's interpretation of a musical composition held lessons for legal scholars as they assessed judges' readings of legal rules and statutes. See Jerome Frank, "Words and Music: Some Remarks on Statutory Interpretation," *Columbia Law Review* (1947).

34. Richard Taruskin, *Text and Act: Essays on Music and Performance* (New York: Oxford University Press, 1995), 33.

35. See Weisbrod. See also Richard Taruskin, "Is There A Baby in the Bathwater (Part I)," *Archiv für Musikwissenschaft* 63.3 (2006): 163–85.

36. Weisbrod.

37. Robert Cover, *Narrative, Violence, and the Law: The Essays of Robert Cover,* ed. Martha Minow, Michael Ryan, and Austin Sarat (Ann Arbor: University of Michigan Press, 1992), 99 and 103.

38. Quoted in Austin Sarat, Matthew Anderson, and Catherine O. Frank, "Introduction," in *Law and the Humanities: An Introduction,* ed. Austin Sarat, Matthew Anderson, and Catherine O. Frank (Cambridge: Cambridge University Press, 2010), 9.

39. Manderson, 27. Manderson writes, "First, aesthetics affect the values of our communities, values which are in their turn given form and symbolism within the legal system. In the law, then, we find not only evidence of our beliefs but traces of the aesthetic concerns that have propelled them. But the converse also holds."

40. Aaron R. S. Lorenz, *Lyrics and the Law: The Constitution of Law in Music* (Lake Mary, FL: Vandeplas, 2007), 2. Lorenz further writes, "As musicians construct truth and justice, law's images of truth and justice change." Lorenz, 15.

41. Manderson and Caudill.

42. Lorenz, 4. Lorenz also writes "Many philosophers including Plato, Rousseau, Nietzsche, and Adorno have drawn distinctions between music and law."

43. In general, music scholars have ignored legal valuations of music, despite their unique perspective and interest in musical issues within the law as well as cases that directly concern music. A unique exception is Alexander J. Fisher's "Song Confession, and Criminality: Trial Records as Sources for Popular Musical Culture in Early Modern Europe," *Journal of Musicology* 18.4 (Autumn 2001): 616–57.

44. Lydia Goehr, *The Imaginary Museum of Musical Works: An Essay in the Philosophy of Music* (Oxford: Clarendon Press, 1992), 80.

45. See a similar conclusion, based on study of the reception of ten influential rock albums, in Jones, 139.

46. Goehr, 245.

47. See, for example, James Lawrence Sernoe, "'It's the Same Old Song': A History of Legal Challenges to Rock-and-Roll and Black Music" (PhD diss., University of Iowa, 2000).

48. See also Lawrence Grossberg, "The Framing of Rock: Rock and the New Conservatism," in *Rock and Popular Music: Politics, Policies, Institutions,* ed. Tony Bennett, Simon Frith, Lawrence Grossberg, John Shepherd and Graeme Turner (London: Routledge, 1993), 206.

49. Christian D. Rutherford, "'Gangsta' Culture in a Political State: the Crisis in Legal Ethics Formation Amongst Hip-hop Youth," *Columbia University National Black Law Journal* (2004), *LexisNexis Academic,* 5 February 2010, http://www.lexis nexis.com.

50. Other articles extend this concern to popular music in general. Reilly writes, ". . . music's messages and lyrics that resonate in the ears and minds of the masses are

not simply off-base, dissonant, or unpopular; rather, they have become the antithesis of any measure of growth, self-confidence, and self-examination that music in civilized society should strive to seek." Tracy Reilly, "The 'Spiritual Temperature' of Contemporary Popular Music: An Alternative to the Legal Regulation of Death-Metal and Gangsta-Rap Lyrics," *Vanderbilt Journal of Entertainment and Technology Law* (Winter 2009), *LexisNexis Academic,* 5 February 2010, http://www.lexisnexis.com.

CHAPTER I

1. Bernard Lagan, "Q: How Do You Get Rid of a Gang of Boy Racers? A: Play Barry Manilow at full volume," *Times* (London), 18 July 2006, 6.

2. "Manilow to drive out 'hooligans,'" *news.bbc,* 15 January 2004, http://news.bbc.co.uk/1/hi/world/asia-pacific/5047610.

3. Andrew Tijs, "Manilow to Challenge Rockdale Yobbos," 6 June 2006, http://www.undercover.com.au/news/2006/jun06/20060606_barrymanilow.html.

4. "Top 10 artists for the Terminally Uncool," *top40,* 24 January 2007, http://top40.about.com/od/top10lists/ss/uncoolpop_10.htm.

5. Quoted in "Manilow unhappy with music-as-weapon-ploy," *soundgenerator,* 19 July 2006, http://www.soundgenerator.com/news/showarticle.cfm?articleid=8038.

6. Ibid.

7. Clint McKay, telephone conversation with the author, 17 January 2007.

8. Chris Smith, "The Kids on the Square: Teen Loiterers in SR's Downtown Have City Worried," *Press Democrat,* 19 May 1996, A1.

9. "Classical Music on West Palm Corner Deters Crime," *USA Today,* 8 July, 2001, http://www.usatoday.com/news/nation/2001/07/08/music.htm.

10. See I. Bennett Capers, "Crime Music," *Ohio State Journal of Criminal Law* (2010), *LexisNexis Academic,* 22 September 2011, http://www.lexisnexis.com.

11. Quoted in Joseph Lanza, *Elevator Music: A Surreal History of Muzak, Easy-Listening, and Other Moodsong* (Ann Arbor: University of Michigan Press, 2004), 17–18.

12. Lanza, 23; and Stephen H. Barnes, *Muzak: The Hidden Messages in Music* (Lewiston, NY: Mellen, 1988), 4.

13. Quoted in Barnes, 12.

14. Anahid Kassabian, "Ubiquitous Listening," in *Popular Music Studies,* ed. David Hesmondhalgh and Keith Negus (London: Arnold, 2002), 134, 137.

15. See Jonathan Sterne, "Sounds Like the Mall of America: Programmed Music and the Architectonics of Commercial Space," *Ethnomusicology* 41.1 (1997): 23, 35–36.

16. Quoted in Pierre Ruhe, "Classical Music Said to Increase Spending and Deter Crime," *Chicago Tribune,* 6 September 2006, http://articles.chicagotribune.com/2006-9-06/features/0609060025.

17. Sterne, 43.

18. Richard Severo, "Mitch Miller, Maestro of the Singalong, Dies at 99," *New York Times,* 3 August 2010, A16.

19. Jan Benzel and Allessandra Stanley, "1990: The Agony and the Ecstasy," *New York Times,* 30 December 1990, H1.

20. Lola Sherman, "The Homeless hate Handel . . . ," 5 January 2005, http://strangeobservations.tribe.net/thread/0c1f5a8f-90e9-4229-857a-1090d59296cb.

21. Margaret Chabris, email to author, 24 January 2007.

22. Scott Timberg, "Classical music as crime stopper," *Los Angeles Times,* 18 February 2005, http://www.freenewmexican.com/artsfeatures/10701.html.

23. "Classical Music on West Palm Corner."

24. "Group Thinks Classical Music Will Deter Hartford Crime," 6 March 2006, http://www.nbc30.com/news/7742633/detail.html?subid=10101541.

25. Nigel Duara, "Portland police employ classical music at light rail stations to chase off loiterers," *StarTribune.com,* 3 April 2011, http://www.startribune.com/nation/119121109.html.

26. Timberg.

27. Quoted in Timberg.

28. Quoted in ibid.

29. Liane Hansen, "Profile: Using classical music to help deter teen-agers from causing trouble at Boston subway stations," *Weekend Edition Sunday* (NPR), 22 September 2002, http://web.ebscohost.com/login.aspx?direct=true&dp=nfh&AN=6XN200209221306&site=ehost-live&scope=site.

30. Edward Lippman, *A History of Western Musical Aesthetics* (Lincoln: University of Nebraska Press, 1992), 10.

31. Plato, *Laws,* quoted in Warren D. Anderson, *Ethos and Education in Greek Music: The Evidence of Poetry and Philosophy* (Cambridge: Harvard University Press, 1966), 74.

32. Anderson, 83.

33. Peter Blecha, *Taboo Tunes: A History of Banned Bands & Censored Songs* (San Francisco: Backbeat, 2004), 2.

34. See Lippman, 11.

35. Quoted in Matthew Riley, "Civilizing the Savage: Johann Georg Sulzer and the 'Aesthetic Force' of Music," *Journal of the Royal Musical Association* 127.1 (2002): 7.

36. Quoted in Riley, 14.

37. Quoted in ibid., 20.

38. Lippman, 235.

39. See Leon Botstein, "The Aesthetics of Assimilation and Affirmation: Reconstructing the Career of Felix Mendelssohn," in *Mendelssohn and his World,* ed. R. Larry Todd (Princeton: Princeton University Press, 1991), 33.

40. Botstein, 33.

41. Quoted in Mark Evan Bonds, "Idealism and the Aesthetics of Instrumental Music at the Turn of the Nineteenth Century," *Journal of the American Musicological Society* 50.2–3 (Summer–Autumn 1997): 390.

42. Ibid., 397.

43. Beethoven to "Emile M. in H[amburg]," 17 July 1819, letter quoted in Bonds,

398; see also Richard Taruskin, "Review: Resisting the Ninth," *19th-Century Music* 12.3 (Spring 1989): 249.

44. For a more rigorous explanation of Schopenhauer's conception of music, see Philip Alperson, "Schopenhauer and Musical Revelation," *Journal of Aesthetics and Art Criticism* 40.2 (Winter 1981): 155–66. See also Lippman, 203–7.

45. James H. Donelan, *Poetry and the Romantic Musical Aesthetic* (New York: Cambridge University Press, 2008), xiv.

46. See also Lippman, 20.

47. Richard Taruskin, "Is There A Baby in the Bathwater (Part I)?," *Archiv für Musikwissenschaft* 63.3 (2006), 167.

48. Scott Timberg, "Halt . . . or I'll Play Vivaldi," *Toronto Star* 20 Feburary 2005, C5.

49. Scott Simon, "Profile: London has found classical music to be a cheap and easy way to deter loitering teens who harass subway riders and staff," *Weekend Edition Saturday* (NPR), 22 January 2005, http://search.ebscohost.com/login.aspx?direct=true&db=nfh&AN=6XN200501221208&site=ehost-live&scope=site.

50. R. Murray Schafer, *The Tuning of the World* (New York: Knopf, 1977), 95.

51. Paul Vitello, "A Ring Tone Meant to Fall on Deaf Ears," *New York Times,* 12 June 2006, A1.

52. See also Jonathan Sterne, "Urban Media and the Politics of Sound Space," *Open* 9: Sound, 2004–2006, http://www.skor.nl/article-2853-en.html.

53. Timothy D. Crowe, *Crime Prevention Through Environmental Design: Applications of Architectural Design and Space Management Concepts* (Boston: Butterworth-Heinemann, 1991), 1.

54. Crowe, 28.

55. Ibid., 3.

56. Ibid., 29.

57. Quoted in C. Ray Jeffrey, *Crime Prevention Through Environmental Design* (Beverly Hills, CA: Sage, 1971).

58. Randall Atlas, *21st Century Security and CPTED: Designing for Critical Infrastructure Protection and Crime Prevention* (Boca Raton, FL: Taylor and Francis, 2008), 30–33.

59. Crowe, 31.

60. Atlas, 35.

61. Crowe, 79.

62. "Classical Music on West Palm Corner."

63. Henri Lefebvre, *The Production of Space,* trans. Donald Nicholson-Smith (Oxford: Blackwell, 1991), 26, 141.

64. Melissa Jackson, "Music to deter yobs," *BBC News Magazine,* 10 January 2005, http://news.bbc.co.uk/1/hi/magazine/4154711.stm.

65. Quoted in Timberg, "Classical Music as Crime Stopper."

66. Quoted in ibid.

67. Stuart Hall, "Introduction: Who Needs Identity," in *Questions of Cultural Identity,* ed. Stuart Hall and Paul du Gay (London: Sage, 1996), 4.

68. See for example, Martin Stokes, ed., *Ethnicity, Identity and Music: The Musical Construction of Place* (Oxford: Berg, 1994).

69. Symbolic power is "a power of constructing reality," which enables one to transform the world, obtaining "the equivalent of what is obtained through force (whether physical or economic) . . ." See Pierre Bourdieu, *Language and Symbolic Power,* ed. John B. Thompson and trans. Gino Raymond and Matthew Adamson (Cambridge: Polity, 1991), 166 and 170.

70. Tia DeNora, *Music in Everyday Life* (Cambridge: Cambridge University Press, 2000), 42.

71. Mark Warr, *Companions to Crime: The Social Aspects of Criminal Conduct* (Cambridge: Cambridge University Press, 2002), 46–55.

72. Peter Martin, "Music, Identity, and Social Control," in *Music and Manipulation: On the Social Uses and Social Control of Music,* ed. Steven Brown and Ulrik Volgsten (New York: Berghahn, 2006), 57.

73. Darla Hernandez, "Folk Devils in Seattle," *Edwardsville Journal of Sociology* 2, 2002, http://www.siue.edu/SOCIOLOGY/journal/v2hernandez2002.htm.

74. Pierre Bourdieu, *Distinction: A Social Critique of the Judgment of Taste,* trans. Richard Nice (Cambridge: Harvard University Press, 1984), 18.

75. See James L. Mursell, *The Psychology of Music* (Westport, CT: Greenwood Press, 1964), 216–17; Jerold Levinson, *Music in the Moment* (Ithaca: Cornell University Press, 1997), 60–61; David J. Hargreaves, *The Developmental Psychology of Music* (Cambridge: Cambridge University Press, 1986), 111. Hargreaves proposes an inverted-U representation of the relationship between familiarity and enjoyment. That is to say, with repeated hearings, a listener's enjoyment of a given piece will typically increase steadily until he or she becomes overexposed to the piece. At this point, enjoyment will steadily decrease (111).

76. Levinson, 60.

77. Sherman.

78. Jacques A. Attali, *Noise: The Political Economy of Music,* trans. Brian Massumi (Minneapolis: University of Minnesota Press, 1985), 6.

79. Ibid., 19–20.

80. Ibid., 87.

81. See also Suzanne G. Cusick, "'You Are in a Place That Is out of the World . . .': Music in the Detention Camps of the 'Global War on Terror'," *Journal of the Society for American Music* 2.1 (February 2008): 1–26.

82. "Sydney, Australia, using Barry Manilow to drive off rowdy teenagers," http://digg.com/music/Sydney,_Australia,_using_Barry_Manilow_to_drive_off_rowdy_teenagers.

83. In *Feminine Endings,* Susan McClary explains of femininity and masculinity in music: "These codes change over time—the 'meaning' of femininity was not the same in the eighteenth century as in the late nineteenth, can musical characterizations differ accordingly." Today, the genre of classical music may be seen as gentle or refined—characteristics that are linked with femininity—while heavy metal and rap are characterized as more masculine. Susan McClary, *Feminine Endings: Music, Gender, and Sexuality* (Minneapolis: University of Minnesota Press, 1991), 7–9.

84. The specific use of antagonistic and loud music is in keeping with Schafer's contention that loud noises historically evoke respect and even fear, in addition to, at times, physical pain. See Barnes, 39.

85. Sterne, "Urban Media."

86. Quoted in Lee Hockstader, "U.S. Rocks Noriega: Troops Blare Music at Papal Nunciature, Tighten Security at Ex-Dictator's Refuge," *Washington Post,* 27 December 1989, A28.

87. Sam Howe Verhovek, "Decibels, Not Bullets, Bombard Texas Sect," *New York Times,* 25 March 1993, A16.

88. Bruce Johnson and Martin Cloonan, *Dark Side of the Tune: Popular Music and Violence* (Aldershot: Ashgate, 2008), 186.

89. Johnson and Cloonan, 186.

90. Kahle is currently president of Kahle Research Solutions, Inc.

91. Mary Ellen Egan, "Move Along," *City Pages* 18.842, 22 January 1997, http://www.citypages.com/databank/18/842/article3195.asp.

92. Sterne, "Urban Media."

93. Ibid.

94. Duara.

95. Clive Coleman and Clive Norris, *Introducing Criminology* (Devon: Willan, 2000), 146–75.

96. Other criminologists argue to the contrary, supporting such focused crime prevention. See Dave Weisburd, Laura A. Wyckoff, Justin Ready, John E. Eck, Joshua C. Hinkle, and Frank Gajewski, "Does Crime Just Move Around the Corner? A Controlled Study of Spatial Displacement and Diffusion of Crime Control Benefits," *Criminology* 44.3 (2006): 549–91.

97. Alecia P. Long, *The Great Southern Babylon: Sex, Race, and Respectability in New Orleans 1865–1920* (Baton Rouge: Louisiana State University Press, 2004), 102–43.

98. Capers.

99. Allegra Wilson, "Unfair Limits," *Press Democrat,* 18 August 1999, B6.

100. Quoted in Timberg, "Classical Music as Crime Stopper."

CHAPTER 2

1. S. P. Singal, *Noise Pollution and Control Strategy* (Oxford: Alpha Science International, 2005), 21; James P. Chambers, "Noise Pollution," in *Advanced Air and Noise Pollution Control,* vol. 2, ed. Lawrence K. Wang, Norman C. Pereira, and Yung-Tse Hung (Totowa, NJ: Humana, 2005), 442; see also Barry Truax, *Acoustic Communication,* 2nd ed. (Westport, CT: Ablex, 2001), 93.

2. See T. Embleton, "Noise Control from the Ancient Past," *Noise News* (March–April 1977): 26.

3. Bruce Johnson and Martin Cloonan, *Dark Side of the Tune: Popular Music and Violence* (Aldershot: Ashgate, 2008), 37.

4. Jacques Attali, *Noise: The Political Economy of Music,* trans. Brian Massumi

(Minneapolis: University of Minnesota Press, 1985), 122. For a brief history of legislation against noise in France, see Attali, 122–124.

5. See Alexander Gillespie, "The No Longer Silent Problem: Confronting Noise Pollution in the 21st Century," *Villanova Environmental Law Journal* (2009), *Lexis-Nexis Academic,* 7 February 2010, http://www.lexisnexis.com.

6. Arthur Schopenhauer, "On Noise," in *The Works of Schopenhauer,* ed. Will Durant (New York: Ungar, 1928), 460.

7. Quoted in John M. Picker, *Victorian Soundscapes* (Oxford: Oxford University Press, 2003), 60–61.

8. Emily Thompson, *The Soundscape of Modernity: Architectural Acoustics and the Culture of Listening in America, 1900–1933* (Cambridge: MIT Press, 2004), 116.

9. Ibid., 125–27.

10. Ibid., 128–29.

11. Quoted in Johnson and Cloonan, 166.

12. Thompson, 128–29.

13. Singal, 21.

14. Stephen H. Barnes, *Muzak: The Hidden Messages in Music: A Social Psychology of Cultures* (Lewiston, NY: Mellen, 1988), 48–50.

15. Quoted in Barnes, 60. See also Barnes, 58–59.

16. See Joseph Lanza, *Elevator Music: A Surreal History of Muzak, Easy-Listening, and Other Moodsong* (Ann Arbor: University of Michigan Press, 2004), 153.

17. Quoted in R. Murray Schafer, *The Soundscape: Our Sonic Environment and the Tuning of the World* (New York: Knopf, 1977), 97.

18. See Joshua Leeds, *The Power of Sound: How to Manage Your Personal Soundscape for a Vital, Productive, and Healthy Life* (Rochester, VT: Healing Arts, 2001), 4, 77–78.

19. Aaron C. Dunlap, "Come on Feel the Noise: The Problem with Municipal Noise Regulation," *University of Miami Business Law Review* (Winter 2006), *Lexis-Nexis Academic,* 9 March 2009, http://www.lexisnexis.com.

20. See Johnson and Cloonan, 163; Jonathan Sterne, "Urban Media and the Politics of Sound Space," *Open* 9: Sound (2004–2006), 6 October 2008, http://www.skor.nl/article-2853-en.html.

21. Gillespie.

22. Chambers, 441.

23. U.S. Office of Noise Abatement and Control, *Summary of Noise Programs in the Federal Government* (Washington, D.C.: U.S. Government Printing Office, 1972), 62.

24. U.S. Office of Noise Abatement and Control, 4–5.

25. Chambers, 443; see also Leeds, 91.

26. U.S. Office of Noise Abatement and Control, 62.

27. Johnson and Cloonan, 181.

28. See Dunlap.

29. Quoted in Johnson and Cloonan, 175.

30. Dunlap; see also Stuart A. Laven, "Turn Down the Volume," *Cleveland State Law Review* (2004), *LexisNexis Academic,* 9 March 2009, http://www.lexisnexis.com.

31. Dunlap.

32. See Laven.

33. Sally T. Hillsman, "The Use of Fines as an Intermediate Sanction," in *Smart Sentencing: the Emergence of Intermediate Sanctions,* ed. James M. Byrne, Arthur J. Lurigio, and Joan Petersilia (Thousand Oaks, CA: Sage, 1992), 124–25.

34. Paul Sacco, email to the author, 22 January 2009.

35. Karen Cade, email to the author 5 January 2009.

36. "Music Immersion Program," Municipal Court, Fort Lupton, Colorado, 5 February 2009, http://www.fortlupton.org/DEPARTMENTS/COURT/music.html.

37. Sacco.

38. Cade, 5 January 2009; Jeff Kass, "Here, lawbreakers listen to Beethoven," *Christian Science Monitor* 19 May 1999, *LexisNexis Academic,* 5 February 2009, http://www.lexisnexis.com.

39. List of selections, courtesy of Karen Cade.

40. See, for example, Susan McClary, "Getting Down Off the Beanstalk: The Presence of a Woman's Voice in Janika Vandervelde's *Genesis II," Feminine Endings: Music, Gender, and Sexuality* (Minneapolis: University of Minnesota Press), 112–131; and the poem "The Ninth Symphony of Beethoven Understood at Last as a Sexual Message," in Adrienne Rich, *Driving into the Wreck: Poems 1971–1972* (New York: Norton, 1973), 43. The novel and especially the film "A Clockwork Orange" should also be mentioned in this regard. For a fascinating discussion of McClary's controversial reading of Beethoven, see Robert Fink, "Beethoven Antihero," in *Beyond Structural Listening? Postmodern Modes of Hearing,* ed. Andrew Dell'Antonio (Berkeley: University of California Press, 2004), 109–53.

41. Quoted in "YouOughtaKnow," *The Denver Post,* 8 March 2009, http://www .denverpost.com/coloradosunday/ci_8824269.

42. "Turn That Noise Down," *CNN,* 25 November 2008, http://www.cnn.com /video/#/video/us/2008/11/25/vanderveen.noise.offenders.Kusa.

43. Cade, 5 January 2009.

44. See "Classical Music as Punishment," *Mark O'Conner Newsletter,* 22 March 2000, http://www.markoconnor.com/index.php?page=bio&family=mark&category =Other_Newsletters_-squo-99--squo-03. There are other reports of schools using music as punishment. See the description of Sinatra's music used as such in Terry Teachout, "Musical Torture Instruments: Can Being Forced to Listen Really Be That Painful?" *Wall Street Journal,* 13 February 2009, http://online.wsj.com/article /SB123456310592185753.html.

45. See Andrew Mueller, "Rhyme and Punishment," *The Guardian,* 21 February 2004, http://www.guardian.co.uk/music/2004/feb/21/classicalmusicandopera.Pop androck.

46. "Judge Sentences Rap Fan to Bach, Beethoven," *MSNBC,* 9 October 2008, http://www.msnbc.msn.com/id/27099954/?GT1=430017.

47. Wayne Miller, telephone conversation with the author, 10 June 2009.

48. "Lift Tunes for Jammer," *Courier-Mail,* 2 November 1991, *LexisNexis Academic,* 5 February 2009, http://www.lexisnexis.com. In conversation with Zachary Brown, he explained his cooperation as necessary; after all, he was "sworn to tell the truth."

49. See Johnson and Cloonan, 180.

50. Lanza, 39.

51. Anna McCarthy, *Ambient Television: Visual Culture and Public Space* (Durham, NC: Duke University Press, 2001), 219.

52. Anahid Kassabian, "Ubiquitous Listening and Networked Subjectivity," *Echo* 3.2, Fall 2001, www.echo.ucla.edu.

53. Barnes, 13.

54. Tia DeNora, *Music in Everyday Life* (Cambridge: Cambridge University Press, 2000), 14.

55. Barnes, 13.

56. DeNora, 9–11.

57. L. V. Ramos (1993) in the *Journal of Music Therapy,* described in Adrian C. North and David J. Hargreaves, "Music in Business Environments," in *Music and Manipulation: On the Social Uses and Social Control of Music,* ed. Steven Brown and Ulrik Volgsten (New York: Berghahn, 2006), 114.

58. See also David Shicher, *The Meaning and Nature of Punishment* (Long Grove, IL: Waveland, 2006), 26.

59. "Judge Uses Barry Manilow Music as Punishment," *Stereotude,* 26 November 2008.

60. Stephen R. Garvey, "Can Shaming Punishments Educate?" *University of Chicago Law Review* (Summer 1998), *LexisNexis Academic,* 12 May 2009, http://www.lexisnexis.com.

61. Andrew von Hirsch, Andrew Ashworth, and Julian Roberts, eds., *Principled Sentencing: Readings on Theory and Policy,* 3rd ed. (Portland, OR: Hart, 2009), 102.

62. DeeDee Correl, "He Writes the Rules That Make Their Eardrums Ring," *Los Angeles Times,* 21 January 2009, http://www.latimes.com/news/nationworld/nation/la-na-music-punishment21-2009jan21,0,1887999.story.

63. "Judge Uses Barry Manilow Music as Punishment." Sacco reiterated this sentiment in our email correspondence.

64. Adam Smith, *The Theory of Moral Sentiments,* ed. D. D. Raphael and A. L. Macfie (Oxford: Clarendon, 1976), 82.

65. See von Hirsch, Ashworth, and Roberts, 103.

66. Music, in this program, also has more direct ties to silence. For example, music here is quite literally "a means of silencing," in Jacques Attali's thinking, obscuring the "monologue of power" (Attali, 8–9, 111). Like the use of music to repel discussed previously, music is used to stop the (present and future) sounds of others by indirectly imposing the authority's will. In practice, the program therefore exploits music as "a manner of silence." The philosopher and musicologist Vladimir Jankélévitch explains: "Music, which is in itself composed of so many noises, is the silence of all other noises, because as soon as music raises its voice, it demands solitude and insists that it occupy vibrating space alone, excluding other sounds." Vladimir Jankélévitch, *Music and the Ineffable,* trans. Carolyn Abbate (Princeton: Princeton University Press, 2003), 139.

67. Thomas P. Roth, "American Corrections: From the Beginning to World War

II," in *Prison and Jail Administration: Practice and Theory,* ed. Peter M. Carlson and Judith Simon (Sudbury, MA: Jones and Bartlett, 1999), 9–10.

68. Quoted in Michel Foucault, *Discipline and Punish: The Birth of the Prison,* trans. Alan Sheridan (New York: Vintage, 1997), 238. The connection between silence and music in rehabilitation can be linked back to early romantic aesthetics of listening that elevated engagement with music, once "idle reception," as a "reflective process" or "reverent contemplation" (*Andacht*). See Mark Evan Bonds, "Idealism and the Aesthetics of Instrumental Music at the Turn of the Nineteenth Century," *Journal of the American Musicological Society* 50.2–3 (Summer–Autumn 1997): 393.

69. See Gethin Chamberlain, "Going Skirl Crazy: Noisy Kids Ordered to Endure Loud Bagpipes," *Daily Record,* 10 May 1999, 16; Kass. Sacco corroborated this basic premise in our email correspondence as well.

70. Sacco.

71. See Joseph Horowitz, *The Post-Classical Predicament: Essays on Music and Society* (Boston: Northeastern University Press, 1995).

72. Robert Fink, "Elvis Everywhere: Musicology and Popular Music Studies at the Twilight of the Canon," *American Music* 16.2 (Summer 1998): 148.

73. Ibid., 156.

74. See, for example, Catherine Gunther Kodat, "Conversing with Ourselves: Canon, Freedom, Jazz," *American Quarterly* 55.1 (March 2003): 1–28; Scott Deveaux, "Constructing the Jazz Tradition: Jazz Historiography," *Black American Literature Forum* 24.3 (1991): 525–60; Carys Wyn Jones, *The Rock Canon: Canonical Values in the Reception of Rock Albums* (Aldershot: Ashgate, 2008); and Motti Regev, "Producing Artistic Value: The Case of Rock Music," *Sociological Quarterly* 35.1 (February 1994): 85–102.

75. Jones, 25–52.

76. Ibid., 122.

77. Ibid., 65–66.

78. See Bethany Bryson, "'Anything but Heavy Metal': Symbolic Exclusion and Musical Dislikes," *American Sociological Review* 61 (October 1996): 884–99.

79. See "Judge Forces Slum Lord to Live in His Own Building," 28 May 2007, http:/www.shortnews.com/start.cfm?id=62714.

80. Garvey.

81. Ibid.

82. Kass, 1.

83. Kass, 1.

84. "The Sentencing Project," 16 March 2009, http://www.sentencingproject .org/Issues.aspx.

85. Correl.

86. Ibid.

87. Kass, 3.

88. There was also one illegible response.

89. "The Most Unwanted Song," 19 March 2009, http://www.diacenter.org/km /musiccd.html.

90. Karen Cade made these forms available to the author.

91. Sacco.

92. Garvey; see also Francis A. Allen, "The Decline of the Rehabilitative Ideal," in *Principled Sentencing: Readings on Theory and Policy*, 3rd ed., ed. Andrew von Hirsch, Andrew Ashworth, and Julian Roberts (Oxford, OR: Hart, 2009), 11. The goal of rehabilitation or education, according to some in the legal profession, is also ultimately doomed in the justice system. The United States court system involves a relationship between government and criminal and thus lacks the emotional bond necessary for rehabilitation or education such as the more intimate bond between family members. Deirdre Golash, *The Case against Punishment: Retribution, Crime Prevention, and the Law* (New York: New York University Press, 2005), 166.

93. Ra Duff, "Punishment, Retribution and Communication?" in *Principled Sentencing: Readings on Theory and Policy*, 3rd ed., ed. Andrew von Hirsch, Andrew Ashworth, and Julian Roberts (Oxford, OR: Hart, 2009), 132; see also Garvey.

94. Suzanne Cusick, "'You Are in a Place That Is out of the World . . .': Music in the Detention Camps of the 'Global War on Terror'," *Journal of the Society for American Music* 2.1 (February 2008), 9.

95. Johnson and Cloonan, 24.

96. Ibid., 24.

97. Ibid., 26, 158.

98. See Elaine Scarry, *The Body in Pain: The Making and Unmaking of the World* (New York: Oxford University Press, 1985), 46; Johnson and Cloonan, 158.

99. Studies of tinnitus, in a way, provide support for such a conclusion. Negative psychological reactions to this condition have to do with perceptions of control rather than perceptions of volume. Jane L. Henry and Peter H. Wilson, *Chronic Tinnitus: A Cognitive-Behavioral Approach* (Boston: Allyn and Bacon, 2001), 20–22.

100. "Judge Offers Loud Rap Music Listening Basketball Player a Break on Fine," 18 March 2009, http://www.fark.com/cgi/comments.pl?IDLink=3931484&cpp=1.

101. "Hip-Hop Fan to Listen to Classical Music," 9 October 2008, http://www.nowpublic.com/strange/judge-sentences-hip-hop-fan-listen-classical-music.

102. Mueller. Music as torture has inspired similarly wide-ranging reactions— from condemnation to condescension. Johnson and Cloonan have discussed these reactions, specifically, for our purposes, the media's humor response to the use of music as torture, in addition to outright dismissals of the very idea of music as torture: for example, Bill O'Reilly, the outspoken host of Fox News, cited the view that music could torture as "just nuts" (188–92).

103. Johnson and Cloonan, 190.

104. Francis Hutcheson, "From *Reflections upon Laughter*," in *The Philosophy of Laughter and Humor*, ed. John Morreal (Albany: State University of New York Press, 1987), 32.

105. John Morreal, "Funny Ha-Ha, Funny Strange, and Other Reactions to Incongruity," in *The Philosophy of Laughter and Humor*, ed. John Morreal (Albany: State University of New York Press, 1987), 188; see also Noel Carrol, "Horror and Humor," *Journal of Aesthetics and Art Criticism* 57.2 (Spring 1999): 146, 154, and 157.

106. "Judge Offers Loud Rap Music Listening Basketball Player a Break on Fine."

107. "Not Corporal but 'Classical' Punishment?" 10 October 2008, http://glo balgrind.com/source/soulbounce.com/156774/not-corporal-but-classical-punish ment.

108. Rachel E. Sullivan, "Rap and Race: It's Got a Nice Beat, but What about the Message," *Journal of Black Studies* 33.5 (May 2003): 605–6. Rap can also promote debauchery as well as an image of women as objects. See Jeanita W. Richardson and Kim A. Scott, "Rap Music and Its Violent Progeny: America's Culture of Violence in Context," *The Journal of Negro Education* 71.3 (Summer 2002): 184.

109. Tricia Rose, *Black Noise: Rap Music and Black Culture in Contemporary American* (Hanover, NH: Wesleyan University Press, 1994), 101.

110. Martin Esslin, *Brecht, a Choice of Evils: A Critical Study of the Man, His Work and His Opinions* (London: Methuen Drama, 1985), 133; see Bertolt Brecht, *Über experimentelles Theater*, ed. Werner Hecht (Frankfurt: Suhrkamp, 1970), 118; and George Ciccariello Maher, "Brechtian Hip-Hop: Didactics and Self-Production in Post-Gangsta Political Mixtapes," *Journal of Black Studies* 36.1 (September 2005): 139.

111. Such a positioning is recognized within the legal community. See Andre L. Smith, "Other People's Property: Hip-Hop's Inherent Clashes with Property Laws and Its Ascendance as Global Counter Culture," *Virginia Sports and Entertainment Law Journal* (Fall 2007). Smith describes hip-hop generally as a part of "an outlaw culture."

112. See Sullivan, 607–8.

113. Tricia Rose, "Hidden Politics: Discursive and Institutional Policing of Rap Music," in *Droppin' Science: Critical Essays on Rap Music and Hip Hop Culture,* ed. William Eric Perkins (Philadelphia: Temple University Press, 1996), 239.

114. This policing of rap concerts was at the heart of the 1995 Supreme Court case in Connecticut, *Marascini v. Sullivan.* See Richardson and Scott, 187.

115. Quoted in Eric Nuzum, *Parental Advisory: Music Censorship in America* (New York: Perennial, 2001), 22.

116. Stan Soocher, *They Fought the Law: Rock Music Goes to Court* (New York: Schirmer, 1999), 132.

117. Eithne Quinn, *Nuthin' but a "G" Thang: The Culture and Commerce of Gangsta Rap* (New York: Columbia University Press, 2005), 149. See also Johnson and Cloonan, 99.

118. Laven. Though there are no national statistics, records from three Ohio municipalities show that a disproportionate number of African Americans "are being cited and or arrested for violation of such ordinances."

119. Charles Hersh, *Subversive Sounds: Race and the Birth of Jazz in New Orleans* (Chicago: University of Chicago Press, 2007), 73.

120. Daniel Ferreira, "Art Should Not Be Punishment," in "Letters to the Editor," *The Modesto Bee,* 5 February 2009, http://www.modbee.com/opinion/letters/story /588847.html.

121. Zachary Brown, telephone conversation with the author, 11 June 2009.
122. Kass.
123. Duff, 133.

CHAPTER 3

1. "Jurors Acquit Rap Musician in Murder Case," *New York Times*, 22 February 1996, A16.
2. Cheryl L. Keyes, *Rap Music and Street Consciousness* (Urbana: University of Illinois Press, 2004), 113.
3. See Edward Helmore, "The Dogg Has His Day in Court," *Independent (London)*, 25 November 1995, 5; Sam Taylor, "Demonic Icon on a Murder Rap," *Observer*, 8 January 1995, 5.
4. Sharon Waxman, "Rapper Acquitted of Murder Charges," *Washington Post*, 21 February 1996, B1.
5. See for example Jeanita W. Richardson and Kim A. Scott, "Rap Music and its Violent Progeny: America's Culture of Violence in Context," *Journal of Negro Education* 71.3 (Summer 2002): 177. See also Eithne Quinn, *Nuthin' but a "G" Thang: The Culture and Commerce of Gangsta Rap* (New York: Columbia University Press, 2005), 10.
6. Andrea L. Dennis, "Poetic (In)Justice? Rap Music Lyrics as Art, Life, and Criminal Evidence," *Columbia Journal of Law and the Arts* (Fall 2007), *LexisNexis Academic*, 5 February 2010, http://www.lexisnexis.com.
7. Michael Brick, "Rap Takes Center Stage at Trial in Killing of Two Detectives," *New York Times*, 12 December 2006, B1.
8. See, for example, *Jones v. State* (2002) or *Doe v. Pulaski County Special School District* (2001), discussed in Sean-Patrick Wilson, "Rap Sheets: The Constitutional and Societal Complications Arising From the Use of Rap Lyrics as Evidence at Criminal Trials," *UCLA Entertainment Law Review* (Spring 2005), *LexisNexis Academic*, 5 February 2010, http://www.lexisnexis.com.
9. *People v. Olguin*, 1994, LEXIS 1325, Nos. G014071, G014235, Court of Appeal of California, Fourth Appellate District, 1355.
10. Ibid.
11. Ibid.
12. Ibid.
13. Ibid.
14. Dennis.
15. Quoted in Dennis.
16. Quoted in ibid.
17. Quoted in Wilson.
18. Wilson.
19. See Wilson; and "Jailed Rapper Changes Names, Hopes New Image Follows," *St. Petersburg Times (Florida)*, 7 April 2005, 2B.

Notes to Pages 54–57 • 155

20. *People v. Richardson*, 2004, LEXIS 699, Court of Appeal of California, Third Appellate District.

21. *People v. Richardson*.

22. See the similar conclusion in *People v. Hilton* (2005).

23. Dennis.

24. *United States v. Stuckey*, 2007, LEXIS 24636, No. 05-1039, United States Court of Appeals for the Sixth District, 468.

25. *United States v. Stuckey*.

26. Wilson.

27. Stuart P. Fischoff, "'Gangsta' Rap and a Murder in Bakersfield," *Journal of Applied Social Psychology* 29.4 (1999): 802.

28. Wilson.

29. Dennis.

30. Aaron A. Fox, *Real Country: Music and Language in Working-Class Culture* (Durham, NC: Duke University, 2004), 318; and Diane Pecknold, *The Selling Sound: The Rise of the Country Music Industry* (Durham, NC: Duke University Press, 2007), 2. Joli Jensen, *Nashville Sound: Authenticity, Commercialization, and Country Music* (Nashville: Country Music Foundation Press and Vanderbilt University Press, 1998), 12–13.

31. See Edward Armstrong, "Eminem's Construction of Authenticity," *Popular Music and Society* 27.3 (2004): 336. Perkins identifies gangsta rap as especially dependent on ideas of authenticity. He writes, "In an age of mass over-consumption and media hype, gangsta rap no doubt represents a religion and ideology of authenticity." William Eric Perkins, "The Rap Attack: An Introduction," in *Droppin' Science: Critical Essays on Rap Music and Hip Hop Culture,* ed. William Eric Perkins (Philadelphia: Temple University Press, 1996), 20.

32. Allan Moore, "Authenticity as Authentication," *Popular Music* 21.2 (May 2002): 210. See also Jensen, 7 and 136; and David Grazian, "The Symbolic Economy of Authenticity in the Chicago Blues Scene," in *Music Scenes: Local, Translocal, and Virtual,* ed. Andy Bennett and Richard A. Peterson (Nashville: Vanderbilt University Press, 2004), 32.

33. See Phillip Vannini's and J. Patrick Williams' discussion of Richard Peterson's conception of authenticity in "Authenticity in Culture, Self, and Society," in *Authenticity in Culture, Self, and Society,* ed. Phillip Vannini and J. Patrick Williams (Burlington, VT: Ashgate, 2009), 2.

34. See, for example, Armstrong, "Eminem's Construction of Authenticity," 337.

35. Ibid., 336.

36. Ibid.

37. Jennifer C. Lena, "Social Context and Musical Content of Rap Music, 1979–1995," *Social Forces* 85.1 (September 2006): 480.

38. Quoted in Quinn, *Nuthin' but a "G" Thang,* 155. Ebony Utley believes Snoop Dogg was more willing to assume the part than he indicates here. Ebony Utley, "Transcendence: The Rhetorical Functions of the Gangsta Rapper's God," (PhD diss., Northwestern University, 2006), 143.

39. Robert J. Brym, "Hip-Hop from Dissent to Commodity: A Note on Consumer Culture," in *Society in Question,* 5th edition, ed. Robert J. Brym (Toronto: Nelson, 2008), 79.

40. Ibid., 79.

41. David Clarke, "Eminem: Difficult Dialogics," *Words and Music* (Liverpool: University of Liverpool, 2005), 82. Dennis also recognizes the role of commerce in the construction of a rapper's persona.

42. Eminem similarly addresses this sort of literal interpretation in "Criminal."

43. Dennis; Cheryl L. Keyes, "Verbal Art Performance in Rap Music: The Conversation of the 80's," *Folklore Forum* 17.2 (1984): 143.

44. Robin D. G. Kelley, "Kickin' Reality, Kickin' Ballistics: Gangsta Rap and Postindustrial Los Angeles," in *Droppin' Science: Critical Essays on Rap Music and Hip Hop Culture,* ed. William Eric Perkins (Philadelphia: Temple University Press, 1996), 129.

45. Imani Perry, *Prophets of the Hood: Politics and Poetics in Hip Hop* (Durham, NC: Duke University Press, 2004), 102–4.

46. Tani Graham Shaffer, "The Shady Side of Hip-Hop: A Jungian and Eriksonian Interpretation of Eminem's Explicit Content" (PhD diss., Pacific Graduate School of Psychology, 2004), 88.

47. Michael Newman, "'That's All Concept; It's Nothing Real': Reality and Lyrical Meaning in Rap," in *Global Linguistic Flows: Hip Hop Cultures, Youth Identities, and the Politics of Language,* ed. H. Samy Alim, Awad Ibrahim, and Alastax Pennycook (New York: Routledge, 2009), 196. For example, a listener can respond to rap with violent lyrics as a form of self-empowerment. However, during the Iraq War, American soldiers responded to lyrical violence more literally. On patrol, they often listened to gangsta rap, as well as heavy metal, in order to prepare for combat by dehumanizing the enemy or oneself. See Jonathan Pieslak, *Sound Targets: American Soldiers and Music in the Iraq War* (Bloomington: Indiana University Press, 2009), 147, 155, and 163.

48. Mitchell-Kernan writes of rap, ". . . complimentary remarks may be delivered in a left-handed fashion. A particular utterance may be an insult in one context and not another. What pretends to be informative may intend to be persuasive. The hearer is thus constrained to attend to all potential meaning carrying symbolic systems in speech events—the total universe." Quoted in Keyes, *Rap Music and Street Consciousness,* 132.

49. Clarke, 86.

50. Ibid., 94.

51. See M. M. Bakhtin, *The Dialogic Imagination: Four Essays,* ed. Michael Lohquist, trans. Caryl Emerson and Michael Holquist (Austin: University of Texas Press, 1981), 263. In this way, rap is in some ways representative of Matthew Wilson Smith's broader conception of the *Gesamtkunstwerk* as the history of "un-reconciled dialectical struggles performed under the sign of aesthetic totality." See Matthew Wilson Smith, *The Total Work of Art: From Bayreuth to Cyberspace* (New York: Routledge, 2007), 3.

52. Steen Kaargard Nielsen, "Wife Murder as Child's Game: Analytical Reflections on Eminem's Performative Self-Dramatization," *Danish Yearbook of Musicology* 34 (2006): 33.

53. Nielsen, 32.

54. Quoted in Quinn, "'Never shoulda been let out the penitentiary': Gangsta Rap and the Struggle over Racial Identity," *Cultural Critique* 34 (Autumn 1996): 85. Some recurring characters include: the hustler, baaadman, and pimp. See for example Lena, 486. Keyes, citing sociologist Eugene Perkins, sees these characters in street culture, adding to this the street man, hustler, pimp (or mack), working-class man, and militant. Keyes, *Rap Music and Street Consciousness,* 125.

55. Ta-Nehisi Coates, "The Mask of Doom: A Nonconformist Rapper's Second Act," *New Yorker,* 21 September 2009, 52.

56. Ibid., 54. Such engagement with the idea of voice in rap similarly extends to popular music in general. One representative example is Gorillaz, "the first entirely virtual pop band," created by Damon Albarn and Jamie Hewlett. See Lars Eckstein, "Torpedoing the Authorship of Popular Music: A Reading of Gorillaz' 'Feel Good Inc.'," *Popular Music* 28.2 (2009): 239–55.

57. Simon Frith, *Performing Rites: On the Values of Popular Music* (Cambridge: Harvard University Press, 1996), 175.

58. Keyes, "Verbal Art Performance in Rap Music: The Conversation of the 80's," 145.

59. Doug E. Fresh, quoted in Keyes, *Rap Music and Street Consciousness,* 126.

60. Keyes, *Rap Music and Street Consciousness,* 127.

61. Ibid., 126–27.

62. Frith, 181.

63. Greg Dimitriadis, *Performing Identity/Performing Culture: Hip Hop as Text, Pedagogy, and Lived Practice* (New York: Peter Lang, 2001), 16.

64. Ibid., 17.

65. Ibid., 23.

66. Frith, 169–70.

67. Ibid., 166.

68. Carolyn Abbate, *Unsung Voices: Opera and Musical Narrative in the Nineteenth Century* (Princeton: Princeton University Press, 1991), 12.

69. Abbate, 28.

70. Jones recognizes similar affinity between constructions of "perceived truth" in rock and notions of the Romantic artist. See Carys Wyn Jones, *The Rock Canon: Canonical Values in the Reception of Rock Albums* (Aldershot: Ashgate, 2008), 34–35.

71. Richard Taruskin, "Is There A Baby in the Bathwater (Part I)?," *Archiv für Musikwissenschaft* 63.3 (2006): 166.

72. Lydia Goehr, *The Imaginary Museum of Musical Works: An Essay in the Philosophy of Music* (Oxford: Clarendon, 1992), 162.

73. E. T. A. Hoffmann, "Beethoven's Instrumental Music (1813)," in *German Essays on Music,* ed. Jost Hermand and Michael Gilbert (New York: Continuum, 1994), 61.

74. Taruskin, 167.

75. Johann Adam Peter Schulz (1775/92), quoted in Mary Hunter, "'To Play as if from the Soul of the Composer': The Idea of the Performer in Early Romantic Aesthetics," *Journal of the American Musicological Society* 58.2 (2005): 364.

76. Edward Lippman, *A History of Western Musical Aesthetics* (Lincoln: University of Nebraska Press, 1992), 234.

77. These lectures were published posthumously in 1835. G. W. F. Hegel, *Aesthetics: Lectures on Fine Art,* trans. T. M. Knox, vol. 2 (Oxford: Clarendon, 1975), 891.

78. Johann Georg Sulzer, "Expression in Music" (1792–1794), in *German Essays on Music,* ed. Jost Hermand and Michael Gilbert (New York: Continuum, 1994), 27. "Expression in Music" appeared originally in Sulzer's *Allgemeine Theorie der Schönen Künste,* first published in 1771, and subsequently published in its second edition in 1792.

79. Hoffmann, "Beethoven's Instrumental Music (1813)," 60.

80. Edward T. Cone, *The Composer's Voice* (Berkeley: University of California Press, 1974), 18 and 23.

81. Stephen Davies, *Musical Meaning and Expression* (Ithaca: Cornell University Press, 1994), 170.

82. Stephen Davies, *The Philosophy of Art* (Malden, MA: Blackwell, 2006), 169.

83. See Dwight Macdonald, "Masscult & Midcult," in *Popular Culture Theory and Methodology: A Basic Introduction,* ed. Harold E. Hinds, Marilyn Ferris Motz, and Angela M. S. Nelson (Madison: University of Wisconsin Press, 2006), 9–15; Barry D. Riccio, "Popular Culture and High Culture: Dwight Macdonald, His Critics and the Ideal of Cultural Hierarchy in Modern America," *Journal of American Culture* 16.4 (1993): 13; and Charles Hersch, *Democratic Artworks: Politics and the Arts from Trilling to Dylan* (Albany: State University of New York Press, 1998), 42–44.

84. See Catherine Gunther Kodat, "Conversing with Ourselves: Canon, Freedom, Jazz," *American Quarterly* 55.1 (March 2003): 2. See also Jones, 123–24.

85. Jones, 36.

86. Jones, 34–36. See also Hersch, 140–41.

87. Moore, 213.

88. Davies, *The Philosophy of Art,* 147.

89. Davies, *Musical Meaning and Expression,* 171.

90. Stephen Davies, "Philosophical Perspectives on Music's Expressiveness," in *Music and Emotion: Theory and Research,* ed. Patrik N. Juslin and John A. Sloboda (New York: Oxford Univesity Press, 2000), 29.

91. Philip Glass, "When Language Fails the World Is Revealed," in *The Voice of Music: Conversations with Composers of Our Time,* ed. Anders Beyer, trans. Jean Christensen and Anders Beyer (Burlington, VT: Ashgate, 2000), 278.

92. Helmore, 5.

93. Quinn, *Nuthin' but a "G" Thang,* 146–47.

94. Edward Armstrong, "The Rhetoric of Violence in Rap and Country Music," *Sociological Inquiry* 63.1 (February 1993): 67.

95. Ralph M. Rosen and Donald R. Mark, "Comedies of Transgression in Gang-

sta Rap and Ancient Classical Poetry," *New Literary History,* 30.4 (Autumn 1999): 910. Keyes similarly recognizes the role of humor and irony in rap. See Keyes, "Verbal Art Performance in Rap Music: The Conversation of the 80's," 147.

96. Dennis.

97. Wilson.

98. See Martin Cloonan, "Call That Censorship? Problems of Definition," in *Policing Pop,* ed. Martin Cloonan and Reebee Garofalo (Philadelphia: Temple University Press, 2003), 14; and Martin Cloonan, *Banned! Censorship of Popular Music in Britain: 1967–92* (Aldershot: Arena, 1996), 91.

99. See this understanding of how consumption relates to identity in Martha A. Starr, "Consumption, Identity, and the Sociocultural Constitution of 'Preferences': Reading Women's Magazines," in *Consuming Symbolic Goods: Identity and Commitment, Values and Economics,* ed. Wilfred Dolfsma (London: Routledge, 2008), 21.

100. Helen A. Anderson, "The Freedom to Speak and the Freedom to Listen: The Admissability of the Criminal Defendant's Taste in Entertainment," *Oregon Law Review* (2004), *LexisNexis Academic,* 5 February 2010, http://www.lexisnexis .com.

101. See Wilson.

102. Armstrong, "The Rhetoric of Violence in Rap and Country Music," 80.

103. See explanation in Tricia Rose, *The Hip Hop Wars: What We Talk about When We Talk about Hip Hop—and Why It Matters* (New York: Basic Books, 2008), 37.

CHAPTER 4

1. Richard Shusterman, "The Fine Art of Rap," *New Literary History* 22.3 (Summer 1991): 613.

2. Ibid., 614. The legendary jazz drummer Max Roach similarly states, "Hip hop lives in the world of sound—not the world of music—and that's why it's so revolutionary. . . . There are many areas that fall outside the narrow Western definition of music and hip-hop is one of them." Quoted in Cheryl L. Keyes, *Rap Music and Street Consciousness* (Urbana: University of Illinois Press, 2002), 145.

3. Jonathan D. Kramer, "The Nature and Origins of Musical Postmodernism," in *Postmodern Music/Postmodern Thought,* ed. Judith Lockhead and Joseph Auner (New York: Routledge, 2002), 14–15.

4. Shusterman, 614. See also David Bracket, "'Where's It At?': Postmodern Theory and the Contemporary Musical Field," in *Postmodern Music/Postmodern Thought,* ed. Judith Lockhead and Joseph Auner (New York: Routledge, 2002), 221. This idea, as Bracket discusses, has also been challenged.

5. Robert Walser, "Rhythm, Rhyme, and Rhetoric in the Music of Public Enemy," *Ethnomusicology* 39.2 (Spring/Summer 1995): 195–98.

6. Ibid., 199–200.

7. See "CNN Student News Transcript," 28 October 2009, http://www.cnn.com

/2009/LIVING/studentnews/10/27/transcript.wed/index.html; and "NYU Names Swizz Beatz its producer-in-residence," *Yahoo! News,* 5 November 2010, http://news .yahoo.com/s/ap/20101105/ap_en_mu/us_swizz_beatz_nyu.

8. Carys Wyn Jones, *The Rock Canon: Canonical Values in the Reception of Rock Albums* (Aldershot: Ashgate, 2008), 10.

9. See Nakeyshaey M. Tille Allen, "Exploring Hip-hop Therapy with High-Risk Youth," *Praxis* 5 (Fall 2005); "Rap Therapy: Hip Hop Psychotherapy," http://www .beatsrhymesandlife.org/brl/raptherapy.html; Don Elligan, *Rap Therapy: A Practical Guide for Communicating with Youth and Young Adults Through Rap Music* (New York: Kensington, 2004); and Edgar H. Tyson, "Hip Hop Therapy: An Exploratory Study of a Rap Music Intervention with At-Risk and Delinquent Youth," *Journal of Poetry Therapy* 15.3 (Spring 2002): 131–43. In Tyson's version of the therapy, this unease is most evidence in his recommendation that practitioners avoid "negative rap" and, instead, work with "positive rap," which "invariably refers to rap that depicts solutions and self-protective concepts and skills, as well as inspires to improve unwanted conditions" (135).

10. Walser, 193.

11. See Sandra Davidson, "Two Perspectives on Ice-T: 'Can't Touch Me': Musical Messages and Incitement Law," in *Bleep! Censoring Rock and Rap Music,* ed. Betty Houchin Winfield and Sandra Davidson (Westport, CT: Greenwood, 1999), 27. See also summary in David R. Dow, "The Moral Failure of the Clear and Present Danger Test," *William and Mary Bill of Rights Journal* (Summer 1998); Geordie Greig, "American Widow Sues for 'Murder under the Influence of Rap'," *Sunday Times (London),* 25 October 1992; Greg Beets, "Jury Weighing Rap as an Accomplice to Murder of a Trooper," *Billboard,* 3 July 1993, 12.

12. Davidson, 27.

13. *Davidson v. Time Warner, Inc.,* 1997, LEXIS 21559, NO. V-94-06, United States District Court for the Southern District of Texas.

14. Ibid.

15. Ibid.

16. See Davidson, 23.

17. Ibid., 23.

18. *Davidson v. Time Warner, Inc.*

19. Stan Soocher, *They Fought the Law: Rock Music Goes to Court* (New York: Schirmer, 1999), 158–60. See also Peter Alan Block, "Modern-Day Sirens: Rock Lyrics and the First Amendment," *Southern California Law Review* (March 1990).

20. Soocher, 153–56.

21. Quoted in Soocher, 157. See also Block.

22. Judith Becker, "Music and Trance," *Leonardo Music Journal* 4 (1994): 41.

23. Ibid., 46 and 49.

24. Block.

25. Quoted in Betty Houchin Winfield, "Because of the Children: Decades of Attempted Controls of Rock 'n' Rap Music," in *Bleep! Censoring Rock and Rap Music,* ed. Betty Houchin Winfield and Sandra Davidson (Westport, CT: Green-

wood, 1999), 12. Dow similarly wrote, "Not every idea is an incitement, but every idea might be, and any idea can be."

26. "Symposium: Forward: A Panel Discussion: Potential Liability Arising From the Dissemination of Violent Music," *Loyola of Los Angeles Entertainment Law Review* 2.2 (2002).

27. Block.

28. See both articles on "Rapping about Cop Killing," sponsored by the Institute for Jewish Policy Research, 2004, http//:www.axt.org.uk/HateMusic/Rappin.htm. See also Davidson, 23. For a list of other lesser known works on this theme, see Peter Blecha, *Taboo Tunes: A History of Banned Bands and Censored Songs* (San Francisco: Backbeat, 2004), 126.

29. Quoted in Eric Nuzum, *Parental Advisory: Music Censorship in America* (New York: Perennial, 2001), 10.

30. Ibid.

31. Block.

32. Dow, "The Moral Failure."

33. Ibid.

34. Ibid.

35. Ibid.

36. Becker, 41.

37. See the chapters on incitement and arousal, and the distinctions within, in Johnson and Cloonan.

38. Cited in Block. In the "The Cult of Violence," Tipper Gore similarly references Plato in her discussion of the perceived harm of music with explicit content: "Plato wrote that music had the power to shape society." Tipper Gore, "The Cult of Violence," in *The Rock History Reader*, ed. Theo Cateforis (New York: Routledge, 2007), 231. In an alternate translation of Tribe's citation from Book IV of *Republic*, Plato wrote, "Musical styles are nowhere altered without (changes in) the most important laws of the state." Quoted in Warren D. Anderson, *Ethos and Education in Greek Music: The Evidence of Poetry and Philosophy* (Cambridge: Harvard University Press, 1966), 41. Also "The ways of poetry and music are not changed anywhere without changes in the most important laws of the city . . ." Plato, *Republic,* trans. G. M. A. Grube (Indianapolis: Hackett, 1974), 90. This change in translation clarifies meaning (substituting "style" for "mode," also a means of organizing music theoretically).

39. Plato, excerpt from Republic II, in *Music Education: Source Readings from Ancient Greece to Today,* ed. Michael L. Mark (New York: Routledge, 2002), 6.

40. See Göran Sörbom, "Aristotle on Music as Representation," *Journal of Aesthetics and Art Criticism* 52.1 (Winter 1994): 37 and 41. See also Anderson, 88.

41. Quoted in Sörbom, 37.

42. Plato, *Republic,* 68–69.

43. See for explanation Anderson, 72–73.

44. See Aristotle, *Politica,* Book VIII, in *Music Education: Source Readings from Ancient Greece to Today,* ed. Michael L. Mark (New York: Routledge, 2002), 15.

45. Ibid., 16.

46. Aristotle, 16. Plato, *Republic,* 69. See also Anderson, 66.

47. Anderson, 9; and James Davidson, "Making a Spectacle of Her(self): The Greek Courtesan and the Art of the Present," in *The Courtesan's Arts: Cross-Cultural Perspectives,* ed. Martha Feldman and Bonnie Gordon (New York: Oxford University Press, 2006), 37.

48. Joseph Lanza, *Elevator Music: A Surreal History of Muzak, Easy-Listening, and Other Moodsong* (Ann Arbor: University of Michigan Press, 2004), 7.

49. Quintilian, in *Music Education: Source Readings from Ancient Greece to Today,* ed. Michael L. Mark (New York: Routledge, 2002), 22.

50. Maria Korpe, Ole Reitov, and Martin Cloonan, "Music Censorship from Plato to the Present," in *Music and Manipulation: On the Social Uses and Social Control of Music,* ed. Steven Brown and Ulrik Volgsten (New York: Berghahn, 2006), 241.

51. Korpe, Reitov, and Cloonan, 243.

52. Blecha, 41.

53. Charles Hersh, *Subversive Sounds: Race and the Birth of Jazz in New Orleans* (Chicago: University of Chicago Press, 2007), 55–67.

54. Charles Hersch, *Democratic Artworks: Politics and the Arts from Trilling to Dylan* (Albany: State University of New York Press, 1998), 129.

55. Cyril Scott, *The Influence of Music on History and Morals: A Vindication of Plato* (London: Philosophical, 1928), 6.

56. Ibid., 9 and 17.

57. Tracy Reilly, "The 'Spiritual Temperature' of Contemporary Popular Music: An Alternative to the Legal Regulation of Death-Metal and Gangsta-Rap Lyrics," *Vanderbilt Journal of Entertainment and Technology Law* (Winter 2009), *LexisNexis Academic,* 5 February 2010, http://www.lexisnexis.com.

58. See Winfield, 9–20, 12; and S. Davidson, "Two Perspectives on Ice-T," 82.

59. "The concept of obscenity is unique in criminal law because it requires a subjective descision of guilt or innocence." Nuzum, 180.

60. Bob Woodward and Scott Armstrong, *The Brethren: Inside the Supreme Court* (New York: Avon, 1979), 227.

61. Ibid., 228.

62. Ibid., 229.

63. Quoted in Woodward and Armstrong, 230.

64. Quoted in ibid., 237.

65. Quoted in ibid., 230.

66. Ibid., 230.

67. Ibid., 237.

68. See Anne L. Clark, "'As Nasty as They Wanna Be': Popular Music on Trial," *New York University Law Review* (December 1990).

69. Kathleen M. Sullivan, "2 Live Crew and the Cultural Contradictions of Miller," in *The Rock Reader,* ed. Theo Cateforius (New York: Routledge, 2007), 272.

70. Ibid., 273.

71. Clark.

72. Ibid.

73. Cited in Soocher, 137.

74. Andre L. Smith, "Other People's Property: Hip-Hop's Inherent Clashes with Property Laws and Its Ascendance as Global Counter Culture," *Virginia Sports and Entertainment Law Journal* (Fall 2007).

75. Olufunmilayo B. Arewa, "From J. C. Bach to Hip Hop: Musical Borrowing, Copyright and Cultural Context," *North Carolina Law Review* (January 2006). See also Smith, "Other People's Property." This ambivalence can give way to outright hostility.

76. See Richard L. Schur, *Parodies of Ownership: Hip-Hop Aesthetics and Intellectual Property Law* (Ann Arbor: University of Michigan Press, 2009), 35–40, and 101.

77. Jones, 30–31.

78. Ronald S. Rosen, *Music and Copyright* (Oxford: Oxford University Press, 2008), 5–6.

79. Suzannah Clark and Elizabeth Eva Leach, "Learning, Citation, and Authority in Musical Culture before 1600," in *Citation and Authority in Medieval and Renaissance Musical Culture: Learning from the Learned,* ed. Suzannah Clark and Elizabeth Eva Leach (Suffolk: Boydell, 2005), xxii–xxiii. See also Honey Meconi, ed., *Early Musical Borrowing* (New York: Routledge, 2004).

80. Rosen, 5.

81. Quoted in J. Peter Burkholder, "Borrowing," *Oxford Music Online.*

82. J. Peter Burkholder, "The Use of Existing Music: Musical Borrowing as a Field," *Notes* 50.3 (March 1994): 851–70.

83. Lydia Goehr, *The Imaginary Museum of Musical Works: An Essay in the Philosophy of Music* (Oxford: Clarendon, 1992), 223.

84. Arewa.

85. Smith. There are similar critiques of laws' idea of creativity in regards to visual art. See Christine Haight Farley, "Imagining the Law: Art," in *Law and the Humanities: An Introduction,* ed. Austin Sarat, Matthew Anderson, and Catherine O. Frank (Cambridge: Cambridge University Press, 2010), 300–304. Beboppers transformed this practice into an artistic challenge. By quoting the music of classical composers, for example, boppers spotlighted the cracks in categories of high and low art. See Krin Gabbart, "The Quoter and His Culture," in *Jazz in Mind: Essays on the History and Meanings of Jazz,* ed. Reginald T. Buckner and Steven Weiland (Detroit: Wayne State University Press, 1991), 93.

86. Soocher, 139–40.

87. Ibid., 141.

88. Ibid., 143.

89. See Clark.

90. Quoted in Soocher, 152.

91. See Robert Walser, *Running with the Devil: Power, Gender, and Madness in Heavy Metal Music* (Hanover, NH: University Press of New England, 1993), 140.

92. Walser, 141.

93. Bruce Johnson and Martin Cloonan, *Dark Side of the Tune: Popular Music and Violence* (Aldershot: Ashgate, 2008), 112–15. The organization FreeMuse, the World Forum on Music and Censorship, is uniquely aware of the connection between censorship and fear and works to expose and combat music censorship in various contexts. See http://www.freemuse.org/sw305.asp.

94. Block, "Modern-Day Sirens."

95. *Davidson v. Time Warner, Inc.* Still, Ozzy Osbourne claimed in regard to his suit, "The backlash from the suicide suits has been that bands are more apt to use these types of lyrics to draw attention to themselves" (Soocher, 170).

CHAPTER 5

1. Arnold Shapiro, telephone conversation with the author, 25 January 2011.

2. Kathy Boccella, "Show on Jail Bands Stirs Outrage," *The Philadelphia Inquirer,* 11 October 2002, B1.

3. Quoted in ibid.

4. Quoted in Michael McGough, "Midweek Perspectives: A Pinhead Editorial Writer's Adventure in the No Spin Zone," *Post-Gazette* (Pittsburgh), 20 November 2002, http://www.post-gazette.com/forum/comm/20021120edmcg20p1.asp.

5. Bill O'Reilly, "Talking Points: VH1 Disgraces Itself," *Fox News,* 18 October 2002, http://www.foxnews.com/story/0,2933,65942,00.html.

6. Lisa de Moraes, "O'Reilly, Convicting VH1 for Its Prison Music Show," *Washington Post,* 19 October 2002, C7.

7. Peter Hart, *The Oh Really? Factor: Unspinning Fox News Channel's Bill O'Reilly* (New York: Seven Stories, 2003), 30.

8. Marla Lehner, "Murder Victim's Family Sues VH1," *Fox News,* 6 March 2003, http://www.foxnews.com/story/0,2933,80369,00.html.

9. See info at http://www.arnoldshapiro.com/.

10. Quoted in Lehner.

11. Shapiro, telephone conversation with the author.

12. Shapiro.

13. Quoted in Shapiro.

14. Boccella.

15. Quoted in Randy Lewis, "New VH1 Series Explores Jailhouse Rock," *Los Angeles Times,* 18 October 2002, http://articles.latimes.com/2002/oct/18/entertainment/et-lewis18.

16. Shapiro.

17. Quoted in Lewis.

18. Moraes.

19. Quoted in Boccella.

20. Moraes.

21. Quoted in Cheryl Wetzstein, "VH1 Angers Victims' Families with Plans for 'Jailhouse Rock'," *Washington Times,* 18 October 2002, A12.

22. Quoted in Moraes.

23. *Young v. Beard,* 2008, LEXIS 14315, United States Court of Appeals for the Third Circuit.

24. Ibid.

25. *Herlein v. Higgins,* 1999, LEXIS 7624, the United States Court of Appeals for the Eighth Circuit.

26. Michel Foucault, *Discipline and Punish: The Birth of the Prison,* trans. Alan Sheridan (New York: Vintage, 1977), 33–48.

27. Marianne Fisher-Giorlando, "Prison Culture: Using Music as Data" (Ph.D. diss., Ohio State University, 1987), 60–69.

28. Caleb Smith, *The Prison and the American Imagination* (New Haven: Yale University Press, 2009), 2.

29. Ibid., 11–12.

30. Quoted in Fisher-Giorlando, 74–75.

31. Smith argues that punishment in the United States has always been dependent on "a foundation of violence dehumanization" (208).

32. Fisher-Giorlando, 75–85.

33. John Bugg, "Close Confinement: John Thelwall and the Romantic Prison," *European Romantic Review* 20.1 (January 2009): 39.

34. See Victor Brombert, *The Romantic Prison: The French Tradition* (Princeton: Princeton University Press, 1978), 5.

35. Suzanne Keen, *Empathy and the Novel* (Oxford: Oxford University Press, 2007), 70–71.

36. See Stephen Meyer, "Terror and Transcendence in the Operatic Prison, 1790–1815," *Journal of the American Musicological Society* 55.3 (2002): 478–80.

37. Brombert, 19.

38. See Meyer, 478–80.

39. Quoted in Sanna Pederson, "Beethoven and Freedom: Historicizing the Political Connection," *Beethoven Forum* 12.1 (2005): 3.

40. Quoted in Edward Lippman, *A History of Western Musical Aesthetic* (Lincoln: University of Nebraska, 1992), 234.

41. Pederson, 5.

42. Quoted in Pederson, 1.

43. Coltrane, quoted in Charles Hersch, *Democratic Artworks: Politics and the Arts from Trilling to Dylan* (Albany: State University of New York Press, 1998), 101.

44. Hersch, 99–109. See also Scott Deveaux, "Constructing the Jazz Tradition: Jazz Historiography," *Black American Literature Forum* 24.3 (1991): 550.

45. Brombert, 3–4.

46. Lydia Goehr, *The Imaginary Museum of Musical Works: An Essay in the Philosophy of Music* (Oxford: Clarendon, 1992), 208.

47. See Mikael Elsila, "Music behind Bars: Liberatory Musicology in Two Michigan Prisons" (M.A. thesis, University of Michigan, 1995), 2.

48. Benjamin J. Harbert, "I'll Keep on Living after I Die: Musical Manipulation and Transcendence at Louisiana State Pentitentiary," *International Journal of Community Music* 3.1 (2010): 66.

49. Similarly, Robert Perkinson wrote, "African American convicts, in particular,

drew on slavery's cultural memory to compose thousands of field hollers and work songs that would eventually coalesce into an original body of music." Robert Perkinson, "'Hell Exploded': Prisoner Music and Memoir and the Fall of Convict Leasing in Texas," *Prison Journal* 89.1 (March 2009): 58.

50. Bruce Jackson, ed., *Wake Up Dead Man: Hard Labor and Southern Blues* (Athens: University of Georgia Press, 1999), vii.

51. Ibid., xxv.

52. Fisher-Giorlando, 358.

53. See similar conclusion in Harbert, 69.

54. Elsila, 3.

55. Mary L. Cohen, "Christopher Small's Concept of Musicking: Toward a Theory of Choral Singing Pedagogy in Prison Contexts" (Ph.D. thesis, University of Kansas, 2007), 269. For information on music making in prison historically, see Roc Lee, "Music Education in Prisons: A Historical Overview," *International Journal of Community Music* 3.1 (March 2010): 7–18.

56. Cohen, 275.

57. James Thompson, "Doubtful Principles in Arts in Prisons," in *Teaching the Arts Behind Bars,* ed. Rachel Marie-Crane Williams (Boston: Northeastern University Press, 2003), 45.

58. William Cleveland, *Art in Other Places: Artists at Work in America's Community and Social Institutions* (Westport, CT: Praeger, 1992), 49.

59. "The Art of Prevention: Arts Serving Youths at Risk in Human Service and Correctional Setting," Hearing Transcript, Joint Committee on the Arts, Chair Henry J. Mello (April 20, 1994), Sacramento, CA.

60. See "The Arts in Corrections Resource List," National Endowment for the Arts, http://www.arts.gov/resources/accessibility/rlists/corrections.html; "Prison Arts Project," William James Association, http://www.williamjamesassociation.org/prison_arts.html.

61. See Mary L. Cohen, "'Mother Theresa, How Can I Help You?': The Story of Elvera Voth, Robert Shaw, and the Bethel College Benefit Sing-Along for Arts in Prison, Inc.," *International Journal of Research in Choral Singing* 3.1 (2008): 10.

62. Kristina Goetz, "Inmates Find Harmony through CDs," *Cincinnati Enquirer,* 16 January 2004, http://www.enquirer.com/editions/2004/01/16/loc_prisonsing16 box0.html.

63. See Kjell Skyllstad, "Music behind Bars: Testimonies of Suffering, Survival, and Transformation," in *Music and Conflict Transformation: Harmonies and Dissonances in Geopolitics,* ed. Olivier Urbain (London: Tauris, 2008), 122.

64. Rachel Marie-Crane Williams, "Introduction," in *Teaching the Arts Behind Bars,* ed. Rachel Marie-Crane Williams (Boston: Northeastern University Press, 2003), 7.

65. Ibid., 4.

66. Alan Lomax, *The Land Where the Blues Began* (New York: New Press, 1993), 285.

67. Ibid., 286.

68. Ibid., 287.

69. See Cleveland, 66.

70. Judith Tannenbaum, *Disguised as a Poem: My Years Teaching Poetry at San Quentin* (Boston: Northeastern University Press, 2000), 21.

71. Ibid., 61.

72. Susan Goldman Rubin, *Art against the Odds: From Slave Quilts to Prison Paintings* (New York: Crown, 2004).

73. Quoted in Mary Hunter, "Opera in Film: Sentiment and Wit, Feeling and Knowing: *The Shawshank Redemption* and *Prizzi's Honor,*" in *Between Opera and Cinema,* ed. Jeongwon Joe and Rose Theresa (New York: Routledge, 2009), 94.

74. Hunter, 97.

75. Phyllis Kornfeld, *Cellblock Visions: Prison Art in America* (Princeton: Princeton University Press, 1997), xiii.

76. See Francis T. Cullen, Edward J. Latessa, Velmer S. Burton, Jr., and Lucien X. Lombardo, "The Correctional Orientation of Prison Wardens," in *Prisons and Jails: A Reader,* ed. Richard Tewksbury and Dean Dabney (Boston: McGraw-Hill, 2009), 222.

77. Fisher-Giorlando, 90.

78. Quoted in Cohen, "Christopher Small's Concept of Musicking," 269–70.

79. See Richard Tewksbury and Elizabeth Ehrhardt Mustaine, "Insiders' Views of Prison Amenities," in *Prison and Jails: A Reader,* ed. Richard Tewksbury and Dean Dabney (New York: McGraw-Hill, 2009), 250; and Michael Santos, *Profiles from Prison: Adjusting to Life Behind Bars* (Westport, CT: Praeger, 2003), 111.

80. Sasha Abramsky, *Hard Time Blues* (New York: St. Martin's, 2002), xiii.

81. Cleveland, 47.

82. Abramsky, xii.

83. Cleveland, 47.

84. Grady Hillman, "The Mythology of the Corrections Community," in *Teaching the Arts Behind Bars,* ed. Rachel Marie-Crane Williams (Boston: Northeastern University Press, 2003), 17.

85. Abramsky, xiv.

86. Smith, 201.

87. Michelle Brown, "'Setting the Conditions' for Abu Ghraib: The Prison Nation Abroad," *American Quarterly* 57.3 (2005): 981–84.

88. Judith Butler, *Precarious Life: The Powers of Mourning and Violence* (London: Verso, 2004), 53.

89. Lehner.

90. Quoted in McGough.

91. Quoted in André Douglas Pond Cummings, "Thug Life: Hip-Hop's Curious Relationship with Criminal Justice," *Santa Clara Law Review* (2009).

92. Quoted in Boccella. One prisoner, Ace, in Mikael Elsila's study of music in two Michigan prisons, recalls prison staffs' similar view of prisoner rights: "You're lucky to even get meals . . . and you want music?" Elsila, 32.

93. "MENS Forums," *The National Association for Music Education,* http://www.menc.org/forums/viewtopic.php?id=402.

94. "Arturo Benedetti Michelangeli," http://www.arturobenedettimichelangeli.com/?l=en&p=home.

95. Elsila, 52.

96. Quoted in Fisher-Giorlando.

97. Quoted in Leslie A. Sprout, "Messiaen, Jolivet, and the Soldier-Composers of Wartime France," *Musical Quarterly* 87.2 (2005): 261.

98. Elsila, 53.

99. Quoted in Cohen, "Mother Theresa," 15.

100. Elsila, 61.

101. Quoted in Cohen, "Christopher Small's Concept of Musicking," 283.

102. Fisher-Giorlando, 280.

103. Quoted in Harbert, 71.

104. Harbert, 70–71.

105. Hans Toch, *Living in Prison: The Ecology of Survival* (New York: Free Press, 1977), 181.

106. Quoted in Elsila, 53.

107. Cohen, "Christopher Small's Concept of Musicking," 285–86.

108. Harbert, 69.

109. Santos, 112.

110. Ibid., 109.

111. Adrian C. North and David J. Hargreaves, "Music in Business Environments," in *Music and Manipulation: On the Social Uses and Social Control of Music,* ed. Steven Brown and Ulrik Volgsten (New York: Berghahn, 2006), 108.

112. Erving Goffman, *Asylums: Essays on the Social Situation of Mental Patients and Other Inmates* (New York: Anchor, 1961), xiii.

113. Goffman, 13.

114. Foucault similarly compares the hierarchy of school and prison. Foucault, 180.

115. Ibid., 180.

116. Santos, 112.

117. Joe Fierro similarly stresses music's role in security in his study of music class at Santa Ana Jail. See Fierro, "Free Inside: The Music Class at Santa Ana Jail," *International Journal of Community Music* 3.1 (March 2010): 144.

118. Quoted in Lewis.

119. Mary L. Cohen, "Conductors' Perspectives of Kansas Prison Choirs," *International Journal of Community Music* 1.3 (2008): 328–29.

120. Cohen, "Christopher Small's Concept of Musicking," 331.

121. Foucault, 164.

122. Ibid., 159.

123. Ibid., 170. (See also dance article.)

124. Ibid., 184.

125. Jeremy Bentham, *The Panopticon Writings,* ed. Miran Božovič (London: Verso, 1995).

126. Foucault, 201.

127. Harbert, 75.

128. Thompson, 57.

129. Lawrence Brewster, "An Evaluation of the Arts-In-Corrections Program of the California Department of Corrections," 1 April 1983, 29, available at http://www .williamjamesassociation.org/reports/Brewster_report_full.pdf.

130. Mello in "The Art of Prevention: Arts Serving Youths at Risk in Human Service and Correctional Setting."

131. Brewster, 25.

132. Paul Katz, "Budget Crisis Finally Killing Program," *Huffington Post,* 15 January 2010, http://www.huffingtonpost.com/paul-katz/california-budget-crisis_b _424298.html.

CHAPTER 6

1. The former Guantanamo detainee, Ibrohim Nasriddinov, quoted in "Ex-Guantanamo Tajik Describes 'Civilized Torture' in U.S. Jail," BBC Monitoring Central Asia Unit, 15 May 2007, http://proxy.ulib.csuohio.edu:2259/hottopics/lnaca demic/.

2. War has also inspired a vast amount of original music composition. See Svanibor Pettan, "Music in War, Music for Peace: Experiences in Applied Ethnomusicology," in *Music and Conflict,* ed. John Morgan O'Connell and Salwa El-Shawan Castelo-Branco (Urbana: University of Illinois Press, 2010), 177.

3. See Bruce Johnson and Martin Cloonan, *Dark Side of the Tune: Popular Music and Violence* (Aldershot: Ashgate, 2008), 32–33; and Steven H. Cornelius, *Music of the Civil War Era* (Westport, CT: Greenwood Press, 2004), 174 and 187.

4. Jonathan Pieslak, *Sound Targets: American Soldiers and Music in the Iraq War* (Bloomington: Indiana University Press, 2009), 79.

5. Ibid., 83.

6. Quoted in ibid., 84.

7. Cusick, "'You Are in a Place That Is out of the World . . .': Music in the Detention Camps of the 'Global War on Terror'," *Journal of the Society for American Music* 2.1 (2008): 1–26.

8. Quoted in Pieslak, 86.

9. Adam Piore, "The Love's Not Mutual," *Newsweek,* 26 May 2003, 13.

10. Moustafa Bayoumi, "Disco Inferno," *The Nation,* 26 December 2005, 32.

11. Quoted in Cusick, "You are . . . ," 9.

12. Ibid., 11–13.

13. See "Secret ORCON: Interrogation Log Detainee 063," http://en.wikisource .org/wiki/Secret_ORCON:_Interrogation_Log_Detainee_063; Cusick, "You are...," 11–13. The designation "Secret ORCON" is a military acronym for a document that is supposed to remain within the originating organization.

14. Bellman and Ford, *Dial "M" for Musicology,* http://musicology.typepad.com /dialm/music-and-torture/.

15. Suzanne Cusick, "Musicology, Torture, Repair, *Radical Musicology* 3 (2008), http://www.radical-musicology.org.uk/2008/Cusick.htm.

16. See Cusick, "You are . . . ," 3.

17. See Alfred McCoy, *A Question of Torture: CIA Interrogation, from the Cold War to the War on Terror* (New York: Metropolitan, 2006), 7–26; and R. Matthew Gildner, "Psychological Torture as a Cold War Imperative," in *The Trauma of Psychological Torture,* ed. Almerindo E. Ojeda (Westport, CT: Praeger, 2008), 23.

18. See Alfred McCoy, "Legacy of a Dark Decade: CIA Mind Control, Classified Behavioral Research, and the Origins of Modern Medical Ethics," in *The Trauma of Psychological Torture,* ed. Almerindo E. Ojeda (Westport, CT: Praeger, 2008), 40–69, 55–56.

19. Quoted in McCoy, *A Question of Torture,* 9. Regarding music's use in interrogation, the vice president of PSYOPS, Rick Hoffman, believes the tactic has "no lasting effect on prisoners." Pieslak, 89.

20. See also Cusick, "Music as Torture/Music as Weapon."

21. Pieslak, 87.

22. Quoted in Johnson and Cloonan, 149.

23. Cusick, "You are . . . ," 3.

24. See Almerindo E. Ojeda, "What Is Psychological Torture?" in *The Trauma of Psychological Torture,* ed. Almerindo E. Ojeda (Westport, CT: Praeger, 2008), 9–17.

25. Quoted in Johnson and Cloonan, 151.

26. Johnson and Cloonan, 151.

27. Amnon Shiloah, *Music in the World of Islam: A Socio-Cultural Study* (Detroit: Wayne State University Press, 1995), 34–43.

28. Quoted in John Baily, "Music and Censorship in Afghanistan, 1973–2003," in *Music and the Play of Power in the Middle East, North Africa and Central Asia,* ed. Laudan Nooshin (Burlington, VT: Ashgate, 2009), 155. See also Baily, 144–55.

29. Ibid., 160.

30. See Cusick, "You are . . . ," 11–13.

31. Quoted in Mark Levine, *Heavy Metal Islam: Rock, Resistance, and the Struggle for the Soul of Islam* (New York: Three Rivers, 2008), 272. See also Levine, 175–82.

32. Cusick, "Music as Torture/Music as Weapon."

33. Steve Goodman, *Sonic Warfare: Sound, Affect, and the Ecology of Fear* (Cambridge: MIT Press, 2010), 65.

34. See Cusick, "You are . . . ," 11–13.

35. "Inside the Interrogation of Detainee 063," *Time,* 12 June 2005, http://www.time.com/time/printout/0,8816,1071284,00.html.

36. "Secret ORCON: Interrogation Log Detainee 063."

37. Pieslak, 83.

38. Ibid., 84.

39. Quoted in ibid., 89.

40. Johnson and Cloonan, 158.

41. See Jennifer Senior, "PsyOps Rock!" *New York Magazine,* 23 October 2009, http://nymag.com/news/intelligencer/60310; Ismael AbduSalaam, "Artists Sue Government for Using Music for Torture," *AllHipHop,* 23 Octoter 2009, http://allhiphop.com/stories/news/archive/2009/10/23/21994124.aspx.

42. Elaine Scarry, *The Body in Pain: The Making and Unmaking of the World* (Oxford: Oxford University Press, 1985), 46 and 49.

43. David Sussman, "What's Wrong with Torture," in *The Phenomenon of Torture: Readings and Commentary*, ed. William F. Schulz (Philadelphia: University of Pennsylvania Press, 2007), 178–79.

44. Dori Laub, "The Narrativization of Traumatic Experiences through Testimony," Presentation at the National Conference of the German Studies Association, 10 October 2010. See also Dori Laub, "September 11, 2001—An Event without a Voice," in *Trauma at Home: After 9/11*, ed. Judith Greenberg (Lincoln: University of Nebraska Press, 2003), 209.

45. "Secret ORCON: Interrogation Log Detainee 063."

46. Vance, quoted in Cusick, "You are . . . ," 23.

47. Oliver Sacks, *Musicophilia: Tales of Music and the Brain* (New York: Knopf, 2007), 41–42.

48. See the discussion of earworms in Goodman, 146–47.

49. Karen Lury, "Chewing Gum for the Ears: Children's Television and Popular Music," *Popular Music* 21.3 (October 2002), 298–303. See also Kenneth M. McGuire, "The Use of Music on *Barney and Friends:* Implications for Music Therapy Practice and Research," *Journal of Music Therapy* 38.2 (Summer 2001): 114–48; and Robert Fink, *Repeating Ourselves: American Minimal Music as Cultural Practice* (Berkeley: University of California Press, 2005), 3–4.

50. Sacks, *Musicophilia*, 43.

51. Judith Becker, "Music and Trance," *Leonardo Music Journal* 4 (1994): 41.

52. Becker, 47.

53. Laub, "The Narrativization."

54. Cusick notes that accounts of such torture involve men, almost exclusively, rather than women. Cusick, "You are . . . ," 2.

55. Moazzam Begg with Victoria Brittain, *Enemy Combatant: My Imprisonment at Guantánamo, Bagram, and Kandahar* (New York: New Press, 2006), 111.

56. Ibid., 287.

57. Ibid., 290.

58. Quoted in Senior.

59. Quoted in Cusick, "You are . . . ," 1.

60. "Secret ORCON: Interrogation Log Detainee 063."

61. Quoted in "Ex-Guantanamo Tajik."

62. See McCoy, *A Question of Torture*, 10.

63. Quoted in Jody Enders, *The Medieval Theater of Cruelty: Rhetoric, Memory, Violence* (Ithaca: Cornell University Press, 1999), 7.

64. Many have written about the connection between sound and music. See for example, Karin Bijsterveld, *Mechanical Sound: Technology, Culture and Public Problems of Noise in the Twentieth Century* (Cambridge: MIT Press, 2008), 35.

65. For such a description of terrorism, see Cindy C. Combs, *Terrorism in the Twenty-First Century* (Boston: Longman, 2011), 6.

66. Quoted in Bayoumi, 33.

67. See Ashby Jones, "Too Much Rockin' in the Not-So-Free World" and responses in *Law Blog,* 22 October 2009, http://blogs.wsj.com.law/2009/10/22/too-much-rockin-in-the-not-so-free-world/.

68. Quoted in Sean Michaels, "Music as Torture May Incur Royalty Fees," *guardian.co.uk,* 9 July 2008, http://www.guardian.co.uk/music/2008.jul/09/news.culture3/print.

69. Michael Booker, "Rap Torture: Eminem Will Sue; Star to Take on U.S. Government," *Sunday Star,* 5 March 2006, 29.

70. Quoted in Senior.

71. Quoted in Andy Worthington, "A History of Music Torture in the 'War on Terror'," *Huffington Post,* 15 December 2008, http://www.huffingtonpost.com/andy-worthington/a-history-of-music-tortur_b_151109.html.

72. See Joe Heim, "Torture Songs Spur a Protest Most Vocal," *Washington Post,* 22 October 2009, 2.

73. *AMS Newsletter* 38.2 (August 2008): 5.

74. "Ethnomusicologists Against Music as Torture," 9 February 2006, http://themusicissue.blogspot.com.

75. Quoted in Lara Pellegrinelli, "Scholarly Discord," *Chronicle of Higher Education* 55.35, 8 May 2009, http://web.ebscohost.com/ehost/delivery?vid=6&hid=106&sid=c20c0054-12f8-4131-9b60.

76. David Cole, ed., *The Torture Memos: Rationalizing the Unthinkable* (New York: New Press, 2009), 7.

77. See Marcy Strauss, "Torture," *New York Law School Law Review* (2003), *LexisNexis Academic.* http://www.lexisnexis.com.

78. See Cole, 41.

79. Ibid., 77.

80. Cusick, "Musicology, Torture, Repair."

81. Goodman (see pages 5–13 for an overview of purpose).

82. Cusick, "Music as Torture/Music as Weapon."

83. Jonathan Pieslak, "Soundtracking Iraq," *The Journal of Music* (October/November 2009), http://journalofmusic.com/article/1053.

84. Cusick, "Musicology, Torture, Repair."

85. "Musicology/Ethnomusicology" (2010–2011), 16 March 2011, http://www.wikihost.org/w/academe/music_history_musicology_ethnomusicology.

86. "Artists Revolt Against Gitmo Using Songs for Torture," *The Vibe,* http://thevibe.socialvibe.com/index.php/2009/10/23/artists-revolt-against-gitmo-using . . .

87. Quoted in Timberg, "Classical Music as Crime Stopper."

88. Daniel Ferreira, "Art Should Not Be Punishment," in "Letters to the Editor," *The Modesto Bee,* 5 February 2009, http://www.modbee.com/opinion/letters/story/588847.html.

89. Szymon Laks, *Music of Another World,* trans. Chester A. Kisiel (Evanston, IL: Northwestern University Press, 2000), 118, 7.

90. Stephen H. Barnes, *Muzak: The Hidden Messages in Music: A Social Psychology of Cultures* (Lewiston, NY: Mellen, 1988), 16.

91. Barnes, 21.

92. Quoted in Taruskin, *Danger of Music,* 217–18.

93. See Theodor W. Adorno and Max Horkheimer, *Dialectic of Enlightenment* trans. John Cumming (New York: Herder and Herder, 1972), 120–67.

94. See Dwight Macdonald, "Masscult & Midcult," in *Popular Culture Theory and Methodology: A Basic Introduction,* ed. Harold E. Hinds, Marilyn Ferris Motz, Angela M. S. Nelson (Madison: University of Wisconsin Press, 2006), 9–15.

95. Jacques A. Attali, *Noise: The Political Economy of Music,* trans. Brian Massumi (Minneapolis: University of Minnesota Press, 1985), 6.

96. Johnson and Cloonan, 26.

97. Gilles Deleuze and Félix Guattari, *A Thousand Plateaus: Capitalism and Schizophrenia,* trans. Brian Massumi (Minneapolis: University of Minnesota Press, 1987), 299.

98. Richard Taruskin, *The Danger of Music and Other Anti-Utopian Essays* (Berkeley: University of California Press, 2009), 173.

99. See Mark Evan Bonds, "Idealism and the Aesthetics of Instrumental Music at the Turn of the Nineteenth Century," *Journal of the American Musicological Society* 50.2–3 (Summer–Autumn 1997): 387–420.

100. As Johnson and Cloonan demonstrate in their work, the use of music's negative possibilities "is mundane and ubiquitous" (73).

101. See, for example, Christopher Small, *Musicking: The Meanings of Performing and Listening* (Middletown, CT: Wesleyan University Press, 1998).

102. Philip Fisher, *Making and Effacing Art: Modern American Art in a Culture of Museums* (Cambridge: Harvard University Press, 1991), 3.

103. Ibid., 5.

104. Ibid., 11.

105. Tobias Rapp, "The Pain of Listening: Using Music as a Weapon at Guantanamo," *Spiegel Online,* 14 January 2010, http://www.spiegel.de/international/world /0,1518,672177,00.html.

106. Arthur C. Danto, "Dangerous Art," in *Eretica: The Transcendent and the Profane in Contemporary Art,* ed. Demetrio Paparoni (Milan: Skira, 2007), 180.

EPILOGUE

1. See Jeff Kass, "Here, Lawbreakers Listen to Beethoven," *Christian Science Monitor,* 19 May 1999, *LexisNexis Academic,* 5 February 2009, http://www.lexisnexis .com.

2. See Mary Hunter, "'To Play as if from the Soul of the Composer': The Idea of the Performer in Early Romantic Aesthetics," *Journal of the American Musicological Society* 58.2 (2005): 357–98; see also Lydia Goehr, *The Imaginary Museum of Musical Works: An Essay in the Philosophy of Music* (Oxford: Clarendon, 1992), 231.

3. Goehr, 243.

4. Carys Wyn Jones, *The Rock Canon: Canonical Values in the Reception of Rock*

Albums (Aldershot: Ashgate, 2008); and Motti Regev, "Producing Artistic Value: The Case of Rock Music," *The Sociological Quarterly* 35.1 (February 1994): 42.

5. Erica Schroeder, "Sounds of Prejudice: Background Music During Victim Impact Statements," *The University of Kansas Law Review* (January 2010), *LexisNexis Academic,* 12 March 2010, http://www.lexisnexis.com.

6. Christine Haight Farley, "Imagining the Law: Art," in *Law and the Humanities: An Introduction,* ed. Austin Sarat, Matthew Anderson, and Catherine O. Frank (Cambridge: Cambridge University Press, 2010), 306.

7. See Edgard H. Tyson, "Rap Music in Social Work Practice with African-American and Latino Youth: A Conceptual Model with Practical Applications," *Journal of Human Behavior in the Social Environment* 8.4 (2003); and Kevin Klinger, "Hip Hop Wisdom for White Therapists" (MA thesis, Pacifica Graduate University, 2010); Winfrey, *Healing Young People thru Empowerment.*

8. See Helen A. Anderson, "The Freedom to Speak and the Freedom to Listen: The Admissability of the Criminal Defendant's Taste in Entertainment," *Oregon Law Review* (2004), *LexisNexis Academic,* 5 February 2010, http://www.lexisnexis .com.

9. Ken Stewart, "The World is Enamored with All Things Celtic," *Billboard,* 109.27, 5 July 1997.

10. See for example, "Popular Songs That Can Be Played Anytime during a Funeral or Memorial Service," http://www.heavenlywhitedoves.net/funeral_songs .html#funeralsongs.

11. Anna Maria Dore, "How Can I Keep from Singing? Enya and the Female Myth of Ireland" (MA thesis, University of Limerick, 2003), 5.

12. See, for example, http://kaystreet.wordpress.com/2011/09/10/911-memo rial-video-enya-only-time/.

13. Dore, 26.

14. Ibid., 24.

15. James McCarthy and Euan Hague, "Race, Nation, and Nature: The Cultural Politics of 'Celtic' Identification in the American West," *Annals of the Association of American Geographers* 94.2 (2004): 389.

16. *The People v. Kelly,* 2007, LEXIS 13795, S049973, Supreme Court of California, 763.

17. Austin Sarat and Thomas R. Kearns, "Responding to the Demands of Difference: An Introduction," in *Cultural Pluralism, Identity Politics, and the Law,* ed. Austin Sarat and Thomas R. Kearns (Ann Arbor: University of Michigan Press, 1999), 13.

18. For more information on Lady Justice, see Matthew B. Robinson, *Justice Blind? Ideals and Realities of American Criminal Justice,* 2nd ed. (Upper Saddle River, NJ: Prentice Hall, 2005), 25–27.

Sources Consulted

PERSONAL COMMUNICATIONS

Brown, Zachary. Telephone conversation with the author. 11 June 2009.
Cade, Karen. Email to the author. 5 January 2009.
Chabris, Margaret. Email to the author. 24 January 2007.
McKay, Clint. Telephone conversation with the author. 17 January 2007.
Miller, Wayne. Telephone conversation with the author. 10 June 2009.
Sacco, Paul. Email to the author. 22 January 2009.
Shapiro, Arnold. Telephone conversation with the author. 25 January 2011.

LEGAL TRANSCRIPTS

Davidson v. Time Warner, Inc. 1997. LEXIS 21559, No. V-94-006, U.S. District Court for the Southern District of Texas.
Herlein v. Higgins. 1999. LEXIS 7624, U.S. Court of Appeals for the Eighth Circuit.
People v. Kelly. 2007. LEXIS 13795, S049973, Supreme Court of California, 763.
People v. Olguin. 1994. LEXIS 1325, Nos. G014071, G014235, Court of Appeal of California, Fourth Appellate District, 1355.
People v. Prince. 2007. LEXIS 4272, Supreme Court of California.
People v. Richardson. 2004. LEXIS 699, Court of Appeal of California, Third Appellate District.
Salazar v. State. 2002. LEXIS 230, No. 2180-01, Court of Criminal Appeals of Texas.
United States v. Stuckey. 2007. LEXIS 24636, No. 05-1039, U.S. Court of Appeals for the Sixth District, 468.
Young v. Beard. 2008. LEXIS 14315, U.S. Court of Appeals for the Third Circuit.

PUBLISHED WORKS

Abbate, Carolyn. *Unsung Voices: Opera and Musical Narrative in the Nineteenth Century.* Princeton: Princeton University Press, 1991.

AbduSalaam, Ismael. "Artists Sue Government for Using Music for Torture." *AllHipHop,* 23 October 2009, http://allhiphop.com/stories/news/archive/2009/10/23/21994124.aspx.

Abramsky, Sasha. *Hard Time Blues.* New York: St. Martin's, 2002.

Adorno, Theodor W., and Max Horkheimer. *Dialectic of Enlightenment.* Trans. John Cumming. New York: Herder and Herder, 1972.

Allen, Francis A. "The Decline of the Rehabilitative Ideal." In *Principled Sentencing: Readings on Theory and Policy,* 3rd ed., ed. Andrew von Hirsch, Andrew Ashworth, and Julian Roberts, 11–15. Oxford, OR: Hart, 2009.

Allen, Nakeyshaey M. Tille. "Exploring Hip-Hop Therapy with High-Risk Youth." *Praxis* 5.1. (2005): 31.

Alperson, Philip. "Schopenhauer and Musical Revelation." *Journal of Aesthetics and Art Criticism* 40.2 (1981): 155–66.

"AMS Board Condemns the Use of Music in Physical or Psychological Tortures." *AMS Newsletter* 38.2 (2008): 5.

Anderson, Helen A. "The Freedom to Speak and the Freedom to Listen: The Admissibility of the Criminal Defendant's Taste in Entertainment." *Oregon Law Review* (2004). *LexisNexis Academic.* http://www.lexisnexis.com.

Anderson, Warren D. *Ethos and Education in Greek Music: The Evidence of Poetry and Philosophy.* Cambridge: Harvard University Press, 1966.

Arewa, Olufunmilayo B. "From J. C. Bach to Hip Hop: Musical Borrowing, Copyright and Cultural Context." *North Carolina Law Review* 84.2 (2006): 547–645.

Armstrong, Edward. "Eminem's Construction of Authenticity." *Popular Music and Society* 27.3 (2004): 335–55.

Armstrong, Edward. "The Rhetoric of Violence in Rap and Country Music." *Sociological Inquiry* 63.1 (1993): 64–83.

"The Art of Prevention: Arts Serving Youths at Risk in Human Service and Correctional Setting." Hearing Transcript, Joint Committee on the Arts, Chair Henry J. Mello, 20 April 1994, Sacramento, CA.

"Artists Revolt against Gitmo Using Songs for Torture." *Vibe,* 23 October 2009. http://thevibe.socialvibe.com/index.php/2009/10/23/artists-revolt-against-gitmo-using-songs-for-torture/.

Atlas, Randall. *21st Century Security and CPTED: Designing for Critical Infrastructure Protection and Crime Prevention.* Boca Raton, FL: Taylor and Francis, 2008.

Attali, Jacques A. *Noise: The Political Economy of Music.* Trans. Brian Massumi. Minneapolis: University of Minnesota Press, 1985.

Baily, John. "Music and Censorship in Afghanistan, 1973–2003." In *Music and the Play of Power in the Middle East, North Africa, and Central Asia,* ed. Laudan Nooshin, 143–63. Burlington, VT: Ashgate, 2009.

Bakhtin, M. M. *The Dialogic Imagination: Four Essays*. Ed. Michael Lohquist. Trans. Caryl Emerson and Michael Holquist. Austin: University of Texas Press, 1981.

Bandes, Susan A. "Exploring the Interaction between Emotions and Legal Institutions: Repellent Crimes and Rational Deliberation: Emotion and the Death Penalty." *Vermont Law Review* (2009). *LexisNexis Academic*. http://www.lexis nexis.com.

Barnes, Stephen H. *Muzak: The Hidden Messages in Music: A Social Psychology of Cultures*. Lewiston, NY: Mellen, 1988.

Baumeister, Roy F., C. Nathan DeWall, and Liqing Zhang. "Do Emotions Improve or Hinder the Decision Making Process?" In *Do Emotions Help or Hurt Decision Making?: A Hedgefoxian Perspective*, ed. Kathleen D. Vohs, Roy F. Baumeister, and George Loewenstein, 11–34. New York: Sage, 2007.

Bayoumi, Moustafa. "Disco Inferno." *The Nation*, 26 December 2005, 32–35.

Becker, Judith. "Music and Trance." *Leonardo Music Journal* 4 (1994): 41–51.

Beets, Greg. "Jury Weighing Rap as an Accomplice to Murder of a Trooper." *Billboard*, 3 July 1993, 12.

Begg, Moazzam, with Victoria Brittain. *Enemy Combatant: My Imprisonment at Guantánamo, Bagram, and Kandahar*. New York: New Press, 2006.

Bellman, Jonathan, and Phil Ford. *Dial "M" for Musicology*. 2007. http://musicol ogy.typepad.com/dialm/music-and-torture/.

Bentham, Jeremy. *The Panopticon Writings*. Ed. Miran Božovič. London: Verso, 1995.

Benzel, Jan, and Alessandra Stanley. "1990: The Agony and the Ecstasy." *New York Times*, 30 December 1990, H1.

Bijsterveld, Karin. *Mechanical Sound: Technology, Culture, and Public Problems of Noise in the Twentieth Century*. Cambridge: MIT Press, 2008.

Blecha, Peter. *Taboo Tunes: A History of Banned Bands and Censored Songs*. San Francisco: Backbeat, 2004.

Block, Peter Alan. "Modern-Day Sirens: Rock Lyrics and the First Amendment." *Southern California Law Review* 63.3 (1990): 777–832.

Blumenthal, Jeremy A. "A Moody View of the Law: Looking Back and Looking ahead at Law and the Emotions." In *Emotion and the Law: Psychological Perspectives*, ed. Brian Bronstein and Richard Wiener, 185–210. New York: Springer, 2010.

Boccella, Kathy. "Show on Jail Bands Stirs Outrage." *Philadelphia Inquirer*, October 11, 2002, B1.

Bonds, Mark Evan. "Idealism and the Aesthetics of Instrumental Music at the Turn of the Nineteenth Century." *Journal of the American Musicological Society* 50.2–3 (1997): 387–420.

Booker, Michael. "Rap Torture: Eminem Will Sue; Star to Take on U.S. Government." *The Daily Star*, 5 March 2006, 29.

Bork, Robert H. *The Tempting of America: The Political Seduction of the Law*. New York: Free Press, 1990.

Bornstein, Brian, and Richard Wiener. "Emotion and the Law: A Field Whose Time Has Come." In *Emotion and the Law: Psychological Perspectives*, ed. Brian Bornstein and Richard Wiener, 1–12. New York: Springer, 2010.

Botstein, Leon. "The Aesthetics of Assimilation and Affirmation: Reconstructing the Career of Felix Mendelssohn." In *Mendelssohn and His World*, ed. R. Larry Todd, 5–42. Princeton: Princeton University Press, 1991.

Bourdieu, Pierre. *Distinction: A Social Critique of the Judgment of Taste*. Trans. Richard Nice. Cambridge: Harvard University Press, 1984.

Bourdieu, Pierre. *Language and Symbolic Power*. Ed. John B. Thompson. Trans. Gino Raymond and Matthew Adamson. Cambridge: Polity, 1991.

Bracket, David. "'Where's It At?': Postmodern Theory and the Contemporary Musical Field." In *Postmodern Music/Postmodern Thought*, ed. Judy Lochhead and Joseph Auner, 207–31. New York: Routledge, 2002.

Brecht, Bertolt. *Über experimentelles Theater*. Ed. Werner Hecht. Frankfurt: Suhrkamp, 1970.

Brewster, Lawrence. "An Evaluation of the Arts-in-Corrections Program of the California Department of Corrections." 1 April 1983. http://www.williamjames association.org/reports/Brewster_report_full.pdf.

Brick, Michael. "Rap Takes Center Stage at Trial in Killing of Two Detectives." *New York Times*, 12 December 2006, B1.

Brombert, Victor. *The Romantic Prison: The French Tradition*. Princeton: Princeton University Press, 1978.

Brown, Michelle. "'Setting the Conditions' for Abu Ghraib: The Prison Nation Abroad." *American Quarterly* 57.3 (2005): 973–97.

Brym, Robert J. "Hip-Hop from Dissent to Commodity: A Note on Consumer Culture." In *Society in Question*, 5th ed., ed. Robert J. Brym, 76–80. Toronto: Nelson, 2008.

Bryson, Bethany. "'Anything but Heavy Metal': Symbolic Exclusion and Musical Dislikes." *American Sociological Review* 61.5 (1996): 884–99.

Bugg, John. "Close Confinement: John Thelwall and the Romantic Prison." *European Romantic Review* 20.1 (2009): 37–56.

Burkholder, J. Peter. "Borrowing." *Oxford Music Online*. http://www.oxfordmusic online.com/subscriber/article/grove/music/52918#552918.

Burkholder, J. Peter. "The Use of Existing Music: Musical Borrowing as a Field." *Notes* 50.3 (1994): 851–70.

Butler, Judith. *Precarious Life: The Powers of Mourning and Violence*. London: Verso, 2004.

Capers, I. Bennett. "Crime Music." *Ohio State Journal of Criminal Law* (2010). *LexisNexis Academic*. http://www.lexisnexis.com.

Carrol, Noel. "Horror and Humor." *Journal of Aesthetics and Art Criticism* 57.2 (1999): 145–60.

Chamberlain, Gethin. "Going Skirl Crazy: Noisy Kids Ordered to Endure Loud Bagpipes." *Daily Record*, Glasgow, Scotland, 10 May 1999, 16.

Chambers, James P. "Noise Pollution." In *Advanced Air and Noise Pollution Control*, ed. Lawrence K. Wang, Norman C. Pereira, and Yung-Tse Hung, 441–52. Totowa, NJ: Humana, 2005.

Clapp, James E. *Webster's Pocket Legal Dictionary*. New York: Random House, 2007.

Clark, Anne L. "'As Nasty as They Wanna Be': Popular Music on Trial." *New York University Law Review* 65 (1990): 1481–1531.

Clark, Suzannah, and Elizabeth Eva Leach, eds. *Citation and Authority in Medieval and Renaissance Musical Culture: Learning from the Learned.* Suffolk: Boydell, 2005.

Clarke, David. "Eminem: Difficult Dialogics." In *Words and Music,* ed. John Williamson, 73–102. Liverpool: University of Liverpool Press, 2005.

"Classical Music as Punishment." *Mark O'Connor Newsletter,* 22 March 2000. http://www.markoconnor.com/index.php?page=bio&family=mark&category=Other_Newsletters_-squo-99--squo-03.

"Classical Music on West Palm Corner Deters Crime." *USA Today,* 8 July 2001. http://www.usatoday.com/news/nation/2001/07/08/music.htm.

Cleveland, William. *Art in Other Places: Artists at Work in America's Community and Social Institutions.* Westport, CT: Praeger, 1992.

Cloonan, Martin. *Banned! Censorship of Popular Music in Britain, 1967–92.* Aldershot: Arena, 1996.

Cloonan, Martin. "Call That Censorship?: Problems of Definition." In *Policing Pop,* ed. Martin Cloonan and Reebee Garofalo, 13–29. Philadelphia: Temple University Press, 2003.

"CNN Student News Transcript." 28 October 2009. http://www.cnn.com/2009/LIVING/studentnews/10/27/transcript.wed/index.html.

Coates, Ta-Nehisi. "The Mask of Doom: A Nonconformist Rapper's Second Act." *New Yorker,* 21 September 2009, 52–57.

Cohen, Mary L. "Christopher Small's Concept of Musicking: Toward a Theory of Choral Singing Pedagogy in Prison Contexts." Ph.D. diss., University of Kansas, 2007.

Cohen, Mary L. "Conductors' Perspectives of Kansas Prison Choirs." *International Journal of Community Music* 1.3 (2008): 319–33.

Cohen, Mary L. "'Mother Theresa, How Can I Help You?': The Story of Elvera Voth, Robert Shaw, and the Bethel College Benefit Sing-Along for Arts in Prison, Inc." *International Journal of Research in Choral Singing* 3.1 (2008): 4–22.

Cole, David, ed. *The Torture Memos: Rationalizing the Unthinkable.* New York: New Press, 2009.

Coleman, Clive, and Clive Norris. 2000. *Introducing Criminology.* Devon: Willan, 2000.

Combs, Cindy C. *Terrorism in the Twenty-First Century.* Boston: Longman, 2011.

Cone, Edward T. *The Composer's Voice.* Berkeley: University of California Press, 1974.

Cornelius, Steven H. *Music of the Civil War Era.* Westport, CT: Greenwood, 2004.

Correl, DeeDee. "He Writes the Rules That Make Their Eardrums Ring." *Los Angeles Times,* 21 January 2009. http://www.latimes.com/news/nationworld/nation/la-na-music-punishment21-2009jan21,0,1887999.story.

Cover, Robert. *Narrative, Violence, and the Law: The Essays of Robert Cover.* Ed. Martha Minow, Michael Ryan, and Austin Sarat. Ann Arbor: University of Michigan Press, 1992.

Crowe, Timothy D. *Crime Prevention through Environmental Design: Applications of Architectural Design and Space Management Concepts.* Boston: Butterworth-Heinemann, 1991.

Cullen, Francis T., Edward J. Latessa, Velmer S. Burton Jr., and Lucien X. Lombardo. "The Correctional Orientation of Prison Wardens." In *Prisons and Jails: A Reader,* ed. Richard Tewksbury and Dean Dabney, 221–36. Boston: McGraw-Hill, 2009.

Cummings, André Douglas Pond. "Thug Life: Hip-Hop's Curious Relationship with Criminal Justice." *Santa Clara Law Review* (2009). http://works.bepress.com/andre_cummings/1/.

Cusick, Suzanne G. "Music as Torture/Music as Weapon." *Transcultural Music Review* 10 (2006). http://www.sibetrans.com/trans/trans10/cusick_eng.htm.

Cusick, Suzanne G. "Musicology, Torture, Repair." *Radical Musicology* (2008). http://www.radical-musicology.org.uk/2008/Cusick.htm.

Cusick, Suzanne G. "'You Are in a Place That Is out of the World . . .': Music in the Detention Camps of the 'Global War on Terror.'" *Journal of the Society for American Music* 2.1 (2008): 1–26.

Danto, Arthur C. "Dangerous Art." In *Eretica: The Transcendent and the Profane in Contemporary Art,* ed. Demetrio Paparoni, 173–208. Milan: Skira, 2007.

Davidson, James. "Making a Spectacle of Her(Self): The Greek Courtesan and the Art of the Present." In *The Courtesan's Arts: Cross-Cultural Perspectives,* ed. Martha Feldman and Bonnie Gordon, 29–51. New York: Oxford University Press, 2006.

Davidson, Sandra. "Two Perspectives on Ice-T: 'Can't Touch Me': Musical Messages and Incitement Law." In *Bleep! Censoring Rock and Rap Music,* ed. Betty Houchin Winfield and Sandra Davidson, 21–34. Westport, CT: Greenwood, 1999.

Davies, Stephen. *Musical Meaning and Expression.* Ithaca: Cornell University Press, 1994.

Davies, Stephen. "Philosophical Perspectives on Music's Expressiveness." In *Music and Emotion: Theory and Research,* ed. Patrik N. Juslin and John A. Sloboda, 23–44. New York: Oxford University Press, 2000.

Davies, Stephen. *The Philosophy of Art.* Malden, MA: Blackwell, 2006.

De Carlo, Alonzo, and Elaine Hockman. "RAP Therapy: A Group Work Intervention Method for Urban Adolescents." *Social Work with Groups* 26.3 (2003): 45–59.

Deleuze, Gilles, and Félix Guattari. *A Thousand Plateaus: Capitalism and Schizophrenia.* Trans. Brian Massumi. Minneapolis: University of Minnesota Press, 1987.

Demers, Joanna. *Steal This Music: How Intellectual Property Law Affects Musical Creativity.* Athens: University of Georgia Press, 2006.

Dennis, Andrea L. "Poetic (In)Justice?: Rap Music Lyrics as Art, Life, and Criminal Evidence." *Columbia Journal of Law and the Arts* (2007). *LexisNexis Academic.* http://www.lexisnexis.com.

DeNora, Tia. *Music in Everyday Life.* Cambridge: Cambridge University Press, 2000.

Deveaux, Scott. "Constructing the Jazz Tradition: Jazz Historiography." *Black American Literature Forum* 24.3 (1991): 525–60.

Dimitriadis, Greg. *Performing Identity/Performing Culture: Hip Hop as Text, Pedagogy, and Lived Practice.* New York: Lang, 2001.

Donelan, James H. *Poetry and the Romantic Musical Aesthetic.* New York: Cambridge University Press, 2008.

Dore, Anna Maria. "How Can I Keep from Singing? Enya and the Female Myth of Ireland." Master's thesis, University of Limerick, 2003.

Dow, David R. "The Moral Failure of the Clear and Present Danger Test." *William and Mary Bill of Rights Journal* (1998). http://scholarship.law.wm.edu/wmborj/vol6/iss3/4.

Duara, Nigel. "Portland Police Employ Classical Music at Light Rail Stations to Chase Off Loiterers." *StarTribune.com,* 3 April 2011. http://www.startribune.com/nation/119121109.html.

Duff, Ra. "Punishment, Retribution, and Communication?" In *Principled Sentencing: Readings on Theory and Policy,* 3rd ed., ed. Andrew von Hirsch, Andrew Ashworth, and Julian Roberts, 127–34. Oxford, OR: Hart, 2009.

Dunlap, Aaron C. "Come on Feel the Noise: The Problem with Municipal Noise Regulation." *University of Miami Business Law Review* (Winter 2006). *LexisNexis Academic.* http://www.lexisnexis.com.

Eckstein, Lars. "Torpedoing the Authorship of Popular Music: A Reading of Gorillaz' 'Feel Good Inc.'" *Popular Music* 28.2 (2009): 239–55.

Egan, Mary Ellen. "Move Along." *City Pages,* 22 January 1997. http://www.citypages.com/databank/18/842/article3195.asp.

Elligan, Don. *Rap Therapy: A Practical Guide for Communicating with Youth and Young Adults through Rap Music.* New York: Kensington, 2004.

Elsila, Mikael. "Music behind Bars: Libratory Musicology in Two Michigan Prisons." Master's thesis, University of Michigan, 1995.

Embleton, T. "Noise Control from the Ancient Past." *Noise News* (March–April 1977): 26.

Enders, Jody. *The Medieval Theater of Cruelty: Rhetoric, Memory, Violence.* Ithaca: Cornell University Press, 1999.

Esslin, Martin. *Brecht, a Choice of Evils: A Critical Study of the Man, His Work, and His Opinions.* London: Methuen Drama, 1985.

"Ethnomusicologists against Music as Torture." 9 February 2006. http://themusicissue.blogspot.com.

"Ex-Guantanamo Tajik Describes 'Civilized Torture' in U.S. Jail." BBC Monitoring Central Asia Unit, 15 May 2007. http://proxy.ulib.csuohio.edu:2259/hottopics/lnacademic/.

Farley, Christine Haight. "Imagining the Law: Art." In *Law and the Humanities: An Introduction,* ed. Austin Sarat, Matthew Anderson, and Catherine O. Frank, 292–312. Cambridge: Cambridge University Press, 2010.

Ferreira, Daniel. "Art Should Not Be Punishment" (Letter to the Editor). *Modesto Bee,* 5 February 2009. http://www.modbee.com/opinion/letters/story/588847.html.

Fierro, Joe. "Free Inside: The Music Class at Santa Ana Jail." *International Journal of Community Music* 3.1 (2010): 143–50.

Fink, Robert. "Beethoven Antihero." In *Beyond Structural Listening? Postmodern Modes of Hearing,* ed. Andrew Dell'Antonio, 109–53. Berkeley: University of California Press, 2004.

Fink, Robert. "Elvis Everywhere: Musicology and Popular Music Studies at the Twilight of the Canon." *American Music* 16.2 (1998): 135–79.

Fink, Robert. *Repeating Ourselves: American Minimal Music as Cultural Practice.* Berkeley: University of California Press, 2005.

Fischoff, Stuart P. "'Gangsta' Rap and a Murder in Bakersfield." *Journal of Applied Social Psychology* 29.4 (1999): 795–805.

Fisher, Alexander J. "Song, Confession, and Criminality: Trial Records as Sources for Popular Musical Culture in Early Modern Europe." *Journal of Musicology* 18.4 (2001): 616–57.

Fisher, Philip. *Making and Effacing Art: Modern American Art in a Culture of Museums.* Cambridge: Harvard University Press, 1991.

Fisher-Giorlando, Marianne. "Prison Culture: Using Music as Data." Ph.D. diss., Ohio State University, 1987.

Foucault, Michel. *Discipline and Punish: The Birth of the Prison.* Trans. Alan Sheridan. New York: Vintage, 1997.

Fox, Aaron A. *Real Country: Music and Language in Working-Class Culture.* Durham, NC: Duke University Press, 2004.

Frank, Jerome. "Words and Music: Some Remarks on Statutory Interpretation." *Columbia Law Review* 47.8 (1947): 1259–78.

Frith, Simon. *Performing Rites: On the Values of Popular Music.* Cambridge: Harvard University Press, 1996.

Gabbart, Krin. "The Quoter and His Culture." In *Jazz in Mind: Essays on the History and Meanings of Jazz,* ed. Reginald T. Buckner and Steven Weiland, 92–111. Detroit: Wayne State University Press, 1991.

Garvey, Stephen R. "Can Shaming Punishments Educate?" *University of Chicago Law Review* (1998). *LexisNexis Academic.* http://www.lexisnexis.com.

Gildner, R. Matthew. "Psychological Torture as a Cold War Imperative." In *The Trauma of Psychological Torture,* ed. Almerindo E. Ojeda, 23–39. Westport, CT: Praeger, 2008.

Gillespie, Alexander. "The No Longer Silent Problem: Confronting Noise Pollution in the 21st Century." *Villanova Environmental Law Journal* (2009). *LexisNexis Academic.* http://www.lexisnexis.com.

Glass, Philip. "When Language Fails the World Is Revealed." In *The Voice of Music: Conversations with Composers of Our Time,* ed. Anders Beyer, trans. Jean Christensen and Anders Beyer, 267–80. Burlington, VT: Ashgate, 2000.

Goehr, Lydia. *The Imaginary Museum of Musical Works: An Essay in the Philosophy of Music.* Oxford: Clarendon, 1992.

Goetz, Kristina. "Inmates Find Harmony through CDs." *Cincinnati Enquirer,* 16 January 2004. http://www.enquirer.com/editions/2004/01/16/loc_prisonsing16 box0.html.

Goffman, Erving. *Asylums: Essays on the Social Situation of Mental Patients and Other Inmates.* New York: Anchor, 1961.

Golash, Deirdre. *The Case against Punishment: Retribution, Crime Prevention, and the Law.* New York: New York University Press, 2005.

Goodman, Steve. *Sonic Warfare: Sound, Affect, and the Ecology of Fear.* Cambridge: MIT Press, 2010.

Grazian, David. "The Symbolic Economy of Authenticity in the Chicago Blues Scene." In *Music Scenes: Local, Translocal, and Virtual,* ed. Andy Bennett and Richard A. Peterson, 31–47. Nashville: Vanderbilt University Press, 2004.

Greig, Geordie. "American Widow Sues for 'Murder under the Influence of Rap.'" *Sunday Times (London),* October 25, 1992. *LexisNexis Academic,* http://www.lexis nexis.com.

Gore, Tipper. "The Cult of Violence." In *The Rock History Reader,* ed. Theo Cateforis, 227–34. New York: Routledge, 2007.

Grossberg, Lawrence. "The Framing of Rock: Rock and the New Conservatism." In *Rock and Popular Music: Politics, Policies, Institutions,* ed. Tony Bennett, Simon Frith, Lawrence Grossberg, John Shepherd, and Graeme Turner, 193–209. London: Routledge, 1993.

"Group Thinks Classical Music Will Deter Hartford Crime." 6 March 2006. http://www.nbc30.com/news/7742633/detail.html?subid=10101541.

Hall, Perry A. "African-American Music: Dynamics of Appropriation and Innovation." In *Borrowed Power: Essays on Cultural Appropriation,* ed. Bruce Ziff and Pratima V. Rao, 31–51. New Brunswick: Rutgers University Press, 1997.

Hall, Stuart. "Introduction: Who Needs Identity?" In *Questions of Cultural Identity,* ed. Stuart Hall and Paul du Gay, 1–17. London: Sage, 1996.

Hansen, Liane. "Profile: Using Classical Music to Help Deter Teen-Agers from Causing Trouble at Boston Subway Stations." *Weekend Edition Sunday,* 22 September 2002. http://web.ebscohost.com/login.aspx?direct=true&dp=nfh&AN=6XN200209221306&site=ehost-live&scope=site.

Harbert, Benjamin J. "I'll Keep on Living after I Die: Musical Manipulation and Transcendence at Louisiana State Penitentiary." *International Journal of Community Music* 3.1 (2010): 65–76.

Harden, Alicia N. "Drawing the Line at Pushing 'Play': Barring Video Montages as Victim Impact Evidence at Capital Sentencing Trials." *Kentucky Law Journal* (2010–11). *LexisNexis Academic.* http://www.lexisnexis.com.

Hargreaves, David J. *The Developmental Psychology of Music.* Cambridge: Cambridge University Press, 1986.

Hart, Peter. *The Oh Really? Factor: Unspinning Fox News Channel's Bill O'Reilly.* New York: Seven Stories, 2003.

Hegel, G. W. F. *Aesthetics: Lectures on Fine Art.* Trans. T. M. Knox. Vol. 2. Oxford: Clarendon, 1975.

Heim, Joe. "Torture Songs Spur a Protest Most Vocal." *Washington Post,* 22 October 2009, 2.

Helmore, Edward. "The Dogg Has His Day in Court." *Independent (London),* 25 November 1995, 5.

Henry, Jane L., and Peter H. Wilson. *Chronic Tinnitus: A Cognitive-Behavioral Approach.* Boston: Allyn and Bacon, 2001.

Hernandez, Darla. "Folk Devils in Seattle." *Edwardsville Journal of Sociology* (2002). http://www.siue.edu/SOCIOLOGY/journal/v2hernandez2002.htm.

Hersch, Charles. *Democratic Artworks: Politics and the Arts from Trilling to Dylan.* Albany: State University of New York Press, 1998.

Hersch, Charles. *Subversive Sounds: Race and the Birth of Jazz in New Orleans.* Chicago: University of Chicago Press, 2007.

Hillman, Grady. "The Mythology of the Corrections Community." In *Teaching the Arts behind Bars,* ed. Rachel Marie-Crane Williams, 14–27. Boston: Northeastern University Press, 2003.

Hillsman, Sally T. "The Use of Fines as an Intermediate Sanction." In *Smart Sentencing: The Emergence of Intermediate Sanctions,* ed. James M. Byrne, Arthur J. Lurigio, and Joan Petersilia, 123–41. Thousand Oaks, CA: Sage, 1992.

"Hip-Hop Fan to Listen to Classical Music." 9 October 2008. http://www.nowpublic .com/strange/judge-sentences-hip-hop-fan-listen-classical-music.

Hockstader, Lee. "U.S. Rocks Noriega: Troops Blare Music at Papal Nunciature, Tighten Security at Ex-Dictator's Refuge." *Washington Post,* 27 December 1989, A 28.

Hoffmann, E. T. A. "Beethoven's Instrumental Music (1813)." In *German Essays on Music,* ed. Jost Hermand and Michael Gilbert, 59–64. New York: Continuum, 1994.

Horowitz, Joseph. *The Post-Classical Predicament: Essays on Music and Society.* Boston: Northeastern University Press, 1995.

Hunter, Mary. "Opera in Film: Sentiment and Wit, Feeling and Knowing: *The Shawshank Redemption* and *Prizzi's Honor.*" In *Between Opera and Cinema,* ed. Jeongwon Joe and Rose Theresa, 93–119. New York: Routledge, 2009.

Hunter, Mary. "'To Play as If from the Soul of the Composer': The Idea of the Performer in Early Romantic Aesthetics." *Journal of the American Musicological Society* 58.2 (2005): 357–98.

Hutcheson, Francis. "From *Reflections upon Laughter.*" In *The Philosophy of Laughter and Humor,* ed. John Morreal, 26–40. Albany: State University of New York Press, 1987.

"Inside the Interrogation of Detainee 063." *Time,* 12 June 2005. http://www.time .com/time/printout/0,8816,1071284,00.html.

Jackson, Bruce, ed. *Wake Up Dead Man: Hard Labor and Southern Blues.* Athens: University of Georgia Press, 1999.

Jackson, Melissa. "Music to Deter Yobs." *BBC News Magazine,* 10 January 2005. http://news.bbc.co.uk/1/hi/magazine/4154711.stm.

"Jailed Rapper Changes Names, Hopes New Image Follows." *St. Petersburg Times,* 7 April 2005, 2B.

Jankélévitch, Vladimir. *Music and the Ineffable.* Trans. Carolyn Abbate. Princeton: Princeton University Press, 2003.

Jeffrey, C. Ray. *Crime Prevention through Environmental Design.* Beverly Hills, CA: Sage, 1971.

Jensen, Joli. *Nashville Sound: Authenticity, Commercialization, and Country Music.* Nashville: Country Music Foundation Press and Vanderbilt University Press, 1998.

Johnson, Bruce, and Martin Cloonan. *Dark Side of the Tune: Popular Music and Violence*. Aldershot: Ashgate, 2008.

Jones, Ashby. "Too Much Rockin' in the Not-So-Free World," and responses. *Law Blog*, 22 October 2009. http://blogs.wsj.com.law/2009/10/22/too-much-rockin-in-the-not-so-free-world/.

Jones, Carys Wyn. *The Rock Canon: Canonical Values in the Reception of Rock Albums*. Aldershot: Ashgate, 2008.

"Judge Forces Slum Lord to Live in His Own Building." 28 May 2007. http://www.shortnews.com/start.cfm?id=62714.

"Judge Offers Loud Rap Music Listening Basketball Player a Break on Fine." 18 March 2009. http://www.fark.com/cgi/comments.pl?IDLink=3931484&cpp=1.

"Judge Sentences Rap Fan to Bach, Beethoven." *MSNBC*, 9 October 2008. http://www.msnbc.msn.com/id/27099954/?GT1=430017.

"Judge Uses Barry Manilow Music as Punishment." *Stereotude*, 26 November 2008. http://www.stereotude.com/barry-manilow/judge-uses-barry-manilow-music-as-punishment.html.

"Jurors Acquit Rap Musician in Murder Case." *New York Times*, February 22, 1996, A16.

Kass, Jeff. "Here, Lawbreakers Listen to Beethoven." *Christian Science Monitor*, 19 May 1999. *LexisNexis Academic*. http://www.lexisnexis.com.

Kassabian, Anahid. "Ubiquitous Listening." In *Popular Music Studies*, ed. David Hesmondhalgh and Keith Negus, 131–42. London: Arnold, 2002.

Kassabian, Anahid. "Ubiquitous Listening and Networked Subjectivity." *Echo* 3.2 (2001). www.echo.ucla.edu.

Katz, Paul. "Budget Crisis Finally Killing Program." *Huffington Post*, 15 January 2010. http://www.huffingtonpost.com/paul-katz/california-budget-crisis_b_424298.html.

Keen, Suzanne. *Empathy and the Novel*. Oxford: Oxford University Press, 2007.

Kelley, Robin D. G. "Kickin' Reality, Kickin' Ballistics: Gangsta Rap and Postindustrial Los Angeles." In *Droppin' Science: Critical Essays on Rap Music and Hip Hop Culture*, ed. William Eric Perkins, 117–57. Philadelphia: Temple University Press, 1996.

Keyes, Cheryl L. *Rap Music and Street Consciousness*. Urbana: University of Illinois Press, 2004.

Keyes, Cheryl L. "Verbal Art Performance in Rap Music: The Conversation of the 80's." *Folklore Forum* 17.2 (1984): 143–52.

Klinger, Kevin. "Hip Hop Wisdom for White Therapists." Master's thesis, Pacifica Graduate Institute, 2010.

Kodat, Catherine Gunther. "Conversing with Ourselves: Canon, Freedom, Jazz." *American Quarterly* 55.1 (2003): 1–28.

Kornfeld, Phyllis. *Cellblock Visions: Prison Art in America*. Princeton: Princeton University Press, 1997.

Korpe, Maria, Ole Reitov, and Martin Cloonan. "Music Censorship from Plato to the Present." In *Music and Manipulation: On the Social Uses and Social Control of Music,* ed. Steven Brown and Ulrik Volgsten, 239–63. New York: Berghahn, 2006.

Kramer, Jonathan D. "The Nature and Origins of Musical Postmodernism." In *Postmodern Music/Postmodern Thought,* ed. Judy Lochhead and Joseph Auner, 13–26. New York: Routledge, 2002.

Lagan, Bernard. "Q: How Do You Get Rid of a Gang of Boy Racers? A: Play Barry Manilow at Full Volume." *Times* (London), 18 July 2006, 6.

Laks, Szymon. *Music of Another World.* Trans. Chester A. Kisiel. Evanston, IL: Northwestern University Press, 2000.

Lanza, Joseph. *Elevator Music: A Surreal History of Muzak, Easy-Listening, and Other Moodsong.* Ann Arbor: University of Michigan Press, 2004.

Laub, Dori. "The Narrativization of Traumatic Experiences through Testimony." Presentation at the National Conference of the German Studies Association, 10 October 2010.

Laub, Dori. "September 11, 2001—An Event without a Voice." In *Trauma at Home: After 9/11,* ed. Judith Greenberg, 204–22. Lincoln: University of Nebraska Press, 2003.

Laven, Stuart A. "Turn Down the Volume." *Cleveland State Law Review* (2004). *LexisNexis Academic.* http://www.lexisnexis.com.

Lee, Roc. "Music Education in Prisons: A Historical Overview." *International Journal of Community Music* 3.1 (March 2010): 7–18.

Leeds, Joshua. *The Power of Sound: How to Manage Your Personal Soundscape for a Vital, Productive, and Healthy Life.* Rochester, VT: Healing Arts, 2001.

Lefebvre, Henri. *The Production of Space.* Trans. Donald Nicholson-Smith. Oxford: Blackwell, 1991.

Lehner, Marla. "Murder Victim's Family Sues VH1." *Fox News,* 6 March 2003. http://www.foxnews.com/story/0,2933,80369,00.html.

Lena, Jennifer C. "Social Context and Musical Content of Rap Music, 1979–1995." *Social Forces* 85.1 (2006): 479–95.

Leubsdorf, John. "Presuppositions of Evidence Law." *Iowa Law Review* (2006). *LexisNexis Academic.* http://www.lexisnexis.com.

Levine, Mark. *Heavy Metal Islam: Rock, Resistance, and the Struggle for the Soul of Islam.* New York: Three Rivers, 2008.

Levinson, Jerrold. *Music in the Moment.* Ithaca: Cornell University Press, 1997.

Levinson, Sanford, and J. M. Balkin. "Essay/Book Review: Law, Music, and Other Performing Arts." *University of Pennsylvania Law Review* (1991). *LexisNexis Academic.* http://www.lexisnexis.com.

Lewis, Randy. "New VH1 Series Explores Jailhouse Rock." *Los Angeles Times,* 18 October 2002. http://articles.latimes.com/2002/oct/18/entertainment/et-lewis18.

"Lift Tunes for Jammer." *Courier-Mail,* 2 November 1991. *LexisNexis Academic.* http://www.lexisnexis.com.

Lindahl, Hans. "Dialectic and Revolution: Confronting Kelsen and Gadamer on Legal Interpretation." *Cardozo Law Review, Yeshiva University* (2003). *LexisNexis Academic.* http://www.lexisnexis.com.

Lippman, Edward. *A History of Western Musical Aesthetics.* Lincoln: University of Nebraska Press, 1992.

Lomax, Alan. *The Land Where the Blues Began.* New York: New Press, 1993.

Long, Alecia P. *The Great Southern Babylon: Sex, Race, and Respectability in New Orleans, 1865–1920.* Baton Rouge: Louisiana State University Press, 2004.

Long, Alex B. "[Insert Song Lyrics Here]: The Uses and Misuses of Popular Music Lyrics in Legal Writing." *Washington and Lee Law Review* (2007). *LexisNexis Academic.* http://www.lexisnexis.com.

Lorenz, Aaron R. S. *Lyrics and the Law: The Constitution of Law in Music.* Lake Mary, FL: Vandeplas, 2007.

Lury, Karen. "Chewing Gum for the Ears: Children's Television and Popular Music." *Popular Music* 21.3 (October 2002): 291–305.

Macdonald, Dwight. "Masscult and Midcult." In *Popular Culture Theory and Methodology: A Basic Introduction,* ed. Harold E. Hinds, Marilyn Ferris Motz, and Angela M. S. Nelson, 9–15. Madison: University of Wisconsin Press, 2006.

Maher, George Ciccariello. "Brechtian Hip-Hop: Didactics and Self-Production in Post-Gangsta Political Mixtapes." *Journal of Black Studies* 36.1 (September 2005): 129–60.

Manderson, Desmond. *Songs without Music: Aesthetic Dimensions of Law and Justice.* New York: Palgrave Macmillan, 2009.

Manderson, Desmond, and David Caudill. "Symposium: Modes of Law: Music and Legal Theory—An Interdisciplinary Workshop Introduction." *Cardozo Law Review, Yeshiva University* (1999). *LexisNexis Academic.* http://www.lexisnexis.com.

"Manilow to Drive Out 'Hooligans.'" *news.bbc,* 15 January 2004. http://news.bbc.co.uk/1/hi/world/asia-pacific/5047610.

"Manilow Unhappy with Music-as-Weapon-Ploy." *soundgenerator,* 19 July 2006. http://www.soundgenerator.com/news/showarticle.cfm?articleid=8038.

Mansfield, Peter M. "Terrorism and a Civil Cause of Action: Boim, Ungar, and Joint Torts." *Journal of International and Comparative Law* (2003). *LexisNexis Academic.* http://www.lexisnexis.com.

Mark, Michael L., ed. *Music Education: Source Readings from Ancient Greece to Today.* New York: Routledge, 2002.

Martin, Peter. "Music, Identity, and Social Control." In *Music and Manipulation: On the Social Uses and Social Control of Music,* ed. Steven Brown and Ulrik Volgsten, 57–73. New York: Berghahn, 2006.

McCarthy, Anna. *Ambient Television: Visual Culture and Public Space.* Durham, NC: Duke University Press, 2001.

McCarthy, James, and Euan Hague. "Race, Nation, and Nature: The Cultural Politics of 'Celtic' Identification in the American West." *Annals of the Association of American Geographers* 94.2 (2004): 387–408.

McClary, Susan. *Feminine Endings: Music, Gender, and Sexuality.* Minneapolis: University of Minnesota Press, 1991.

McClary, Susan. "Getting Down Off the Beanstalk: The Presence of a Woman's

Voice in Janika Vandervelde's *Genesis II.*" In *Feminine Endings: Music, Gender, and Sexuality,* 112–31. Minneapolis: University of Minnesota Press, 1991.

McCoy, Alfred. "Legacy of a Dark Decade: CIA Mind Control, Classified Behavioral Research, and the Origins of Modern Medical Ethics." In *The Trauma of Psychological Torture,* ed. Almerindo E. Ojeda, 40–69. Westport, CT: Praeger, 2008.

McCoy, Alfred. *A Question of Torture: CIA Interrogation, from the Cold War to the War on Terror.* New York: Metropolitan, 2006.

McGough, Michael. "Midweek Perspectives: A Pinhead Editorial Writer's Adventure in the No Spin Zone." *Post-Gazette* (Pittsburgh), 20 November 2002. http://www.post-gazette.com/forum/comm/20021120edmcg20p1.asp.

McGuire, Kenneth M. "The Use of Music on *Barney and Friends:* Implications for Music Therapy Practice and Research." *Journal of Music Therapy* 38.2 (2001): 114–48.

Meconi, Honey, ed. *Early Musical Borrowing.* New York: Routledge, 2004.

"MENS Forums." *National Association for Music Education.* http://www.menc.org/forums/viewtopic.php?id=402.

Meyer, Stephen. "Terror and Transcendence in the Operatic Prison, 1790–1815." *Journal of the American Musicological Society* 55.3 (2002): 477–523.

Michaels, Sean. "Music as Torture May Incur Royalty Fees." *guardian.co.uk,* 9 July 2008. http://www.guardian.co.uk/music/2008/jul/09/news.culture3?INTCMP=SRCH.

Moore, Allan. "Authenticity as Authentication." *Popular Music* 21.2 (May 2002): 209–23.

Moraes, Lisa de. "O'Reilly, Convicting VH1 for Its Prison Music Show." *Washington Post,* 19 October 2002, C7.

Morreal, John, ed. *The Philosophy of Laughter and Humor.* Albany: State University of New York Press, 1987.

"The Most Unwanted Song." 19 March 2009. http://www.diacenter.org/km/music cd.html.

Mueller, Andrew. "Rhyme and Punishment." *Guardian,* 21 February 2004. http://www.guardian.co.uk/music/2004/feb/21/classical musicandopera.Popandrock?INTCMP=SRCH.

Mursell, James L. *The Psychology of Music.* Westport, CT: Greenwood, 1964.

"Music Immersion Program." Municipal Court, Fort Lupton, Colorado. 5 February 2009. http://www.fortlupton.org/DEPARTMENTS/COURT/music.html.

"Musicology/Ethnomusicology" (2010–11). 16 March 2011. http://www.wikihost.org/w/academe/music_history_musicology_ethnomusicology.

National Endowment for the Arts. "The Arts in Corrections Resource List." N.d. http://www.arts.gov/resources/accessibility/rlists/corrections.html.

Newman, Michael. "'That's All Concept; It's Nothing Real': Reality and Lyrical Meaning in Rap." In *Global Linguistic Flows: Hip Hop Cultures, Youth Identities, and the Politics of Language,* ed. H. Samy Alim, Awad Ibrahim, and Alastair Pennycook, 195–212. New York: Routledge, 2009.

Nielsen, Steen Kaargard. "Wife Murder as Child's Game: Analytical Reflections on

Eminem's Performative Self-Dramatization." *Danish Yearbook of Musicology* 34 (2006): 31–46.

North, Adrian C., and David J. Hargreaves. "Music in Business Environments." In *Music and Manipulation: On the Social Uses and Social Control of Music,* ed. Steven Brown and Ulrik Volgsten, 103–25. New York: Berghahn, 2006.

"Not Corporal but 'Classical' Punishment?" 10 October 2008. http://globalgrind .com/source/soulbounce.com/156774/not-corporal-but-classical-punishment.

Nuzum, Eric. *Parental Advisory: Music Censorship in America.* New York: Perennial, 2001.

"NYU Names Swizz Beatz Its Producer-in-Residence." *Yahoo! News,* 5 November 2010. http://news.yahoo.com/s/ap/20101105/ap_en_mu/us_swizz_beatz_nyu.

Ojeda, Almerindo E. "What Is Psychological Torture?" In *The Trauma of Psychological Torture,* ed. Almerindo E. Ojeda, 1–22. Westport, CT: Praeger, 2008.

O'Reilly, Bill. "Talking Points: VH1 Disgraces Itself." *Fox News,* 18 October 2002. http://www.foxnews.com/story/0,2933,65942,00.html.

Pecknold, Diane. *The Selling Sound: The Rise of the Country Music Industry.* Durham, NC: Duke University Press, 2007.

Pederson, Sanna. "Beethoven and Freedom: Historicizing the Political Connection." *Beethoven Forum* 12.1 (2005): 1–12.

Pellegrinelli, Lara. "Scholarly Discord." *Chronicle of Higher Education* 55.35, 8 May 2009. http://web.ebscohost.com/ehost/delivery?vid=6&hid=106&sid=c20c005 4-12f8-4131-9b60.

Perkins, William Eric. "The Rap Attack: An Introduction." In *Droppin' Science: Critical Essays on Rap Music and Hip Hop Culture,* ed. William Eric Perkins, 1–40. Philadelphia: Temple University Press, 1996.

Perkinson, Robert. "'Hell Exploded': Prisoner Music and Memoir and the Fall of Convict Leasing in Texas." *Prison Journal* 89.1 (March 2009): 54–69.

Perry, Imani. *Prophets of the Hood: Politics and Poetics in Hip Hop.* Durham, NC: Duke University Press, 2004.

Pettan, Svanibor. "Music in War, Music for Peace: Experiences in Applied Ethnomusicology." In *Music and Conflict,* ed. John Morgan O'Connell and Salwa El-Shawan Castelo-Branco, 177–92. Urbana: University of Illinois Press, 2010.

Picker, John M., *Victorian Soundscapes.* Oxford: Oxford University Press, 2003.

Pieslak, Jonathan. *Sound Targets: American Soldiers and Music in the Iraq War.* Bloomington: Indiana University Press, 2009.

Pieslak, Jonathan. "Soundtracking Iraq." *Journal of Music* (2009). http://journalof music.com/article/1053.

Piore, Adam. "The Love's Not Mutual." *Newsweek,* 26 May 2003, 13.

Plato. *Republic.* Trans. G. M. A. Grube. Indianapolis: Hackett, 1974.

Posner, Richard A. *Overcoming Law.* Cambridge: Harvard University Press, 1995.

Quinn, Eithne. *Nuthin' but a "G" Thang: The Culture and Commerce of Gangsta Rap.* New York: Columbia University Press, 2005.

Quinn, Michael. "'Never shoulda been let out of the penitentiary': Gansta Rap and the Struggle over Racial Identity." *Cultural Critique* 34 (Autumn 1996): 65–89.

Rapp, Tobias. "The Pain of Listening: Using Music as a Weapon at Guantanamo." *Spiegel Online,* 14 January 2010. http://www.spiegel.de/international /world/0,1518,672177,00.html.

"Rapping about Cop Killing." 2004. http//:www.axt.org.uk/HateMusic/Rappin .htm.

Regev, Motti. "Producing Artistic Value: The Case of Rock Music." *Sociological Quarterly* 35.1 (February 1994): 85–102.

Reilly, Tracy. "The 'Spiritual Temperature' of Contemporary Popular Music: An Alternative to the Legal Regulation of Death-Metal and Gangsta-Rap Lyrics." *Vanderbilt Journal of Entertainment and Technology Law* (2009). *LexisNexis Academic.* http://www.lexisnexis.com.

Riccio, Barry D. "Popular Culture and High Culture: Dwight Macdonald, His Critics and the Ideal of Cultural Hierarchy in Modern America." *Journal of American Culture* 16.4 (1993): 7–18.

Rich, Adrienne. *Driving into the Wreck: Poems, 1971–1972.* New York: Norton, 1973.

Richardson, Jeanita W., and Kim A. Scott. "Rap Music and Its Violent Progeny: America's Culture of Violence in Context." *Journal of Negro Education* 71.3 (2002): 175–92.

Riley, Matthew. "Civilizing the Savage: Johann Georg Sulzer and the 'Aesthetic Force' of Music." *Journal of the Royal Musical Association* 127.1 (2002): 1–22.

Robinson, Matthew B. *Justice Blind?: Ideals and Realities of American Criminal Justice.* 2nd ed. Upper Saddle River, NJ: Prentice Hall, 2005.

Rolland, Megan. "Oklahoma City's At-Risk Youth Will Learn Vocabulary through Rap." 4 June 2010. http://newsok.com/oklahoma-citys-at-risk-youth-will-learn -vocabulary-through-rap/article/3465911?custom_click=rss.

Rose, Tricia. *Black Noise: Rap Music and Black Culture in Contemporary America.* Hanover, NH: Wesleyan University Press, 1994.

Rose, Tricia. "Hidden Politics: Discursive and Institutional Policing of Rap Music." In *Droppin' Science: Critical Essays on Rap Music and Hip Hop Culture,* ed. William Eric Perkins, 236–57. Philadelphia: Temple University Press, 1996.

Rose, Tricia. *The Hip Hop Wars: What We Talk about When We Talk about Hip Hop— and Why It Matters.* New York: Basic Books, 2008.

Rosen, Ralph M., and Donald R. Mark. "Comedies of Transgression in Gangsta Rap and Ancient Classical Poetry." *New Literary History* 30.4 (Autumn 1999): 897–928.

Rosen, Ronald S. *Music and Copyright.* Oxford: Oxford University Press, 2008.

Roth, Thomas P. "American Corrections: From the Beginning to World War II." In *Prison and Jail Administration: Practice and Theory,* ed. Peter M. Carlson and Judith Simon Garrett, 8–14. Sudbury, MA: Jones and Bartlett, 1999.

Rubin, Susan Goldman. *Art against the Odds: From Slave Quilts to Prison Paintings.* New York: Crown, 2004.

Ruhe, Pierre. "Classical Music Said to Increase Spending and Deter Crime." *Chicago Tribune,* 6 September 2006. http://articles.chicagotribune.com/2006-09-06 /features/0609060025.

Rutherford, Christian D. "'Gangsta' Culture in a Political State: The Crisis in Legal

Ethics Formation amongst Hip-hop Youth." *Columbia University National Black Law Journal* (2004). *LexisNexis Academic.* http://www.lexisnexis.com.

Sacks, Oliver. *Musicophilia: Tales of Music and the Brain.* New York: Knopf, 2007.

Salzmann, Victoria S. "Honey, You're No June Cleaver: The Power of 'Dropping Pop' to Persuade." *Maine Law Review* (2010). *LexisNexis Academic.* http://www.lexisnexis.com.

Santos, Michael. *Profiles from Prison: Adjusting to Life behind Bars.* Westport, CT: Praeger, 2003.

Sarat, Austin, Matthew Anderson, and Catherine O. Frank, eds. *Law and the Humanities: An Introduction.* Cambridge: Cambridge University Press, 2010.

Sarat, Austin, and Thomas R. Kearns. "Responding to the Demands of Difference: An Introduction." In *Cultural Pluralism, Identity Politics, and the Law,* ed. Austin Sarat and Thomas R. Kearns, 1–25. Ann Arbor: University of Michigan Press, 1999.

Scarry, Elaine. *The Body in Pain: The Making and Unmaking of the World.* Oxford: Oxford University Press, 1985.

Schafer, R. Murray. *The Tuning of the World.* New York: Knopf, 1977.

Schopenhauer, Arthur. "On Noise." In *The Works of Schopenhauer,* ed. Will Durant, 460–64. New York: Ungar, 1928.

Schroeder, Erica. "Sounds of Prejudice: Background Music during Victim Impact Statements." *University of Kansas Law Review* (2010). *LexisNexis Academic.* 2010, http://www.lexisnexis.com.

Schur, Richard L. *Parodies of Ownership: Hip-Hop Aesthetics and Intellectual Property Law.* Ann Arbor: University of Michigan Press, 2009.

Scott, Cyril. *The Influence of Music on History and Morals: A Vindication of Plato.* London: Philosophical, 1928.

"Secret ORCON: Interrogation Log Detainee 063." http://en.wikisource.org/wiki /Secret_ORCON:_Interrogation_Log_Detainee_063.

Senior, Jennifer. "PsyOps Rock!" *New York Magazine,* 23 October 2009. http:// nymag.com/news/intelligencer/60310.

"The Sentencing Project." March 16, 2009. http://www.sentencingproject.org /Issues.aspx.

Sernoe, James Lawrence. "'It's the Same Old Song': A History of Legal Challenges to Rock-and-Roll and Black Music." Ph.D. diss., University of Iowa, 2000.

Severo, Richard. "Mitch Miller, Maestro of the Singalong, Dies at 99." *New York Times,* 3 August 2010, A16.

Shaffer, Tani Graham. "The Shady Side of Hip-Hop: A Jungian and Eriksonian Interpretation of Eminem's Explicit Content." Ph.D. diss., Pacific Graduate School of Psychology, 2004.

Sherman, Lola. "The Homeless Hate Handel . . ." 5 January 2005. http://strangeobser vations.tribe.net/thread/0c1f5a8f-90e9-4229-857a-1090d59296cb.

Shicher, David. *The Meaning and Nature of Punishment.* Long Grove, IL: Waveland, 2006.

Shiloah, Amnon. *Music in the World of Islam: A Socio-Cultural Study.* Detroit: Wayne State University Press, 1995.

Shusterman, Richard. "The Fine Art of Rap." *New Literary History* 22.3 (1991): 613–32.

Simon, Scott. "Profile: London Has Found Classical Music to Be a Cheap and Easy Way to Deter Loitering Teens Who Harass Subway Riders and Staff." *Weekend Edition Saturday,* 22 January 2005. http://search.ebscohost.com/login.aspx?direct=true&db=nfh&AN= 6XN200501221208&site=ehost-live&scope=site.

Singal, S. P. *Noise Pollution and Control Strategy.* Oxford: Alpha Science International, 2005.

Skyllstad, Kjell. "Music behind Bars: Testimonies of Suffering, Survival, and Transformation." In *Music and Conflict Transformation: Harmonies and Dissonances in Geopolitics,* ed. Olivier Urbain, 115–27. London: Tauris, 2008.

Small, Christopher. *Musicking: The Meanings of Performing and Listening.* Middletown, CT: Wesleyan University Press, 1998.

Smith, Adam. *The Theory of Moral Sentiments.* Ed. D. D. Raphael and A. L. Macfie. Oxford: Clarendon, 1976.

Smith, Andre L. "Other People's Property: Hip-Hop's Inherent Clashes with Property Laws and Its Ascendance as Global Counter Culture." *Virginia Sports and Entertainment Law Journal* 7 (2007): 59–73.

Smith, Caleb. *The Prison and the American Imagination.* New Haven: Yale University Press, 2009.

Smith, Chris. "The Kids on the Square: Teen Loiterers in SR's Downtown Have City Worried." *Press Democrat,* Santa Rosa, CA, 19 May 1996, A1.

Smith, Matthew Wilson. *The Total Work of Art: From Bayreuth to Cyberspace.* New York: Routledge, 2007.

Soocher, Stan. *They Fought the Law: Rock Music Goes to Court.* New York: Schirmer, 1999.

Sörbom, Göran. "Aristotle on Music as Representation." *Journal of Aesthetics and Art Criticism* 52.1 (1994): 37–46.

Sprout, Leslie A. "Messiaen, Jolivet, and the Soldier-Composers of Wartime France." *Musical Quarterly* 87.2 (2004): 259–304.

Starr, Martha A. "Consumption, Identity, and the Sociocultural Constitution of 'Preferences': Reading Women's Magazines." In *Consuming Symbolic Goods: Identity and Commitment, Values and Economics,* ed. Wilfred Dolfsma, 17–32. London: Routledge, 2008.

Sterne, Jonathan. "Sounds Like the Mall of America: Programmed Music and the Architectonics of Commercial Space." *Ethnomusicology* 41.1 (1997): 22–50.

Sterne, Jonathan. "Urban Media and the Politics of Sound Space." *Open* 9 (n.d.). http://www.skor.nl/article-2853-en.html.

Stewart, Ken. "The World Is Enamored with All Things Celtic." *Billboard,* July 5, 1997, 43–44.

Stokes, Martin, ed. *Ethnicity, Identity, and Music: The Musical Construction of Place.* Oxford: Berg, 1994.

Strauss, Marcy. "Torture." *New York Law School Law Review* (2003). *LexisNexis Academic.* http://www.lexisnexis.com.

Sullivan, Kathleen M. "2 Live Crew and the Cultural Contradictions of Miller." In *The Rock History Reader,* ed. Theo Cateforius, 271–73. New York: Routledge, 2007.

Sullivan, Rachel E. "Rap and Race: It's Got a Nice Beat, but What about the Message." *Journal of Black Studies* 33.5 (2003): 605–22.

Sulzer, Johann Georg. "Expression in Music (1792–1794)." In *German Essays on Music,* ed. Jost Hermand and Michael Gilbert, 26–30. New York: Continuum, 1994.

Sussman, David. "What's Wrong with Torture." In *The Phenomenon of Torture: Readings and Commentary,* ed. William F. Schulz, 178–79. Philadelphia: University of Pennsylvania Press, 2007.

"Sydney, Australia, Using Barry Manilow to Drive Off Rowdy Teenagers." http://digg.com/music/Sydney,_Australia,_using_Barry_Manilow_to_drive_off_rowdy_teenagers.

"Symposium: Forward: A Panel Discussion: Potential Liability Arising from the Dissemination of Violent Music." *Loyola of Los Angeles Entertainment Law Review* 2.2 (2002): 237–62.

Tannenbaum, Judith. *Disguised as a Poem: My Years Teaching Poetry at San Quentin.* Boston: Northeastern University Press, 2000.

Taruskin, Richard. *The Danger of Music and Other Anti-Utopian Essays.* Berkeley: University of California Press, 2009.

Taruskin, Richard. "Is There a Baby in the Bathwater (Part I)?" *Archiv für Musikwissenschaft* 63.3 (2006): 163–85.

Taruskin, Richard. "Review: Resisting the Ninth." *19th-Century Music* 12.3 (1989): 241–56.

Taruskin, Richard. *Text and Act: Essays on Music and Performance.* New York: Oxford University Press, 1995.

Taylor, Sam. "Demonic Icon on a Murder Rap." *Observer,* 8 January 1995, 5.

Teachout, Terry. "Musical Torture Instruments: Can Being Forced to Listen Really Be That Painful?" *Wall Street Journal,* 13 February 2009. http://online.wsj.com/article/SB123456310592185753.html.

Tewksbury, Richard, and Elizabeth Ehrhardt Mustaine. "Insiders' Views of Prison Amenities." In *Prison and Jails: A Reader,* ed. Richard Tewksbury and Dean Dabney, 249–62. New York: McGraw-Hill, 2009.

Thompson, Emily. *The Soundscape of Modernity: Architectural Acoustics and the Culture of Listening in America, 1900–1933.* Cambridge: MIT Press, 2004.

Thompson, James. "Doubtful Principles in Arts in Prisons." In *Teaching the Arts behind Bars,* ed. Rachel Marie-Crane Williams, 40–61. Boston: Northeastern University Press, 2003.

Tijs, Andrew. "Manilow to Challenge Rockdale Yobbos." 6 June 2006. http://www.undercover.com.au/news/2006/jun06/20060606_barrymanilow.html.

Timberg, Scott. "Classical Music as Crime Stopper." *Los Angeles Times,* 18 February 2005. http://www.freenewmexican.com/artsfeatures/10701.html.

Timberg, Scott. "Halt . . . or I'll Play Vivaldi." *Toronto Star,* 20 February 2005, C5.

Toch, Hans. *Living in Prison: The Ecology of Survival.* New York: Free Press, 1977.

"Top 10 Artists for the Terminally Uncool." *top40,* 24 January 2007. http://top40 .about.com/od/top10lists/ss/uncoolpop_10.htm.

Truax, Barry. *Acoustic Communication.* 2nd ed. Westport, CT: Ablex, 2001.

"Turn That Noise Down." *CNN,* 25 November 2008. http://www.cnn.com/video/# /video/us/2008/11/25/vanderveen.noise.offenders.Kusa.

Tyson, Edgar H. "Hip Hop Therapy: An Exploratory Study of a Rap Music Intervention with At-Risk and Delinquent Youth." *Journal of Poetry Therapy* 15.3 (2002): 131–43.

Tyson, Edgar H. "Rap Music in Social Work Practice with African-American and Latino Youth: A Conceptual Model with Practical Applications." *Journal of Human Behavior in the Social Environment* 8.4 (2003): 1–21.

U.S. Office of Noise Abatement and Control. *Summary of Noise Programs in the Federal Government.* Washington, DC: U.S. Government Printing Office, 1972.

Utley, Ebony. "Transcendence: The Rhetorical Functions of the Gangsta Rapper's God." Ph.D. diss., Northwestern University, 2006.

Vannini, Phillip, and J. Patrick Williams. "Authenticity in Culture, Self, and Society." In *Authenticity in Culture, Self, and Society,* ed. Phillip Vannini and J. Patrick Williams, 1–20. Burlington, VT: Ashgate, 2009.

Verhovek, Sam Howe. "Decibels, Not Bullets, Bombard Texas Sect." *New York Times,* 25 March 1993, A16.

Vitello, Paul. "A Ring Tone Meant to Fall on Deaf Ears." *New York Times,* 12 June 2006, A1.

von Hirsch, Andrew, Andrew Ashworth, and Julian Roberts, eds. *Principled Sentencing: Readings on Theory and Policy.* 3rd ed. Portland, OR: Hart, 2009.

Walser, Robert. *Running with the Devil: Power, Gender, and Madness in Heavy Metal Music.* Hanover, NH: University Press of New England, 1993.

Walser, Robert. "Rhythm, Rhyme, and Rhetoric in the Music of Public Enemy." *Ethnomusicology* 39.2 (1995): 193–217.

Warr, Mark. *Companions to Crime: The Social Aspects of Criminal Conduct.* Cambridge: Cambridge University Press, 2002.

Waxman, Sharon. "Rapper Acquitted of Murder Charges." *Washington Post,* 21 February 1996, B1.

Weisbrod, Carol. "Fusion Folk: A Comment on Law and Music." *Cardozo Law Review, Yeshiva University* (1999). *LexisNexis Academic.* http://www.lexisnexis .com.

Weisburd, Dave, Laura A. Wyckoff, Justin Ready, John E. Eck, Joshua C. Hinkle, and Frank Gajewski. "Does Crime Just Move around the Corner? A Controlled Study of Spatial Displacement and Diffusion of Crime Control Benefits." *Criminology* 44.3 (2006): 549–91.

West, Robin L. "Adjudication Is Not Interpretation: Some Reservations about the Law-as-Literature Movement." *Tennessee Law Review* (1986). *LexisNexis Academic.* http://www.lexisnexis.com.

Wetzstein, Cheryl. "VH1 Angers Victims' Families with Plans for 'Jailhouse Rock.'" *Washington Times,* 18 October 2002, A12.

William James Association. "Prison Arts Project." 2004. http://www.williamjames association.org/prison_arts.html.

Williams, Rachel Marie-Crane. Introduction to *Teaching the Arts behind Bars,* ed. Rachel Marie-Crane Williams, 3–13. Boston: Northeastern University Press, 2003.

Wilson, Allegra. "Unfair Limits." *Press Democrat,* Santa Rosa, CA, 18 August 1999, B6.

Wilson, Sean-Patrick. "Rap Sheets: The Constitutional and Societal Complications Arising from the Use of Rap Lyrics as Evidence at Criminal Trials." *UCLA Entertainment Law Review* (2005). *LexisNexis Academic.* http://www.lexisnexis.com.

Winfield, Betty Houchin. "Because of the Children: Decades of Attempted Controls of Rock 'n' Rap Music." In *Bleep! Censoring Rock and Rap Music,* ed. Betty Houchin Winfield and Sandra Davidson, 9–20. Westport, CT: Greenwood, 1999.

Winfrey, Aida McClellan. *Healing Young People Thru Empowerment (H.Y.P.E.).* Self-published, 2009.

Woodward, Bob, and Scott Armstrong. *The Brethren: Inside the Supreme Court.* New York: Avon, 1979.

Worthington, Andy. "A History of Music Torture in the 'War on Terror.'" *Huffington Post,* 15 December 2008. http://www.huffingtonpost.com/andy-worthington /a-history-of-music-tortur_b_151109.html.

"YouOughtaKnow." *Denver Post,* 8 March 2009. http://www.denverpost.com/colo radosunday/ci_8824269.

Index

Abbate, Carolyn, 59–60
Abel, Ben, 112, 115, 118
Abramsky, Sasha, 100
Abramson, Jeffrey, 42
Abu Ghraib scandal, 100
AC/DC, 115
Acrassicauda, 116
Adorno, Theodor, 8, 129
"An Affair to Remember," 34
Afghanistan, 25, 116
African Americans. *See also* race; racial
  bias
  hip-hop therapy, 69, 135–36, 160n9
  prison music and, 94–95, 96–97,
    165–66n49
  rap music and, 45–46
  sampling/borrowing, 81–82
  segregation, 27
  stereotypes of, 67
Aguilera, Christina, 112, 117, 120
Ahmadinejad, Mahmoud, 116
airplanes, music on, 37–38
Akron, Ohio, 103
Albarn, Damon, 157n56
alienation (*Verfremdung*), 46
All in the Family, 34
Alternative Restitution Program, 35

alternative sentencing, 42
amazon.com, 87
American Musicological Society
  (AMS), 25, 125, 128
Anderson, Helen A., 66
"An die Freude" (Schiller), 93
Andy Dufresne (fictional character),
  97
Another Mississippi Murder, 136
Apollo, cult of, 76
Arconti, Ken, 106
Arewa, Olufunmilayo B., 80, 82
Aristotle, 75–76, 140n13
Armstrong, Edward, 56, 67
Arnold, Allison, 66–67
Art against the Odds (Rubin), 97
Arts in Corrections program, 95–96,
  97, 108
Arts in Other Places (Cleveland), 95
Ashhurst-Watson, Carmen, 56–57
As Nasty as They Wanna Be, 80
Attali, Jacques, 24, 129, 150n66
Auburn System, 91–92
aulos, 76
Authenticity and Early Music, 6
authenticity, 56, 58, 60, 62–63, 65, 94,
  129, 134, 155n31

autonomous art, 129
Autry, Gene, 34

"Baby Elephant Walk" (Mancini), 33
Bach, Johann Sebastian, 24, 81
Baghdad International Airport, 120
Bailey v. State, 136
Baker, Greg, 82
Bakhtin, Mikhail, 58
Balkin, J. M., 6–7, 8
Barnes, Stephen H., 128
Barney and Friends, 34, 43, 44, 120
Baroque music, 24
Bass, Michael T., 30
Battle of Waterloo, 111
Bayoumi, Moustafa, 124
Beach Boys, 40
Beard, Jeffrey A., 89
Beatles, 5, 40–41, 73
Beatz, Swizz, 69
Beaumont, Gustave de, 91–92
beboppers, 163n85
Becker, Judith, 74
Beecher, Henry K., 114
Beethoven, Ludwig van, 19, 34, 61, 93
Begg, Moazzam, 122
Belknap, Raymond, 72
Bellman, Jonathan, 113, 125
Bentham, Jeremy, 107
Berlin Philharmonic, 93
Berlioz, Hector, 83
Bernstein, Lee, 120–21
The Best Day Ever, 34
Betts v. McCaughtry, 83
Beyer, Russel Joe, 104
Beyond Scared Straight, 88
"Beyond the Realms of Death" (Judas
    Priest), 72
Bissey, Christopher, 86
Block, Peter Alan, 74, 84
"Bodies," 112
Boim, David, 5
Bomstein, Brian, 140n13
Bonds, Mark Evan, 19
Book of Revelations, 73

*The Book of the Censure of Instruments of
    Diversion* (Dhamm al-malāhī), 115
Bork, Robert H., 6
"Born in the USA" (Springsteen), 118
Boston subways, 17
Botstein, Leon, 18
Bourdieu, Pierre, 23
Boy George, 34
Branch Davidian compound, 25, 73
Brandenburg incitement standard, 71–
    72, 73, 75
Brandenburg v. Ohio, 71
"Brand New Key" (Safka), 34
Bravin, Jess, 124
Brecht, Bertolt, 46
Brennan, William, 78
Brewster, Lawrence, 108
British Columbia, Canada, 16
British subways, 16–17
Broadus, Calvin. *See* Snoop Dog
Brolin, James, 26
Brombert, Victor, 92, 93, 94
Brown, Leotha, 104
Brown, Michelle, 100
Brown, Zachary, 36, 47
Brym, Robert J., 57
Bryson, Bethany, 41
Burger, Warren, 79
Burkholder, J. Peter, 81
Business Owners Association of
    University Avenue, 23
Butler, Judith, 100

Cady, Drew, 24
Calzada, People v., 51
Camp Cropper, 120
Camp Delta, 124
canon formation, 41, 48–49, 69
"Can't Smile without You" (Manilow), 34
Capers, I. Bennett, 14, 27
Capital Transit buses, 31
Captain and Tennille, 33
Carnegie Hall, 93
Carreras, Michael, 35, 45
Carrol, Noel, 45

Carroll, Patrick, 41–42
Cartman, 34, 43
Cash, Rosanne, 124, 127–28
Catholic Church, 91
Caudill, David, 6
CBS, 4, 35
Celtic culture and spirituality, 137, 138
censorship, 18, 46–47, 65, 84, 164n93
Central Intelligence Agency (CIA), 25,
    113–14
Chabris, Margaret, 16
"Chelsea Morning" (Mitchell), 34
Christenson, Peter, 74
Christopher, Charisse, 3
Chung, Connie, 88
CIA (Central Intelligence Agency), 25,
    113–14
Civil War, 111
Clark, Anne, 79–80, 82
Clark, Suzannah, 81
Clarke, David, 57, 58
class and musical taste, 23–24, 26–27
classical music. See also crime
    prevention, classical music in
    associations, 23, 28, 34, 46
    definition of, 8
    elevation of, 17–20, 40
    as punishment, 35–36
    status of, 28
    as a symbolic language, 22
    teens and, 22, 23–24
    waning authority of, 28, 41
Cleveland, William, 95
A Clockwork Orange, 149n40
Cloonan, Martin, 26, 44, 45, 65, 76, 84,
    118, 129–30, 152n102
Club Platinum, 54
C-Murder, 54
CNN, 34, 35, 136
Coates, Ta-Nehisi, 58
Cochran, Johnnie L., 50
Cohen, Mary, 106–7
Coleman, Clive, 26
Collier, M., 106
Collins, Cardiss, 47

Coltrane, John, 93–94
"Come Sail Away," 34
composers
    economic circumstances of, 60–61
    elevation of, 60–63, 81
    familiarity and, 24
    legislature's similarity to, 141n33
    music as reflective of, 60–65
    role of, 133–34
The Composer's Voice (Cone), 61–62
Le Comte de Monte-Cristo (Dumas), 92
concentration camps, 114, 128
concert saloons, 27
Cone, Edward T., 61–62
Congreve, William, 18
Conroy, John, 113
Constitution, U.S., 6, 31
consumerism and, 15
    criticisms of, 28
    discrimination and segregation,
        26–27
    identity construction, 14, 22
    listener, centrality of role of, 134–35
    music as marker of space, 20–22,
        24–26
    selection of classical music, 17, 20,
        22, 25–26
    teen loitering, 12–13, 16–17, 20, 22,
        23–24, 28
"Cop Killer" (Ice-T), 73
copyright cases, 80–81
copyright law, 124
Correctional Education Association, 95
The Count of Monte Cristo (Dumas), 92
country music, 25, 36, 56, 67
Couric, Katie, 88
Court of Appeals of California, 54
Cover, Robert, 7
CPTED (Crime Prevention through
    Environmental Design), 20–21
The Crests, 33
crime prevention, classical music in,
    12–28
Crime Victim Compensation
    Commission, 96

"Crooked Ass Nigga" (Shakur), 71
Crosby, Bing, 34
Crowe, Timothy D., 21
Cruel and Unusual Clause, 44
Cuba, 25
"The cult of violence" (Gore),
    161n38
cultural hegemony, 118
Cummings, André Douglas Pond, 101
Cusick, Suzanne, 25, 113, 116, 126–27,
    171n54

Dachau concentration camp, 114
daily life, music in, 36–38. *See also*
    programmed music
"Dance of the Sugarplum Fairy"
    (Tchaikovsky), 33
Danto, Arthur, 131
Dark Mischief, 86
Dat Nigga Daz, 63
Davidson, Bill, 10, 69–71, 134
Davidson case, 69–71, 78, 82–83, 134
Davies, Stephen, 62
death metal, 77. *See also* heavy metal
    music
Death on the Road, 116
Death Row Records, 50, 57
Defensible Space (Newman), 21
Def Jam Records, 56
Deleuze, Gilles, 130
Demers, Joanna, 4, 8
Dennis, Andrea L., 51, 53, 56, 65
DeNora, Tia, 37–38
Der Freischütz (Weber), 101
Dial "M" for Musicology (blog), 113
Dickens, Charles, 30
Dido, 45
Dimitriadis, Greg, 59
Dion, Celine, 2
Dionysus, cult of, 76
discipline, music and, 105–8
Doggystyle, 50, 64
Dohanich, Mike, 106
Do It for the Children, 96
Dominguez, Frank, 103

Donelan, James H., 19
Dore, Anna Maria, 137
Douglas, William O., 31, 79
Dow, David R., 74, 161n25
"Do You Really Want to Hurt Me?"
    (Boy George), 34
Dre, 56
drug dealers, outlaw positioning of,
    57–58
Duff, R. A., 44, 48
Dumas, Alexandre, 92
Dumile, Daniel (Metal Face Doom/MF
    Doom), 58
Dunwoody, Georgia, 15
Durham, Mamie, 17
Dylan, Bob, 5, 40–41, 62–63
Dyn-Corp, 120

ear worms, 120–21
Eastern Connecticut State University,
    35
East Hill Singers, 96
easy-listening music, 36
EatZi's, 15
Edmond Dantès (fictional character),
    92
Eighth Amendment, 44
elevation
    of classical music, 17–20, 40
    of composers, 60–63, 81
    of jazz music, 40, 48
    of music, 127, 129
    of righteous prisoner, 92–93, 101
    of rock music, 40–41, 48
"elevator music," 15
elevators, 36
Elijah (Mendelssohn), 18
Elsila, Mikael, 95, 102
Eminem, 56, 57, 58, 112, 118, 124,
    156n42
emotions
    impact of music on, 1–4
    role of in legal discourse, 2–3, 132,
        140n13
    in victim impact statements, 140n15

Empathy and the Novel (Keen), 92
England, 81
"Enter Sandman" (Metallica), 112
Environmental Protection Agency
    (EPA), 32
Enya, 1–2, 132, 135, 136–38
escape, music and, 102–3. *See also*
    freedom, music and
Espejo, Edgar, 25
"Essay on the Unification of All the
    Fine Arts and Sciences under the
    Concept of the Perfected Thing in
    Itself" (Moritz), 19
European Court of Human Rights, 126
"expression theory," 62

familiarity and music, 23–24, 146n75
Farley, Christine Haight, 135, 139n4
Faulkner, William, 79
FBI (Federal Bureau of Investigation),
    25, 120
Federal Aviation Act, 32
Federal Aviation Administration, 32
Federal Bureau of Investigation (FBI),
    25, 120
"Feelings" (Gemini), 25
femininity, 146n83
Ferreira, Daniel, 47, 128
Ferrell, Jeff, 73
Fierro, Joe, 168n117
Fifth Amendment, 31
50 Cent, 35, 57
"Fight the Power" (Public Enemy), 46,
    69
"The Fine Art of Rap" (Shusterman), 68
Fink, Robert, 17, 20, 40
First Amendment, 31, 32, 55, 69–70,
    71–72, 78–79, 90
Fischoff, Stuart, 55
Fisher, Philip, 130
Fisher-Giorlando, Marianne, 95, 103
"For All We Know," 37
Ford, Phil, 113, 125, 126–27
Fort Bragg, North Carolina, 112, 114
Fort Lupton, Colorado, 29, 33, 42

Forward Operating Base Tiger, 112
Foucault, Michel, 39, 102, 105, 107
Fourteenth Amendment, 32
France, 81
Frank, Jerome, 141n33
Frankfurt School, 129
freedom, music and, 93–94, 96, 102–3
Freedom of Information Act, 124
free jazz movement, 94
Freeman, Morgan, 97–98
FreeMuse, 164n93
Freese, Douglas W., 54
free will, 74
French Revolution, 93
Fried, Carrie B., 67
Frith, Simon, 58–60
"Fuck the Police" (NWA), 46
Fuller, R. Buckminster, 21
furniture music (*musique
    d'ameublement*), 14

Gacy, John Wayne, 108
Game, 57
gangs, 52, 53
gangsta rap, 50–51, 56–58, 77, 155n31,
    156n47
Ganksta N-I-P, 70
Gebrauchsmusik (music for use), 14
Gehrig, Andrew E., 43, 45
Gemini, 25
"gender coercion," 117
George Washington University, 124
Germany, 81
Gesamtkunstwerk, 156n51
Geto Boys, 70, 136
al-Ghazzālī, Ḥāmid, 115
Ghianda, Ron, 13
Gitlow v. New York, 73
Glass, Philip, 63
Goehr, Lydia, 9, 81, 131, 134
Goffman, Erving, 105
Goldsboro, Bobby, 34
Goldsmith, Jerry, 34
Golgona Trinity Baptist church, 63
Gonzales, Alberto R., 126

"The Good, the Bad, and the Ugly,"
33, 34
Goodman, Steve, 126
Gore, Tipper, 46, 161n38
Gorillaz, 157n56
Grace, Robert, 50
Graterford Prison, 86, 89
Great Britain, 114
Greene, Dennis, 53
Greene v. Commonwealth, 53
Grim Reaper, 116–17
Grisham, C. J., 118
Grossman, Mell, 80
Guantánamo Bay, 110, 112, 169n1
Guattari, Félix, 130

Hadsell, Mark, 112, 113
Hague, Euan, 137
Half Baked, 64
Hamlet (Shakespeare), 73
Hamm, Mark S., 73
Handel, Frideric, 8, 77
"Happy Trails" (Autry), 34
Hara, Leslie, 98
Harbert, Benjamin, 94, 104, 105, 107
Harden, Alicia N., 140n15
Hard Time Blues (Abramsky), 100
Hart, Michael, 86–87, 100–101
Hartford, Connecticut, 17
Harvey, Louisiana, 54
Hassam, Childe, 30, 33
Hawaii Five-O theme song, 34
Haydn, Franz Joseph, 61
*Healing Young People thru Empowerment
(H.Y.P.E.)* (Winfrey), 136
hearing loss, 31
"heat-of-passion" defense, 3
Heavy Metal Baghdad, 116–17
heavy metal music, 25, 41, 83–84, 112,
116, 118, 129, 156n47
Hegel, Georg Wilhelm Friedrich, 18,
61, 93
Hendrix, Jimi, 36, 80
Henthorne, Jason, 86, 99
Herlein, Michael Jon, 90

Herlein v. Higgins, 90
"Heroes End" (Judas Priest), 72
Hetfield, James, 131
Hewlett, Jamie, 157n56
Highway 61 Revisited (Dylan), 40
Hildegard of Bingen, 101
Hillman, Grady, 97, 100
hip hop, 159n2
hip-hop therapy, 69, 135–36, 160n9
"Hip Hop Wisdom for White
Therapists" (Klinger), 136
A History of Western Musical Aesthetics
(Lippman), 61
"Hit Me Baby One More Time"
(Spears), 118
Hobbs, David, 80
Hoffman, E. T. A., 61
Hoffman, Rick, 170n19
Holmes, Oliver Wendell, 73
"Honey (I Miss You)" (Goldsboro), 34
Horkheimer, Max, 129
Hospice di San Michelle, 91
House of Correction in Ghent, Austria,
91
Howard, Rodney Ray, 70–71, 74, 82–
83, 134
Huffington Post, 108
Huggy Bear, 64
Hugo, Victor, 93
humor, 45, 64, 82
Hutcheson, Francis, 45

"I Am Woman" (MC Lyte), 59
Ibn Abī'l-Dunyā, 115
Ice Cube, 70
Ice-T, 73
idealist aesthetic, 19, 40–41, 45, 47
identity
    composers and, 134
    construction and, 14, 22
    culture and, 66–67
    Enya's music, implications of, 137–38
    music and, 11, 74, 84, 103, 119–20
    violation of, 45
"Illegal Search" (L. L. Cool J), 46

"I Love You" (Barney and Friends), 120–21, 122
"Implicit Personality Theory," 55
incitement. *See* legal valuations of music, obscenity and incitement in
Industrial Revolution, 30
intellectual property law, 8
International Music Council, 31
International Noise Awareness Day, 32
Interscope Records, 71, 134
"Invasion of Space by a Female," 117
Iran, 116
Iraq War, 25, 111, 156n47
Irish Republican Army, 114
Iron Maiden, 116–17
"I Shot the Sheriff" (Marley), 73
Italy, 81
"The Itsy Bitsy Spider," 34
"I've Got a Feeling I'm Falling," 37
"I Wanna Be Free" (The Monkees), 34

Jackson, Bruce, 94–95
Jackson, Melissa, 22
Jackson, Michael, 118
Jacobellis v. Ohio, 78–79
Jahn, Friedrich Ludwig, 93
Jake, Jason Jermell, 54
Jankélévitch, Vladimir, 150n66
Jarrell, Tommy, 73
jazz music
    criticism of, 77
    elevation of, 40, 48
    freedom and, 93–94
    policing of, 47
Jeffrey, C. Ray, 20–21
Johnson, Bruce, 26, 44, 45, 84, 118, 129–30, 152n102
Johnson, Gary (G-Bone), 53–54
Jolly, John, 80, 82
Jones, Blake, 66–67
Jones, Carys Wyn, 40–41, 62, 157n70
Jones v. State, 66–67
Journal des Economistes, 39
Journal of International and Comparative Law, 5

Joyce, James, 79
Judaism, 76
Judas Priest, 72–73

Kahle, Robert, 26
Kahle Research Solutions, 26
Kapilow, Rob, 22
Katz, Paul, 108
Kearns, Thomas R., 138
Keen, Suzanne, 92
Kellaris, James, 15, 120, 121
Kelley, Robin D. G., 57
Kelly, Douglas Oliver, 1, 132
Kelly, People v., 1, 3–4, 11, 55, 135, 136–38
Kenyon, Nicholas, 6
Keyes, Cheryl, 59
Key West, Florida, 36
King, Rodney, 50
King, Stephen, 97
Klinger, Kevin, 136
Knight, Suge, 57
Komar and Melamid, 43
Kopf, Howard, 124
Koran, 117–18
Koresh, David, 25
Kornfeld, Phyllis, 99
Korpe, Maria, 76
Kramer, Jonathan, 68
KUBARK Counterintelligence Interrogation Handbook, 113
Ku Klux Klan, 71
Kulani Correctional Facility, 96

Lakewood, Ohio, 42
Laks, Szymon, 128
The Land Where the Blues Began (Lomax), 96–97
Lansing Correctional Facility, 96
Lanza, Joseph, 36
Laub, Dori, 119, 122
Laven, Stuart, 47
law. *See also* legal valuations of music, obscenity and incitement in
    art and, 135, 139n4
    links with music, 5–6

vs. literature, 3–4
role of within culture, 7
"Law, Music, and Other Performing
    Arts" (Levinson and Balkin), 6
Law Blog, 124
Leach, Elizabeth Eva, 81
League for the Hard of Hearing, 32
Lebrecht, Norman, 28, 128
Lefebvre, Henri, 22
legal valuations of music, obscenity and
    incitement in, 68–84
  2 Live Crew case, 80, 82
  arguments against musical
      incitement, 74
  Bradenburg test, 71–72, 73, 75
  Davidson case, 69–71, 78, 82–83, 134
  Judas Priest case, 72–73
  obscenity, standard of, 78–80
  Ozzy Osbourne case, 72, 164n95
  Tupac Shakur case, 10, 69–72, 74, 78,
      83, 134
Léger, Fernand, 14–15
Letters on the Aesthetic Education of Man
    (Schiller), 93
Leubsdorf, John, 3
Levin, Mark, 116
Levinson, Jerrold, 23
Levinson, Sanford, 6–7, 8
Levitin, Daniel, 122
lex talionis, 38–39
Limp Bizkit, 112
Lindhal, Hans, 140n14
Lippman, Edward, 17
listening, mode of, 23, 37
listening habits, use of in court, 66
literature, vs. law, 3–4
L. L. Cool J, 46
Lobgesang Symphony (Mendelssohn),
    18
Lomax, Alan, 94, 96–97
Lomax, John, 94
Long, Alex B., 5
Lord's Prayer, 64
Lorenz, Aaron R. S., 7
Los Angeles riots, 50

Los Angeles Times, 17
loud music, 45, 120, 147n84
Louisiana State Penitentiary, 94

MacCormick, Austin, 95
Macdonald, Dwight, 62, 129
Machaut, Guillaume de, 81
MacIntoch, Lorenzo, 87
Maine State Prison, 106
Majd al-Dīn al-Tūsī al-Ghazālī, 116
Mancera, People v., 51
Mancini, Henry, 33, 34
Manderson, Desmond, 6
Manilow, Barry, 12–13, 25, 33, 34, 40
"Manilow Method," 12–13
"Man of Constant Sorrow," 98
Mansfield, Peter M., 5
Manson, Charles, 73
Marascini v. Sullivan, 153n114
"March of the Pigs" (Nine Inch Nails),
    120
Marks, Donald R., 64
Marley, Bob, 73
The Marriage of Figaro, 97
Martin, Dennis R., 73
Martin, Peter, 23
Martinson, Robert, 99
masculinity, 146n83
"masscult," 62, 129
mass-culture theory, 62
Master P, 54
Mathers, Marshall, 58. *See also* Eminem
Matteson, Johann, 81
Mauer, Marc, 42
Mayer, Jane, 113
McBride, Thomas L., 106
McCarthy, Anna, 37
McCarthy, James, 137
McClary, Susan, 146n83
McCollum, John, 72
McCollum v. CBS Inc., 73
McCoy, Alfred, 113
McDermott, Dylan, 86, 99
McGill, Rosemary, 30
Mckay, Clint, 13

MC Lyte, 59
McManus, Francis, 32
McNally Smith College, 69
"Mele Kalikimaka" (Crosby), 34
Mello, Henry, 95, 108
Memphis, Tennessee, 42
Mendelssohn, Felix, 18–19
Mendelssohn, Moses, 19
"Mendelssohnian Project," 18
Mendoza, Manuel, 42
Menuhin, Yehudi, 31
Merrill, Jeff, 106
mescaline experiments, 114
Messiaen, Olivier, 102–3
Metallica, 112, 131
Meyer, Stephen, 92–93
Miami Herald, 80
Michelangeli, Arturo Benedetti, 102
Milan House of Correction, 91
Military, U.S., 25. *See also* torture,
    music as
Miller, Mitch, 16, 25
Miller, State v., 54
Miller, Wayne, 36, 48
Miller standard, 78, 79, 82
Miller v. California, 79
Mississippi Mafia, 136
Mitchell, Joni, 34, 40
MKUltra, 114
"Modes of Law" (Manderson and
    Caudill), 6
"Moments to Remember" (Murray),
    34
The Monkees, 34, 41
"Moonlight Serenade," 34
Moore, Cynthia, 55–56
Moore, Joshua Adam, 53–54, 55–56, 134
Mora, Francisco Calderon, 51–53
moral reform theory, 44
Morello, Tom, 125
Moritz, Karl Philipp, 19
Morreal, John, 45
Mosquito, 20
"most unwanted music," 43
Mount Olive prison, 98–99, 106

Mount Pleasant Correctional Facility
    (MPCF), 90
The Mourning Bride (Congreve), 18
Mozart, Wolfgang Amadeus, 24
"Mr. Lucky" (Mancini), 33, 34
"Mr. Self-Destruct" (Nine Inch Nails),
    120
Mudgrave, 118
Mueller, Andrew, 45
"Murder Was the Case" (Snoop Dog),
    50, 63–64
Murder Was the Case: The Movie, 50, 57
Murray, Anne, 34
music. *See also specific genres*
    emotional impact of, 1–4
    as the ideal art, 19–20
    law, philosophers on the distinctions
        between, 142n42
    links with the law, 5–6
    vs. noise, 30–31
    as an object, 130–31
    positive and negative potential of,
        70, 75–77, 83, 84, 102–6, 129–30
    as repetition, 24–25
    as a tool, 131
"Music as Torture/Music as Weapon"
    (Cusick), 25
Music behind Bars
    communion through music, 98–99
    criticism of, 88–89
    defense of, 88
    discipline and, 105–7
    effects of, 108
    introduction to, 10
    prisoners on positive functions of
        music, 102–6
    reactions to, 86–88, 100–101
    Young v. Beard, 85, 89
music education, 40, 41–42
music for use (*Gebrauchsmusik*), 14
Music Immersion Program
    choice of music, 41
    criticisms of, 44–48
    feedback forms, 35, 42–44
    introduction to, 33–35

as music education, 40–42
music in daily life vs. as punishment, 38
proportionality, 44–45
reactions to, 45
The Music of Murder (Martin), 73
"Musicology, Torture, Repair" (Cusick), 113
musique d'ameublement (furniture music), 14
musique de table (table music), 14
Muslim societies, role of music in, 115–16
Muzak, 15, 37, 128
"My Heart Will Go On" (Dion), 2

Nasriddinov, Ibrohim, 110, 123, 169n1
The Nation, 124
National Association for Music Education, 101
National Endowment for the Arts, 95
National Security Archive, 124
Navarro, Nick, 80
Nazi Germany, 114, 128
Nebraska Supreme Court, 52
Nelson, Willie, 34
Nevius, Sall, 47
Newman, Michael, 58
Newman, Oscar, 21
New Orleans, 26–27, 47, 77, 104
newsletters as evidence, 52
New Times, 82
Newton, Francis, 30
New York City, 30, 33, 46
New Yorker, 58
New York prisons, 39
New York Times, 16
New York University, 69
"911 Is a Joke" (Public Enemy), 46
Nine Inch Nails, 120, 124
Ninth Symphony (Beethoven), 93
No Frills Prison Act, 99–100
noise
    aircrafts and, 32
    complaints, history of, 29–30

legislation regarding, 32–33
vs. music, 30–31
policing of, 33–35, 47
Noise (Attali), 24
noise violators, punishment of. *See* punishment of noise violators
"Nomos and Narrative" (Cover), 7
"nonaggressive music deterrent," 25, 26
Noriega, Manuel Antonio, 25, 115
Norman, Christina, 86
Norris, Clive, 26
North, Adrian, 20
North, Tyler, 43
"Not Corporal but 'Classical' Punishment?," 46
NWA, 46

Obama, Barack, 125
Obel, Ned, 43
obscenity, 77–80, 162n59. *See also* legal valuations of music, obscenity and incitement in
"Ode to Joy" (Schiller), 93
Ohio State Journal of Criminal Law, 14
Ojito, People v., 51
Old School, 64
Olguin, Cesar Javier, 51–53
Olguin, People v., 51–53
"Only Time" (Enya), 136–37
"Only You" (The Platters), 33
"Ordo Virtutum" (Hildegard of Bingen), 101
O'Reilly, Bill, 86, 88, 152n102
The O'Reilly Factor, 86, 89
originalism, 6
Orlando, Mary, 86, 89, 101
Osbourne, Ozzy, 72, 164n95
Otterman, Michael, 113

parental advisory warning, 47, 90
Parents' Music Resource Center (PMRC), 46–47
Parents of Murdered Children, 89
Parodies of Ownership (Schur), 4, 80–81
parole system, 92

patronage system, 19
Paulus (Mendelssohn), 18
Payne v. Tennessee, 3
Pearl Jam, 124
peer rejection, 23
penal reform, history of, 91–93, 99
Penn, William, 91
Pennsylvania Department of
    Corrections, 89, 90
Pennsylvania prisons, 39
People magazine, 47
People v. Calzada, 51
People v. Kelly, 1, 3–4, 11, 55, 132–33, 135,
    136–38
People v. Mancera, 51
People v. Ojito, 51
People v. Olguin, 51–53
People v. Prince, 2
People v. Richardson, 54
Perkins, William Eric, 155n31
Perkinson, Robert, 165–66n49
Pet Sounds (Beach Boys), 40
Pham, Cheri, 53–54
Phifer, Jerald, 114
Philadelphia Inquirer, 86
Pieslak, Jonathan, 111, 113, 114, 118, 127
Piore, Adam, 112
Plato, 18, 75–76, 161n38
The Platters, 33
"Playing the Part" (Wolters-Fredlund),
    128
PMRC (Parents' Music Resource
    Center), 46–47
*Poetry and the Romantic Musical
    Aesthetic* (Donelan), 19
"Policeman" (Jarrell), 73
Politics (Aristotle), 75
Pope, Zazi, 73
Pope v. Illinois, 79
popular music
    authenticity in, 62–63
    canon formation, 41, 69
    fear of, 142–43n50
    hierarchies within, 41
Portland, Oregon, 17

postmodern art, 68–69
"Potential Liability Arising from the
    Dissemination of Violent Music,"
    73
Potratz, Terri, 45
Prince, People v., 2
prison, music in, 85–109. *See also Music
    behind Bars*
arts in prison programs, 95–96, 97, 108
    change in goals of imprisonment,
        99–101
    communion through music, 97–99,
        103–4
    criticism of *Music behind Bars*, 88–89
    defense of *Music behind Bars*, 88
    discipline and, 105–8
    freedom, music and, 93–94, 96, 102–3
    history of, 90–91
    identity and, 103
    independent band program, 89–90
    introduction to, 85–86
    performance and, 107–8
    practical purposes of, 102–9
    prison education movement, 95
    prisoners as victims, 97–98
    privilege, music as, 101–2, 106
    reactions to *Music behind Bars*, 86–
        88, 100–101
    Romantic image of, 92–93, 96–97,
        105–6
    security and, 89–90, 168n117
    self-esteem, 103–4
    silence in, 39, 92
    "total institution," 105
    virtuous prisoner, 92–93, 101
prison education movement, 95
prisoners
    on positive functions of music, 102–6
    righteous or virtuous, 92–93, 101
    self-identification with, 96–98
    as victims, 97–98
probation system, 92
property law, 80–82
*Prosecuting Gang Cases: What Local
    Prosecutors Need to Know*, 53

prostitution, 27
psychological operations (PsyOps), 112
psychological torture, 113–14
Public Enemy, 46, 69
*Public Utilities Commission of the
    District of Columbia v. Pollack*, 31
punishment
    dehumanization and, 165n31
    goals of, 91, 92, 99–101
    retribution, 38–39, 41–42, 44, 91,
        99–101
    theories of, 38–39
punishment of noise violators, 29–49
    associations, 132
    choice of music, 37, 41
    classical music, 35–36
    deterrent effects of, 42, 44
    as music education, 40, 41–42
    Music Immersion Program, 33–35,
        38–48
    racial issues, 46–47
    rap music, 45–47
    retribution, 38–39, 41–42, 44
Puritans, 76–77

al-Qahtani, Muhammad, 112, 117–18,
    119–20, 123
Quartet for the End of Time (Messiaen),
    102–3
Queen, 118
Quintilian, 76
al-Qutaji, Yasir, 112

race. *See also* African Americans
    communion through music, 97–99
    Enya's music, implications of, 137
    punishment of noise violators, 46–47
    rap music and, 45–46
racial bias, 56, 67, 82, 153n118
Rage against the Machine, 112, 125
ragtime music, 77
Rainey, John D., 71–72, 84
Ramirez, John, 51
rap lyrics as evidence, 50–67

composers' identity, 134
context of performance, 59, 64–65
criteria for admittance, 66–67
defense opposition to, 55
gangs, 52, 53
gangsta rap, 50–51, 56–58, 77, 155n31,
    156n47
Greene v. Commonwealth, 53
introduction to, 50–51
lyrics as speech not art, 56, 59, 64–65
People v. Olguin, 51–53
People v. Richardson, 54
racial bias, 56, 67
repercussions of, 55–56
Snoop Dog and, 50, 54, 57, 63–64,
    155n38
State v. Miller, 54
State v. Rollings, 55
United States v. Stuckey, 55
rap music
    in academic settings, 69
    African Americans and, 45–46
    appropriation of, 49
    associations, 46
    authenticity in, 56, 58, 60, 65
    canon formation, 48–49, 69
    commercial demands of music
        industry, 56–58
    context of performance, 59, 64–65
    copyright cases, 80–81
    as a disliked genre, 41
    gangsta rap, 50–51, 56–58, 77, 155n31,
        156n47
    humor in, 64, 82
    imprisonment, representation of, 101
    in Iran, 116
    in Iraq War, 156n47
    justice system and, 46–47
    layering of multiple voices, 58–59
    negative associations of, 55–56
    outlaw positioning of thugs, 57–58
    policing of, 47, 48–49, 153n114
    as postmodern art, 68–69
    punishment of noise violators, 45–47

race and, 45–46
reception of, 68–70
rhyme in, 59
sampling/borrowing, 80–82
status of, 83–84
use of in torture, 25, 129
"Rapper's Delight," 59
rap therapy, 69. *See also* hip-hop
therapy
recording technology, 24
Red (fictional character), 97–98
redlight districts, 26–27
Redrup v. New York, 78
Reflections upon Laughter (Hutcheson),
45
reggae music, 36
rehabilitation, 91, 99, 151n68, 152n92
Reilly, Tracy, 77, 142–43n50
Reitov, Ole, 76
R.E.M., 124
Republic (Plato), 18, 75
retribution, 38–39, 41–42, 44, 91, 99–101
Revolver (Beatles), 40
Reznor, Trent, 124, 125
Richardson, People v., 54
*Rita Hayworth and Shawshank
Redemption* (King), 97
"River" (Enya), 2
Roach, Max, 159n2
Robbins, Tim, 97
Roberts, Donald, 74
Rockdale, Australia, 12–13
rock music, 40–41, 48, 62, 77
Rollings, State v., 55
Roma, Catherine, 96
Roman Empire, 18
Romantic composers, 18–19
Romantic era
copyright, development of, 81
view of connection between art and
composer, 60–61
The Romantic Prison (Brombert), 92
Romantic thinking
about prison, 92–93, 96–97, 105–6

freedom as link between prison and
creative process, 94, 96
goals of prison reform and, 99
ideal of music, 8–9, 19, 40–41, 45,
47, 93
music as a privilege, 101–2, 106
power and function of music, 132
Room 222 theme song, 34
Rorem, Ned, 128–29
Rose, Tricia, 46
Rosen, Ralph M., 64
Roth v. United States, 79
Rubin, Susan Goldman, 97
Ruhe-Munch, Nancy, 89
Rutherford, Christian D., 10

Sacco, Paul, 29, 33, 34–35, 38–44, 45,
130, 132. *See also* Music Immersion
Program
Sacks, Oliver, 120, 121
sacred music, 76
Safka, Melanie, 34
Saidi, Laid, 123
Salazar v. State, 1–2
Salinas Valley State Prison, 98
sampling/borrowing, 80–82
Sanchez, Ricardo S., 114–15
Sanctuary (Faulkner), 79
San Diego Symphony, 24
San Quentin prison, 97
Santa Ana Jail, 168n117
Santa Rosa, California, 13, 17
Santos, Michael, 104–5
Sarat, Austin, 138
Saravinovski, Bill, 12
Satie, Erik, 14
Saturday Night Live, 87
Scalia, Antonin, 79
Scared Straight! series, 87
Scarry, Elaine, 119, 123
Schafer, R. Murray, 20, 147n84
Schenker, Henrich, 8
Schiller, Friedrich, 93
Schleiermacher, Friedrich, 19

Schopenhauer, Arthur, 19, 30
Schroeder, Erica, 2, 135
Schumann, Robert, 8
Schur, Richard L., 4, 80–81
Schweiker, Mark, 89
Scott, Cyril, 77
Scruggs, John, 26
Seattle, 23
security, music's role in, 89–90, 168n117
SEM (Society for Ethnomusicology), 125
Sentencing Project, 42
SERE (Survival-Evasion-Resistance-Escape) conference, 114
Sesame Street, 112, 120
7-Eleven stores, 16
Shaffer, Tani Graham, 57–58
Shakespeare behind Bars, 95
Shakur, Tupac, 10, 69, 70–72, 74, 78, 83, 134
Shapiro, Arnold, 85–88, 105–6
Shaw, Robert, 96, 103
The Shawshank Redemption, 97–98
Sher, Daniel, 47–48, 132
"She Wore a Yellow Ribbon," 34
Shield Group Security Company, 120
Shusterman, Richard, 68–69
silence, 39, 92, 150n66, 151n68
Simmons, Russell, 64
Simpson, O. J., 50
Sinatra, Nancy, 25
Singal, S. P., 31
"6 Feet Deep" (Geto Boys), 136
"Sixteen Candles" (The Crests), 33
Slim Shady, 58–59
Smith, Adam, 39
Smith, Andre L., 80, 82
Smith, Caleb, 91, 100
Smith, Elouise, 95
Smith, Matthew Wilson, 156n51
Smolla, Rod, 73
Snoop Dog, 47, 50, 54, 57, 63–64, 155n38
Society for Ethnomusicology (SEM), 125

Soldier, Dave, 43
solitary confinement, 91–92
Songs without Words (Manderson), 6
Sonic Warfare (Goodman), 126
"Sounds Like the Mall of America" (Sterne), 15
"Sounds of Prejudice" (Schroeder), 2
South Park, 34, 43
Southwest Correctional Art Network, 95, 97
Speaking of the Devil, 72
Spears, Britney, 112, 118, 124
Spencer, Troy, 86
SpongeBob and the Hi-Seas, 34
Springsteen, Bruce, 112, 118
Squier, George Owen, 15
Stained Class, 72
"Stan" (Eminem), 57
Stanley v. Georgia, 79
Starsky and Hutch, 64
State v. Miller, 54
State v. Rollings, 55
Steal This Music (Demers), 4
Sterne, Jonathan, 15, 25
Stewart, Potter, 78–79
"Storms in Africa" (Enya), 2
"Stormy Weather," 37
Story, Sidney, 27
Storyville, 26–27
Stravinsky, Igor, 8
Street Music in the Metropolis (Bass), 30
Streisand, Barbra, 26
Stuckey, Thelmon F., 55
Stuckey, United States v., 55
"stuck tune syndrome," 120–21
Stuessy, Clarence Joseph, Jr., 82
subliminal messages, 72
suicide, 72–73
"Suicide Solution" (Osbourne), 72
Sullivan, Kathleen M., 79
Sulzer, Johann Georg, 18, 61
Sunday Star, 124
Supreme Court, U.S., 4, 31, 71, 78–79
Survival-Evasion-Resistance-Escape (SERE) conference, 114

Sussman, David, 119
Swartz, Jeffrey, 35
Swizz Beatz, 69
symbolic language, classical music as, 22
symbolic power, 146n69
Symphonie Fantastique (Berlioz), 83
Symphony no. 9 (Beethoven), 34
Symphony no. 40 in G minor (Mozart), 24

table music (*musique de table*), 14
Taliban, 116, 130
Tannenbaum, Judith, 97
Tanner, Allen, 70
Taruskin, Richard, 6, 8, 61, 125, 130
Tchaikovsky, Pyotr Ilyich, 33
Teaching the Arts behind Bars (Williams), 96
Telemann, Georg Philipp, 8, 14
"Tennessee Waltz," 33, 34
"Terrorism and a Civil Cause of Action" (Mansfield), 5
Tesh, John, 34
Texas Court of Criminal Appeal, 1–2
The Theory of Moral Sentiments (Smith), 39
"These Boots Are Made for Walking" (Sinatra), 25
"This Old Man," 121, 122
Thomas, Steve, 54
Thompson, James, 107
Thompson, Kenan, 87
"Those Were the Days," 34
three strikes laws, 99–100
Tillicum, Washington, 16
Timberg, Scott, 17
Time-Warner, 71, 134
tinnitus, 152n99
Tiny Tim, 34
"Tiptoe through the Tulips" (Tiny Tim), 34
"To Be or Not to Be" speech in *Hamlet*, 73
Toch, Hans, 104

Tocqueville, Alexis de, 91–92
torture
    imposition of sound, 44–45
    loud music, 45, 120, 147n84
    men and, 171n54
    prison and, 100
    resistance training, 114–15, 120
torture, music as, 110–31
    dehumanization, 165n31
    detention camps, 25, 111–12
    disorientation, 122–23
    distinction between sound and music, 126, 128
    identity and, 119–20
    introduction to, 110–11
    Islamic devotion questioned, 117–18, 120
    legal justification for, 125–26
    music selection, 116–19, 123–24
    origins of, 113–14
    performance in, 123
    physical repercussions, 116–17
    rap music, 25, 129
    responses to, 124–29, 131, 152–53n102
    role of music in Muslim societies, 115–16
    suppression of thought, 120–21
    trauma of, 119–20
"total institution," 105
trance, 73, 74, 121–22
La Traviata (Verdi), 35
Tribe, Paul, 75
"True North," 38
The Tuning of the World (Schafer), 20
Turner v. Safley, 89, 90
2 Live Crew, 80, 82
2Pacalypse Now, 70–71
Tyson, Edgar H., 136

Ulysses (Joyce), 79
Uncle Dave's Rusty Banjo, 98, 106
UNESCO, 31
United Kingdom, 32
United States v. Stuckey, 55

University of Pennsylvania Law Review, 6
Urbana, Ohio, 35
Urban Safety Program, 26
Utley, Ebony, 155n38
Utopia or Oblivion (Fuller), 21

Vactor, Andrew, 35, 45–46
Vance, Donald, 120
Vance, James, 72
Van Halen, 80
Vatican embassy, 25
Verdi, Giuseppe, 35
Verfremdung (alienation), 46
VH1, 10, 85, 87–88, 95, 98
The Vibe, 127–28
victim impact statements, 1–4, 132, 135, 140n15
Vietnam War, 113
Vitry, Philippe de, 81
Der volkommene Capellmeister (Mattheson), 81
Vorlesung über die Äesthetik (Hegel), 93
Voth, Elvera, 96, 97

Wake Up Dead Man (Jackson), 94
Walser, Robert, 69, 83
war, use of music in, 111–12
war on terror, 100, 110, 111, 114–15, 119, 124, 127
Warren Correctional Institution, 96
Wayne University, 26
"We Are the Champions" (Queen), 118
Weber, Carl Maria von, 101

"Wedding Song (There is Love)" (Captain and Tennille), 33
Weiner, Cy, 86–87, 100–101
Weir, Sara, 1, 132, 137
Weisbrod, Carol, 7
Weiss, Rob, 87–88
Werktreue, 134
West, Robin L., 3–4
West Coast rap, 59
West Palm Beach, Florida, 13, 17, 21
"What Works?: Questions and Answers about Prison Reform" (Martinson), 99
"White America" (Eminem), 118
White Zombie, 26
"Who Wants to Race Me?," 34
Wiener, Richard, 140n13
William James Association, 95–96
Williams, Andy, 25
Williams, Rachel Marie-Crane, 96
Wilson, Mrs. Richard T., 30
Wilson, Sean-Patrick, 51, 65
Winfrey, Adia McClellan, 136
"With a Little Bit of Luck," 37
Woldemariam, Philip, 50
Wolters-Fredlund, Benita, 128
Wong, Brian, 96

Yale Journal of Law and the Humanities, 7
"You Are Always on My Mind" (Nelson), 34
Young, Richard Glenn, 89
Young v. Beard, 85, 89